Copyright © 2025 by HermannPress

All rights reseved.

First edition

ISBN 978-1-964383-18-7

Published by

www.hermannpress.com

All rights reserved. No part of this work may be reproduced in any form or by any means (electronic, mechanical, photocopying, recording, or other methods) without the prior written permission of the copyright holder. This work may not be processed, duplicated, or distributed using electronic systems.

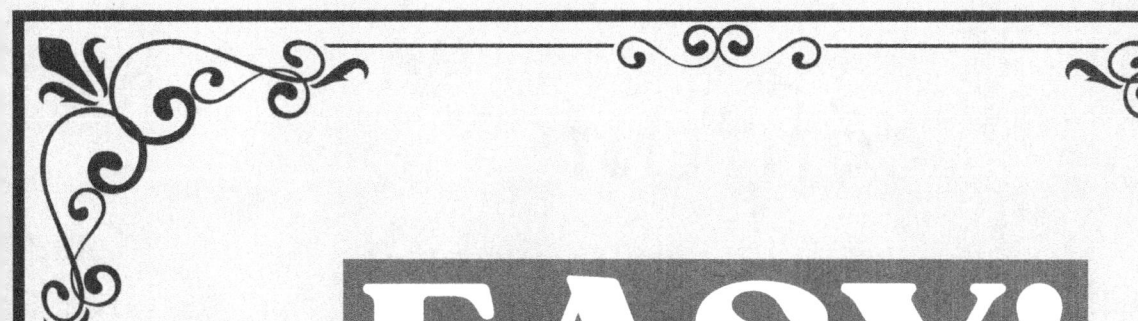

EASY! PIANO

NOTE READING EXERCISES

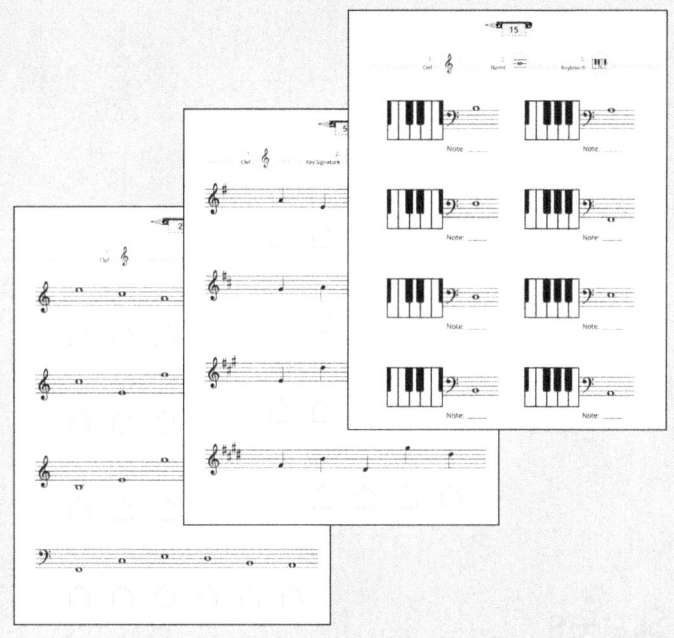

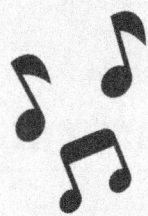

CONTENT

Your Free Gift 1

Introduction

About This Book 3
History of Music Notation 3

Chapter 1: Note Reading Theory

Musical Staff 5
The Clef 5
The Grand Staff 6
    Treble Clef 7
    Bass Clef 7
Pitch 10
Accidentals 11
    Accidentals on the Staff 13
    Accidentals & Key Signature 14
Major & Minor Scales 15
Circle of Fifths 21

Chapter 2: Exercises Natural Notes

Instructions with Example 23

Practice in the Grand Staff.. 24

Exercise Layout with Example.. 37

Practice on Keyboard & Staff.. 38

Chapter 3: Exercises Accidentals

Instructions with Example.. 51

Practice in the Grand Staff.. 52

Exercise Layout with Example.. 65

Practice on Keyboard & Staff.. 66

Chapter 4: Exercises Key Signatures

Instructions with Example.. 79

Practice in the Grand Staff.. 80

Exercise Layout with Example.. 93

Practice on Keyboard & Staff.. 94

Tips for Reading Notes.. 107

Solution to Exercises

Chapter 2 Solutions.. 108

Chapter 3 Solutions.. 112

Chapter 4 Solutions.. 116

Your Free Gift!

Welcome to your continuing journey in the realm of music!

To enhance your experience and provide you with valuable insights, I'm thrilled to present an exclusive bonus available via the **QR code below**.

This special bonus includes 5 pages packed with helpful charts, diagrams, and cheat sheets specifically designed to accompany and simplify the exercises presented in each chapter of this book.

Each cheat sheet has been thoughtfully crafted to serve as a quick reference guide, ideal for assisting you as you progress through your exercises.

These sheets summarize key concepts, making them exceptionally useful to have on hand or printed out for convenient reference while practicing.

In addition to the cheat sheets, you'll find included blank staff music paper, perfect for writing down your own musical notes and ideas or practicing your newly learned skills.

Every chapter of this book offers practical guidance that you can readily follow.
These additional resources are tailored to strenghten your understanding, ensuring you get the most out of your study sessions.

Scan the **QR code** to access and download these carefully curated templates.

This bonus expresses my heartfelt gratitude for your dedication, interest, and enthusiasm for learning.

I truly hope these materials inspire you to confidently turn your musical aspirations into reality safely and enjoyably.

Keep your cheat sheets close, print your music paper, and let your creativity flourish!

About This Book

By learning to read music, you unlock a delightful world of compositions from various composers.

This guide aims to ease your journey into note reading, establishing a strong foundation to boost your confidence in music reading.

In just two pages, you'll be equipped to solve all exercises in Chapter 2.

The additional music theory complements the exercises in subsequent chapters. This book introduces you to the basics of music notation in a clear and accessible manner.

Across 76 exercise sheets, you'll master reading notes, navigating the grand staff, and identifying and understanding accidentals and key signatures.

History of Music Notation

The roots of music notation can be traced back to ancient Greece. It wasn't until the Middle Ages, when writing became prevalent in monasteries and schools, that notation began to take shape.

In the 11th century, Guido of Arezzo transformed music notation by introducing the staff system, which allowed for a more accurate identification of pitches.

Subsequently, rhythmic symbols were incorporated, and by the Baroque period (around 1750), it became standard to notate music for orchestras and ensembles in scores, leading to the modern musical notation we use today.

This development enabled artists and musicians to record their works and share them across distances and generations, allowing for the compositions of renowned figures such as Bach, Mozart, and Beethoven to be passed along to other musicians.

Today, written music is a vital component of music education, playing a significant role not just in classical music, but also in popular music and jazz, where it is used to compose and preserve arrangements and original works.

Chapter 1

Note Reading Theory

Clef & Grand Staff

Pitch & Accidentals

Scales in Major & Minor

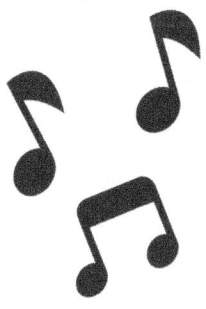

Musical Staff

The staff is made up of five horizontal, parallel lines. Most musical notes are placed either on these lines or in the spaces between them. However, notes can be higher or lower, and additional ledger lines may be added for notes that exceed the normal range of the staff.

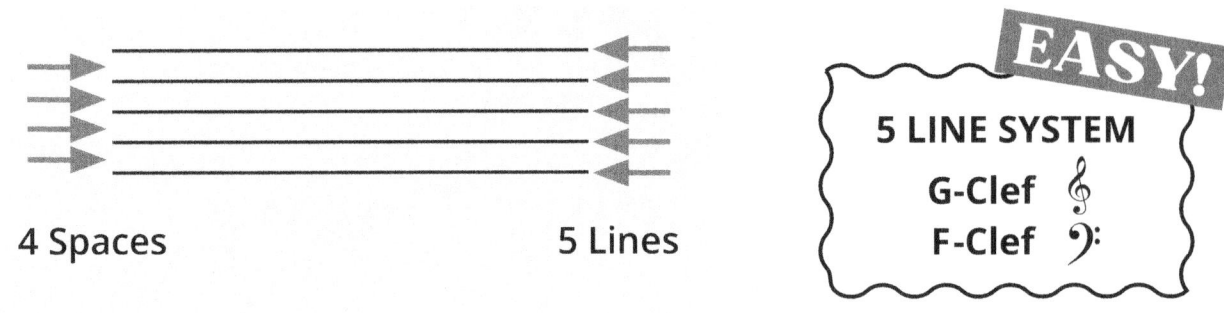

The Clef

At the beginning of each staff, the first symbol is a clef. This symbol is very important because it indicates which note (A, B, C, D, E, F, and G) is placed on each specific line or space.

The Treble Clef

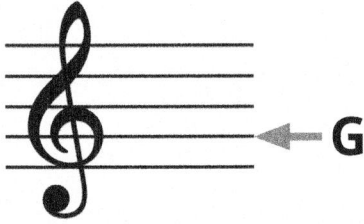

For example, a treble clef indicates that the second line from the bottom (the line around which the symbol curls) represents a "**G**."

On any staff, the notes are always arranged so that the next letter follows on the next higher line or space. After the letter G, the sequence continues with an A.

The Bass Clef

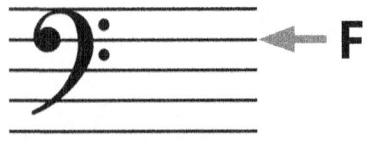

A bass clef indicates that the second line from the top (the one between the two dots of the symbol) represents an "**F**."

The notes still follow an ascending order, but they are positioned differently than in the treble clef.

Grand Staff

A full piano keyboard has **88 keys**, starting with the note '**A**' and ending with the note '**C**'. The letter names are numbered in each octave; therefore, the first A is called A1 and repeats in each octave up to A8. The same applies to all C notes—the first is C1 and the last is C8. The C located near the middle of the keyboard is referred to as "**Middle C**" because it is closest to the center of the keyboard.

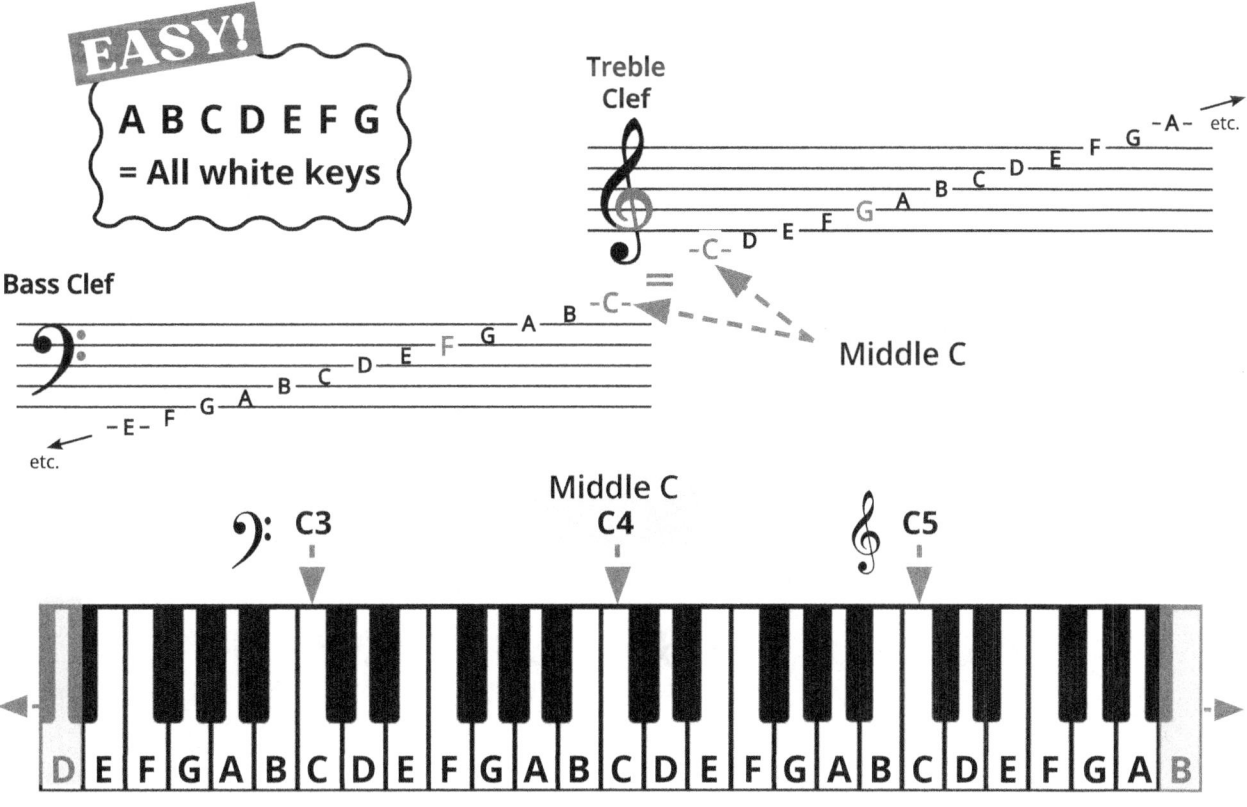

The illustration shows both clefs on the keyboard, with **Middle C** located above the bass clef and below the treble clef. These two staves cover the majority of notes and pitches used by most instruments.

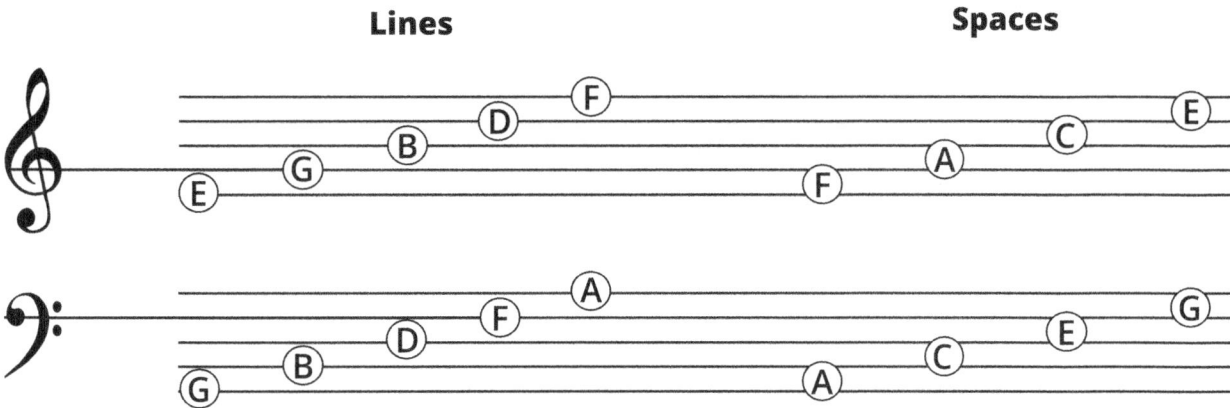

Notes in the Treble Clef (G-Clef)

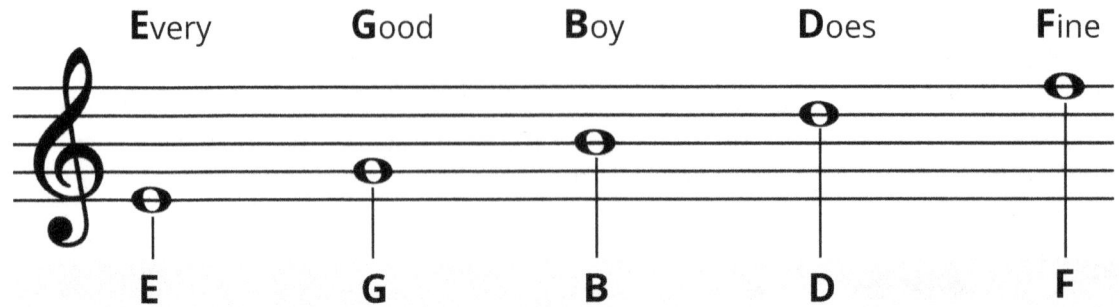

The word **FACE** fits perfectly in the spaces.

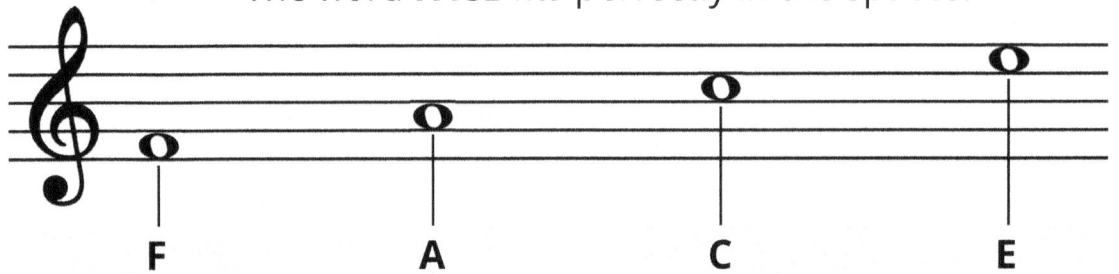

Notes in the Bass Clef (F-Clef)

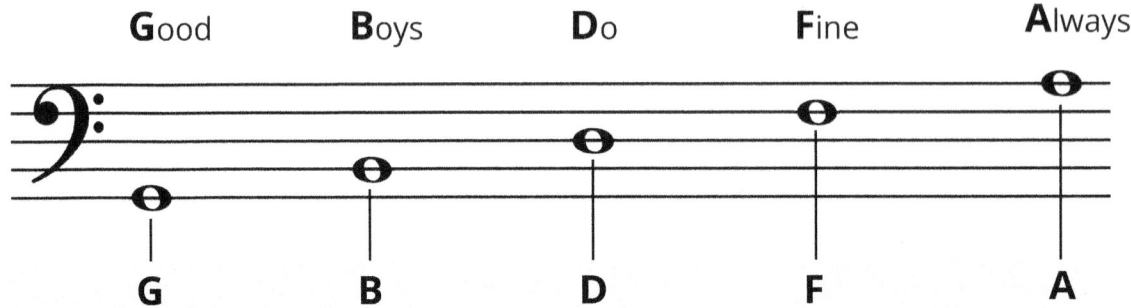

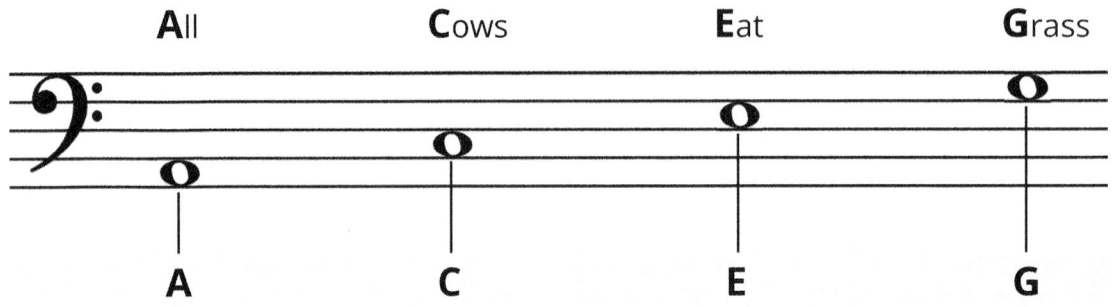

The natural notes correspond to all the white keys on the keyboard.

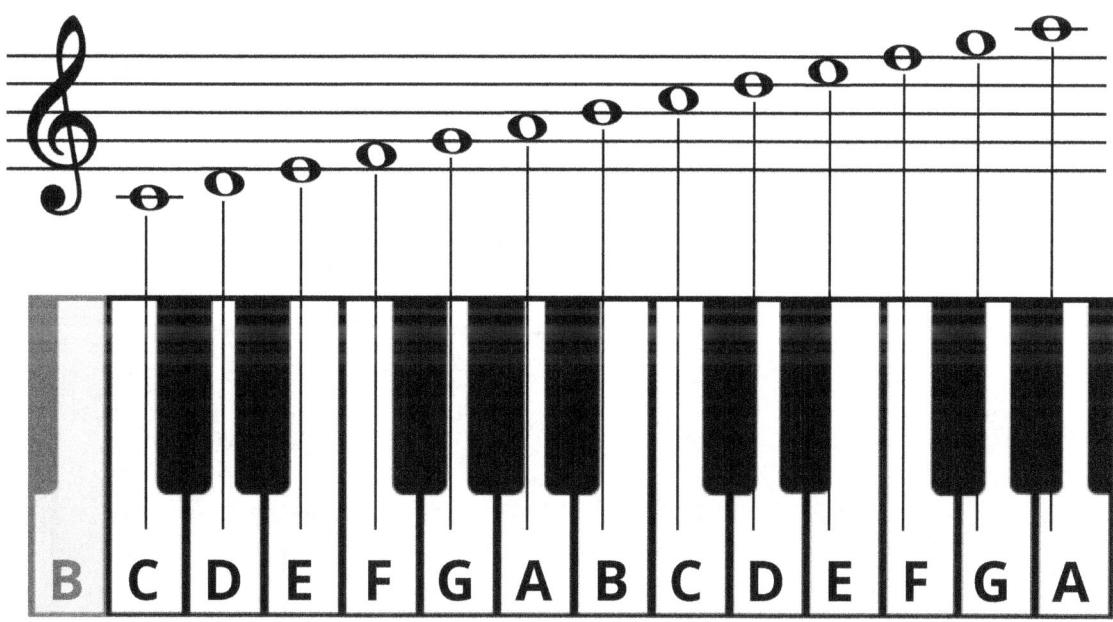

Musical Staff & Keyboard

This practice example illustrates how to complete the exercises on both the musical staff and the piano keyboard:

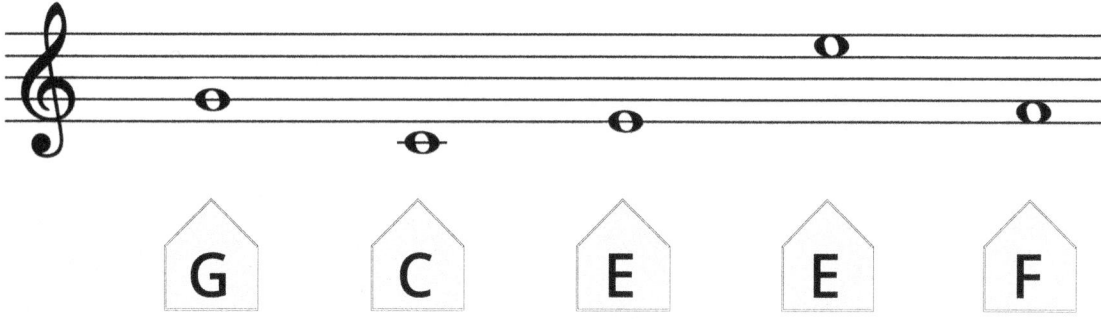

1. **Clef:** The Treble Clef is given. 2. **Draw the Note:** Notes C and E

3. **Keyboard:** Circle the note on the piano keyboard.

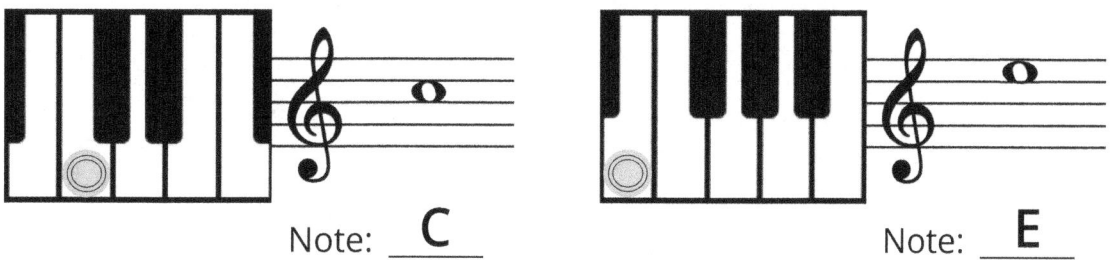

The natural notes correspond to all the white keys on the keyboard.

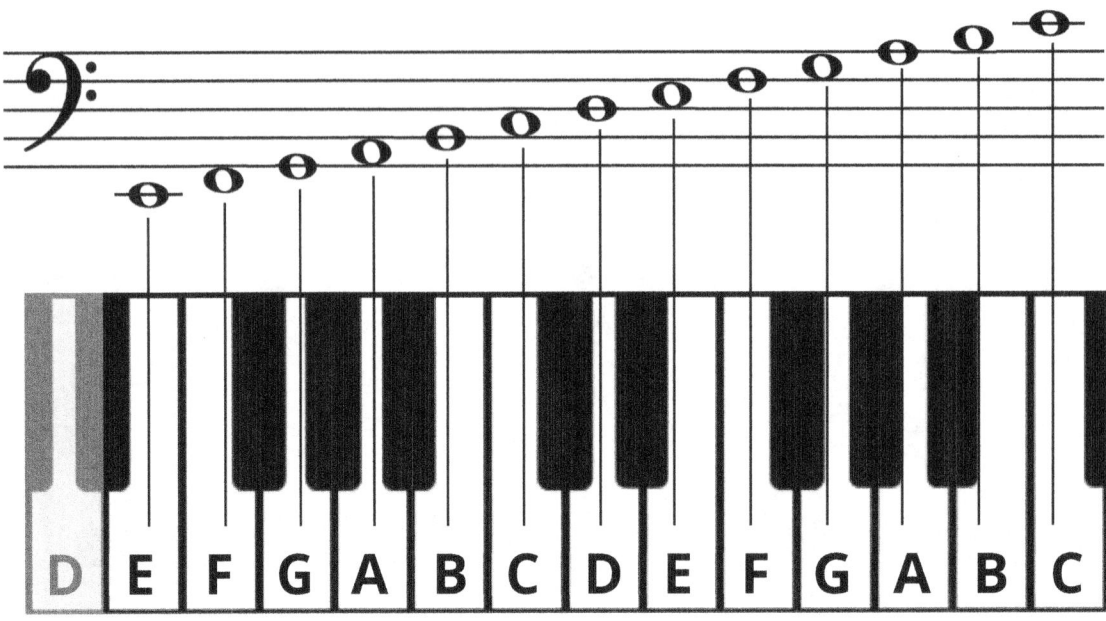

Musical Staff & Keyboard

This practice example illustrates how to complete the exercises on both the musical staff and the piano keyboard:

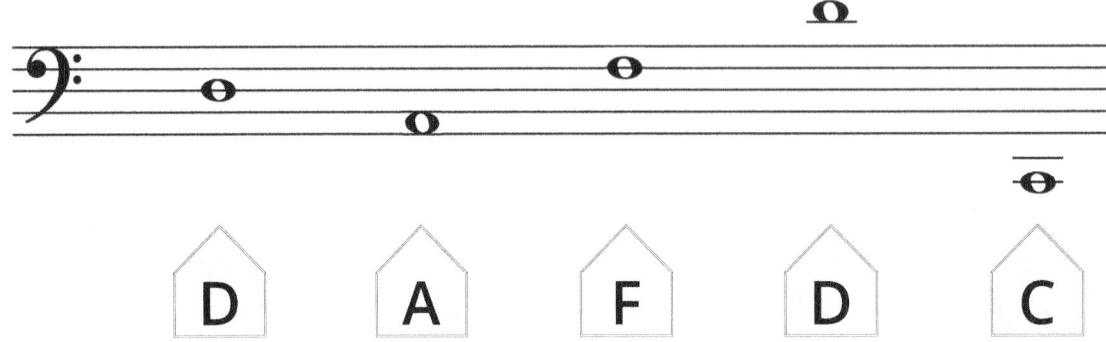

1. **Clef:** The Bass Clef is given.   2. **Draw the Note:** Notes D and A
3. **Keyboard:** Circle the note on the piano keyboard.

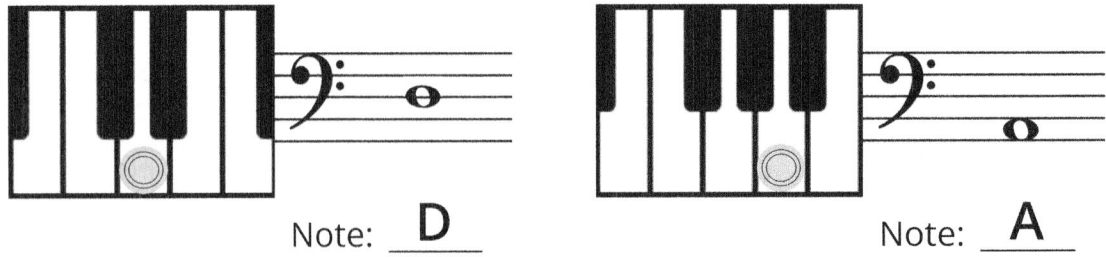

Pitch

The pitch of a note describes how high or low it sounds. Musicians assign different letter names to the various pitches: **C, D, E, F, G, A, and B**.

These seven letters represent all the natural tones (the white keys on a keyboard) within one octave.

An octave is the interval between two notes of the same name. When you reach the eighth natural tone, you begin the next octave with another C.

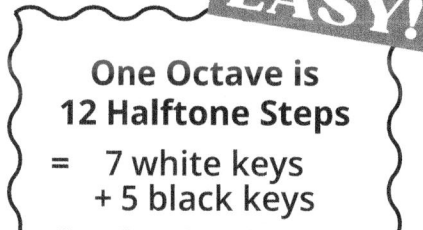

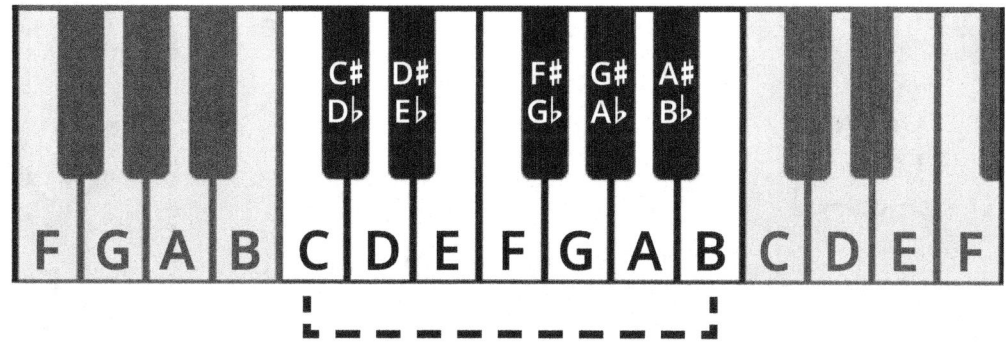

These seven letters represent the natural notes (all the white keys) within an octave. The next 'C' (note 8) marks the beginning of the next octave (from the Latin "octo," meaning eight).

For example from C to C is one octave, from F → F, or from G → G, and so on.

With 12 half (semitone) **steps you get from a note to the next octave.**

What are the names of the other five notes (on a piano, the black keys)?

To illustrate this, we look at an octave, which consists of seven white keys and five black keys.

The seven white keys (natural tones):
C, D, E, F, G, A and B

The five black keys depending on the musical context are called:

C♯, D♯, F♯, G♯, and A♯
(when raised) **or**

D♭, E♭, G♭, A♭ and B♭
(when lowered).

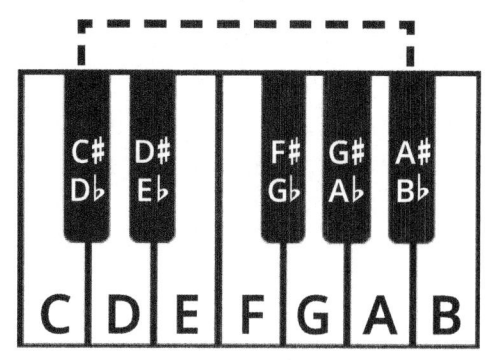

Accidentals

In music notation, there are three important accidentals: the flat sign (♭), the sharp sign (♯), and the natural sign (♮).
These symbols change the pitch of a note and are essential for identifying the black keys on the piano keyboard.

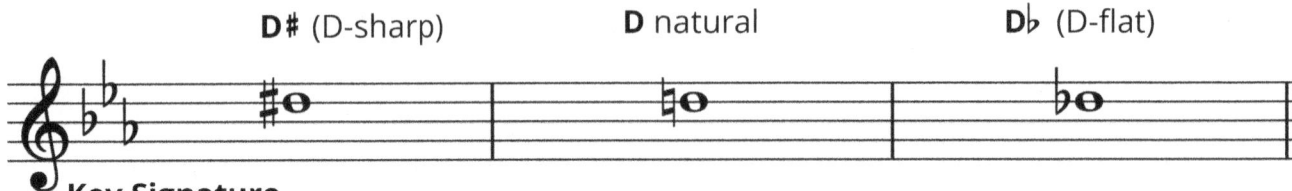

Key Signature
Three ♭'s (E♭-Major)

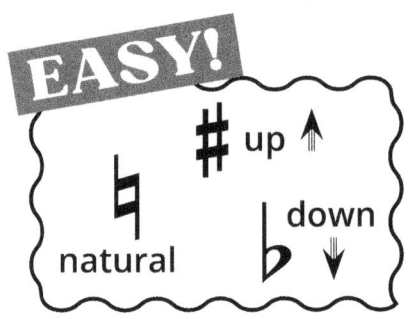

Sharps, flats, and natural signs can appear either in the key signature or directly in front of the notes they modify.

Let's take the note D on the staff as an example:

The sharp (♯) raises it by a half step to D-sharp (D♯).

The natural sign (♮) brings it back to regular D (natural).

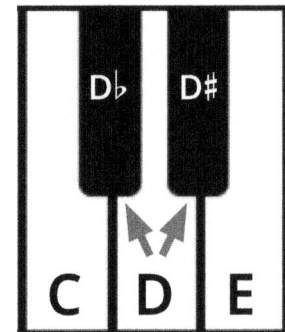

The flat (♭) lowers it by a half step, turning D into D-flat (D♭).

Now let's look at the note C:
There is also a white key called C-flat (C♭).

The sharp (♯) raises it to C-sharp (C♯), the natural sign (♮) brings it back to natural C, and the flat (♭) lowers it to C-flat (C♭). Since there is no black key between C and B, **C♭** is the same as the white key **B**.

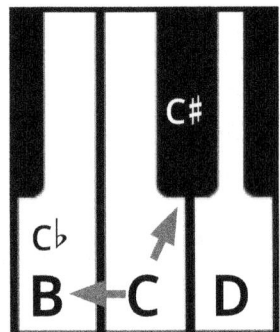

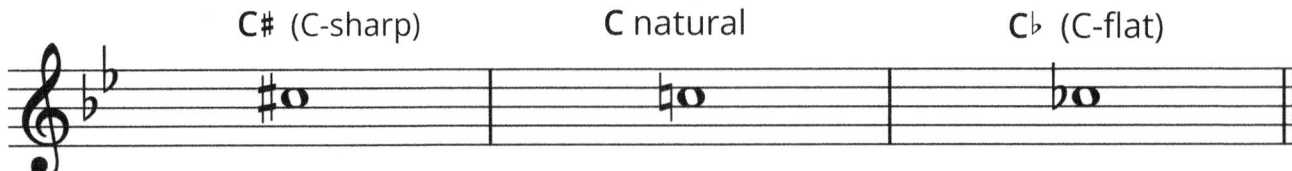

A **half step** on the piano is the smallest distance between two neighboring keys (for example, from a white key to the next black key).
A **whole step** consists of two half steps (for example, from one white key to the next white key, skipping a black key in between).

When two white keys have no black key between them, that also counts as a half step from white to white—**such as from B to C, or from E to F**.

Flat Sign: The flat symbol lowers a note by a half step. Therefore, a note altered by a flat is played a half tone lower.

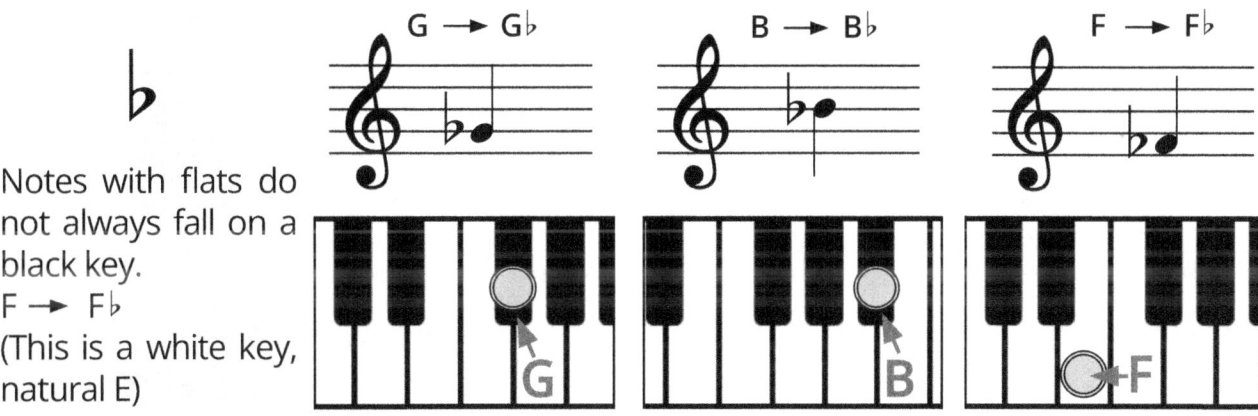

Notes with flats do not always fall on a black key.
F → F♭
(This is a white key, natural E)

Sharp Sign: The sharp symbol increases a note by a half step (semitone). A note altered by a sharp is thus played a half tone higher.

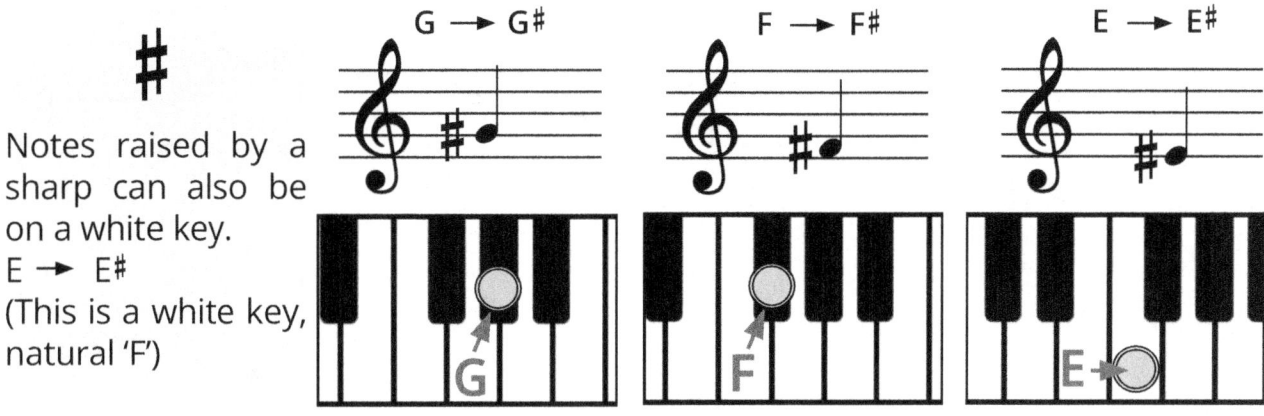

Notes raised by a sharp can also be on a white key.
E → E♯
(This is a white key, natural 'F')

Natural Sign: The natural sign cancels any previous alteration made by a sharp or flat, returning the note to its natural pitch.

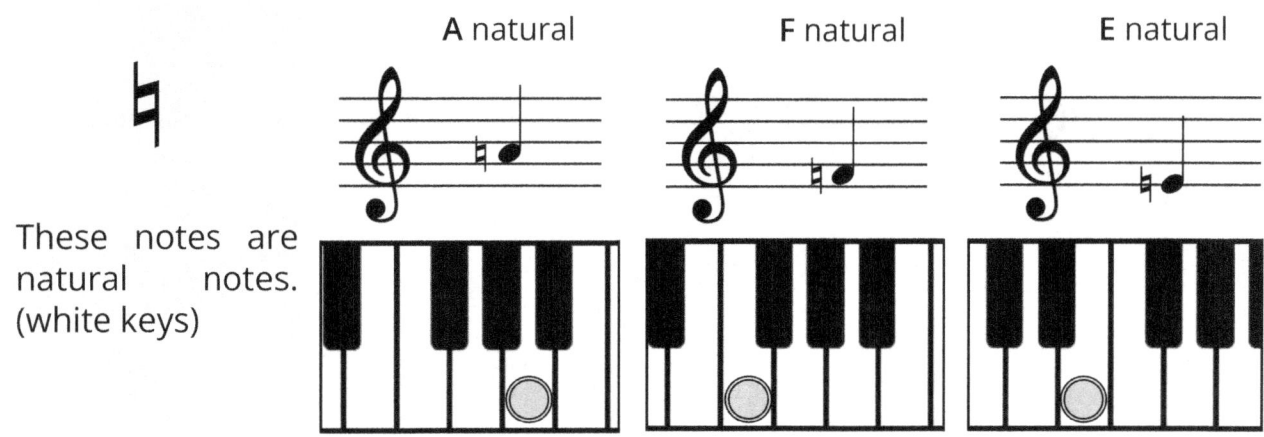

These notes are natural notes. (white keys)

- 12 -

Accidentals on the Staff

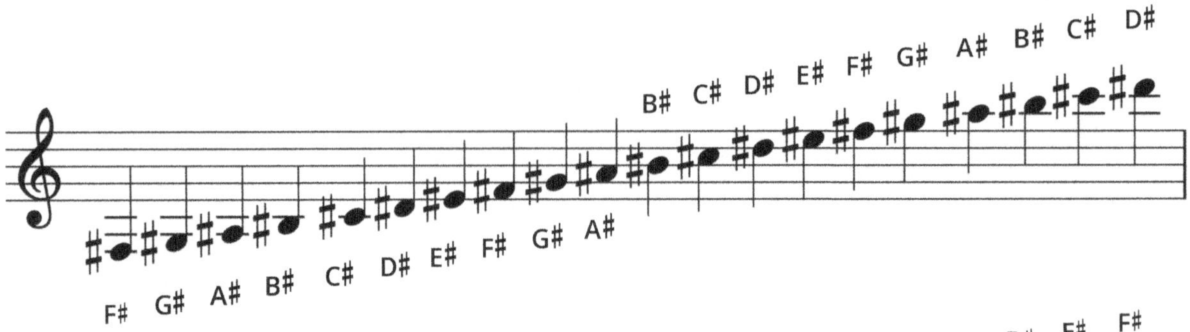

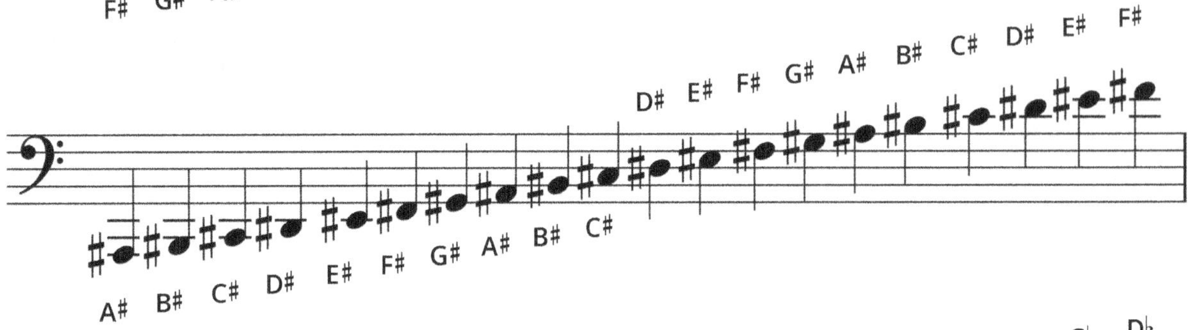

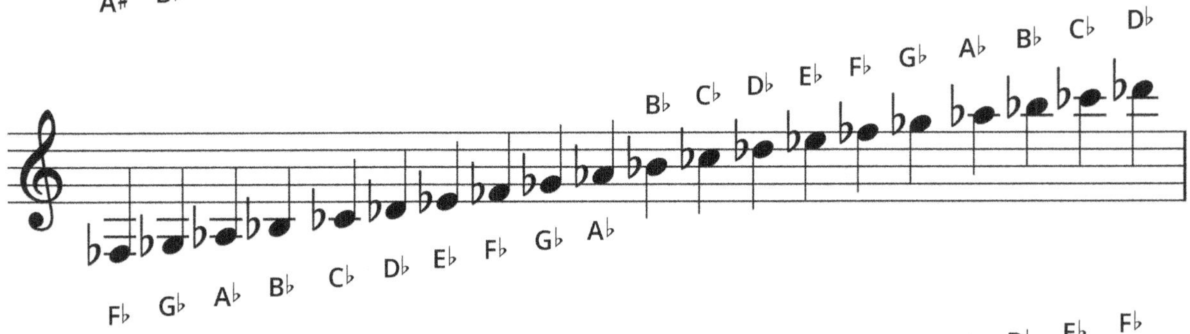

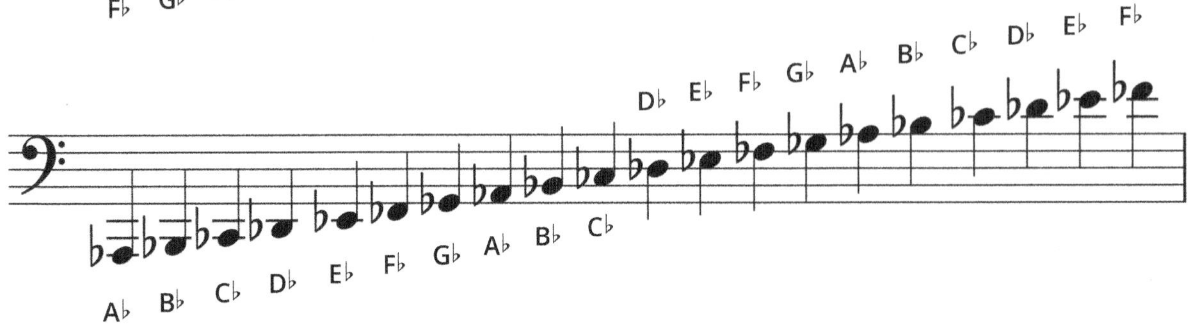

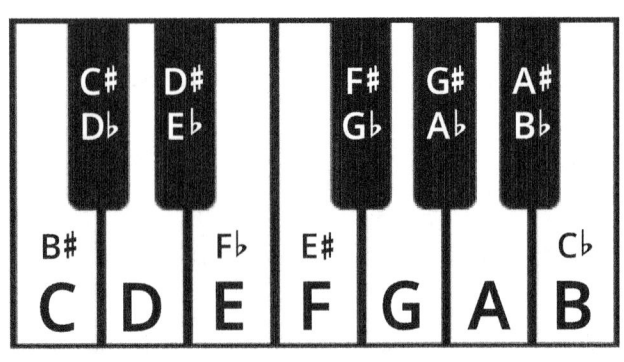

Natural Notes	Sharp-Notes #	Flat-Notes ♭
C	C#	C♭
D	D#	D♭
E	E#	E♭
F	F#	F♭
G	G#	G♭
A	A#	A♭
B	B#	B♭

Accidentals and Key Signature

When accidentals appear after the clef, they represent the key signature. The sequence of sharps or flats is a marker for both major and minor scales.

Sharps and flats are always arranged in the same order across key signatures (up to seven sharps or seven flats, never both).

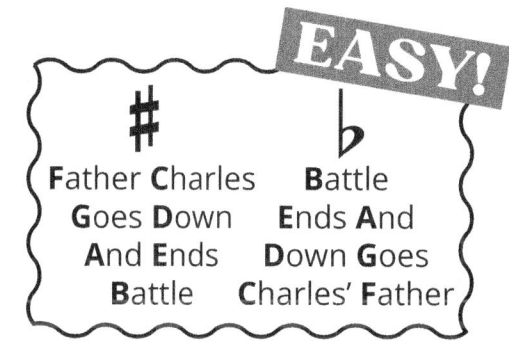

For example, in the key of G major or E minor, which has only one sharp, that sharp will always be F-sharp. Therefore, F-sharp consistently appears as the first sharp in any key signature that contains sharps

Order in the Staff

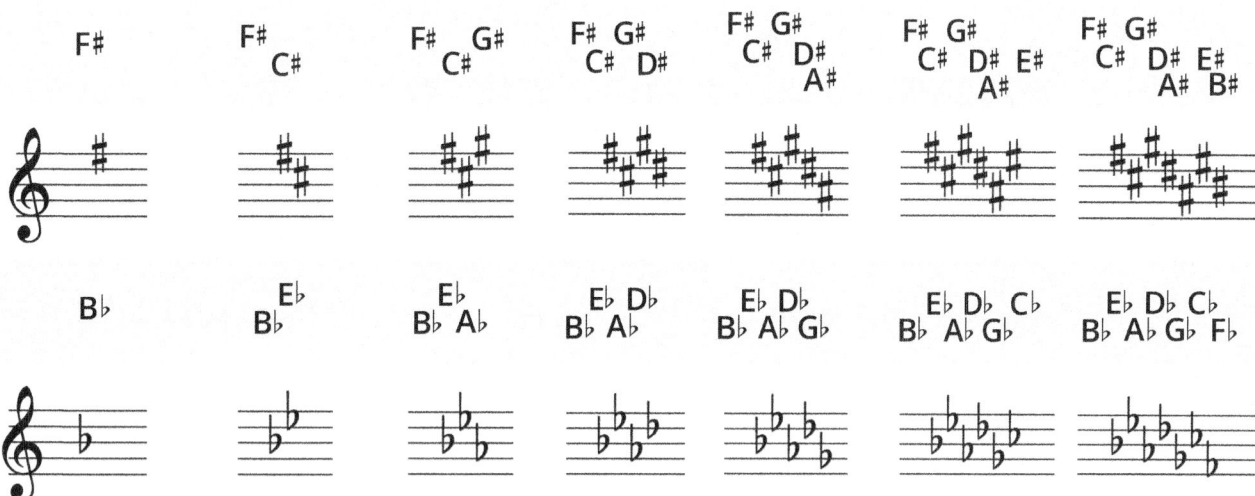

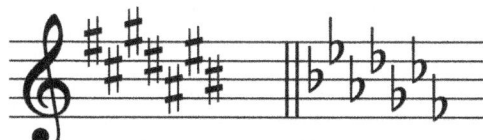

Treble Clef
Order of accidentals

The **order of sharps** is:
F♯, C♯, G♯, D♯, A♯, E♯, B♯.

Key signatures with two sharps (**D major** and **B minor**) have **F♯** and **C♯**, so C♯ is always the second sharp listed, and so on.

The order of flats is the reverse of the order of sharps.

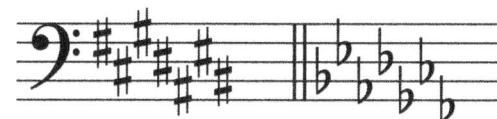

Bass Clef
Order of Accidentals

The **order of flats** is:
B♭, E♭, A♭, D♭, G♭, C♭, F♭.

Therefore the keys with only one flat (**F major** and **D minor**) have **B♭**; keys with two flats (B♭ major and G minor) have B♭ and E♭, and so on.

Major and Minor Scales

A scale always starts on the note it's named after. The order of sharps and flats, along with the arrangement of key signatures, follows a special pattern called the **Circle of Fifths** (see page 21).

Major Scale

To find the notes in a major scale, start on the root note and follow this pattern:
whole step, whole step, half step, whole step, whole step, whole step, half step.
This will bring you to the root note one octave higher than where you began and includes all the notes of the scale within that octave.

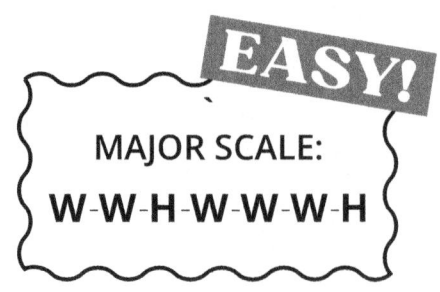

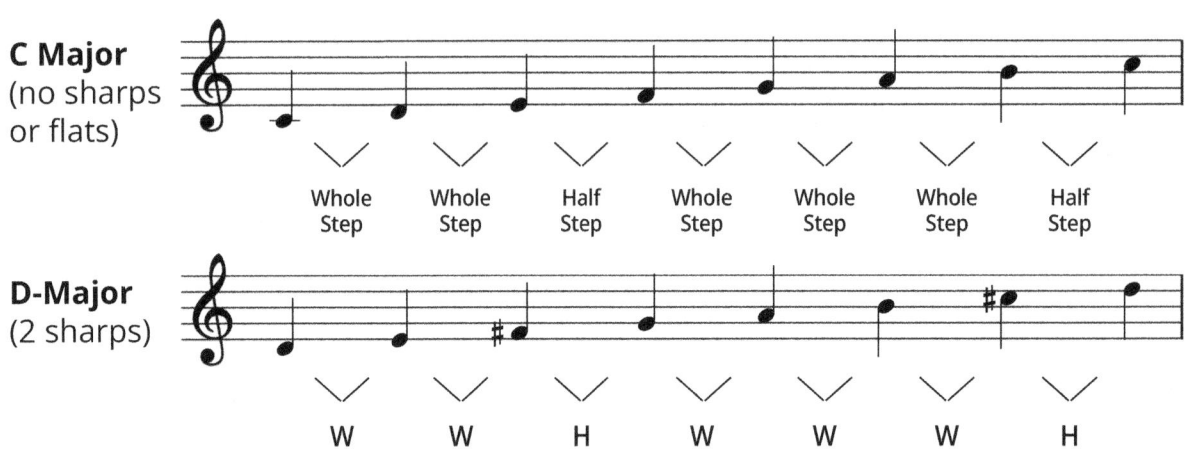

Minor Scale

To find the notes in a minor scale, start on the root note and follow this pattern:
whole step, half step, whole step, whole step, half step, whole step, whole step.
This will also lead you to the root note one octave higher than your starting point.

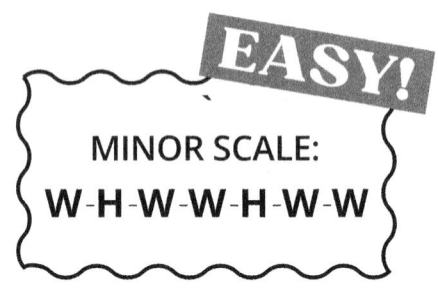

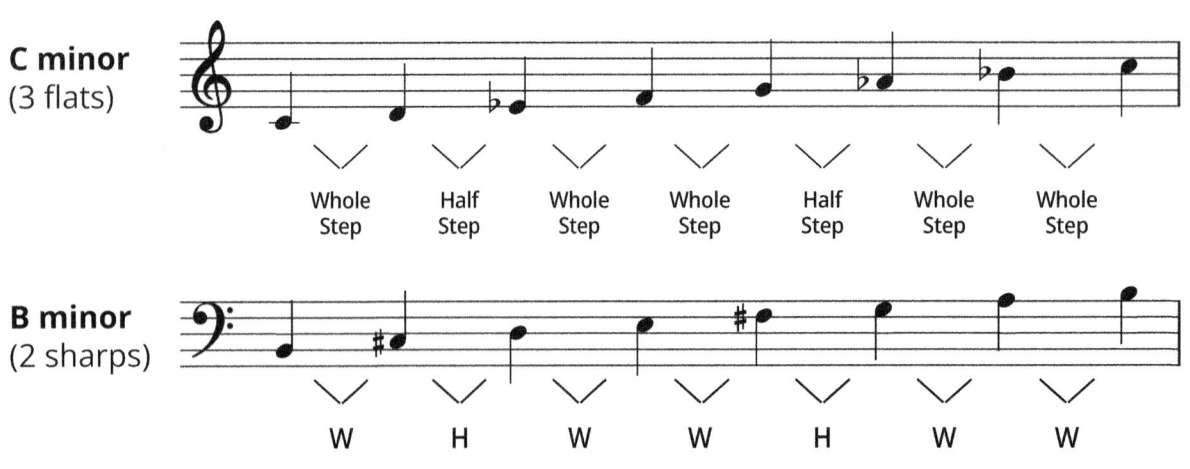

Key Signature Examples

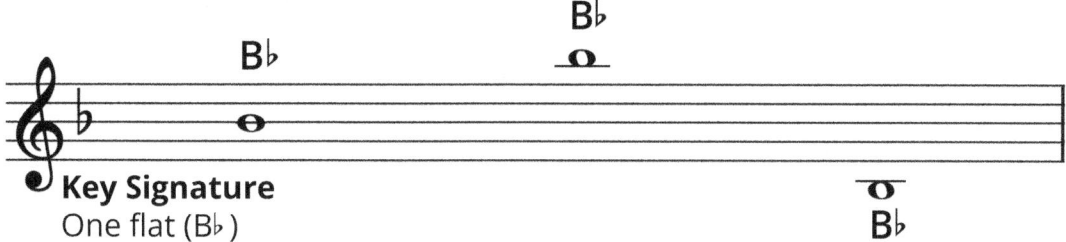

The key signature has a flat on the B line, which means every B note on the staff will have a flat as its accidental.

This makes sense when most of the B notes in the piece are intended to be flat—then it's added to the key signature. If it occurs only occasionally, the individual notes are marked with accidentals instead.

The key signature is placed directly after the clef on the staff. It may include several sharps on specific lines or spaces, or several flats, also placed on specific lines or spaces.
If there are no sharps or flats indicated after the clef symbol, the key signature means "all notes are natural."

The key signature lists all the sharps or flats used in the key of the music.

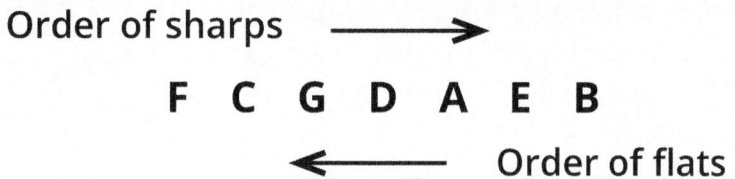

When a sharp (or flat) appears on a specific line or space in the key signature, all notes on that line or space are raised (or lowered), and all other notes with the same letter name in different octaves are also raised (or lowered).

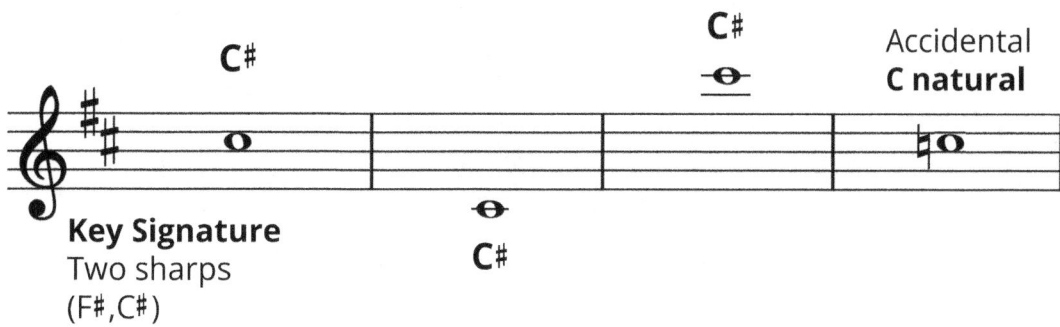

If a sharp appears in the C space on the staff, all C notes become C-sharp (C#) unless an accidental changes them.

The clef and the key signature indicate which note is found on each line and space of the staff. The clef tells you the letter name of the note (C, D, E, etc.), while the key signature indicates whether the note is sharp, flat, or natural.

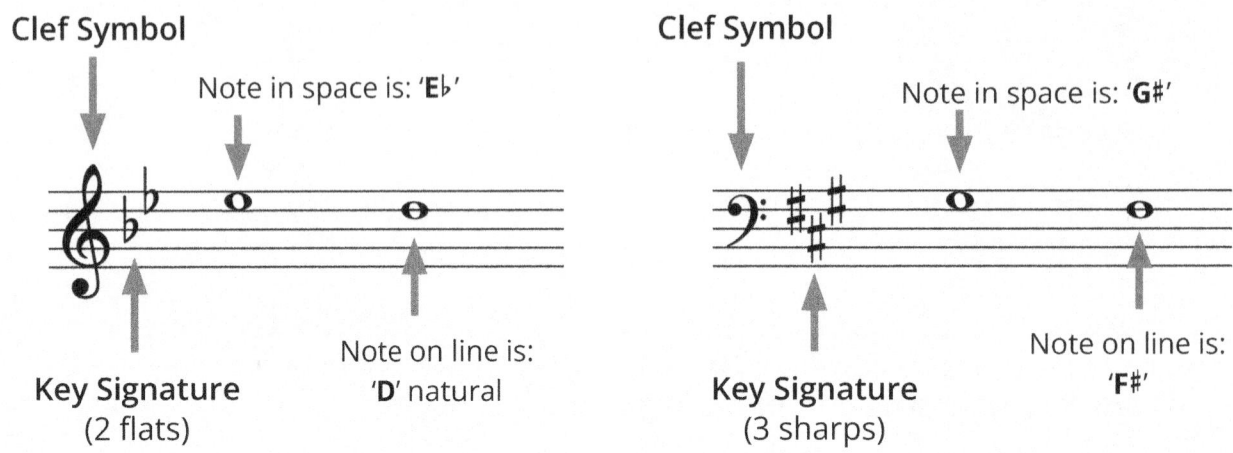

The key signature lists all the sharps or flats used in the key in which the piece is written, avoiding the need to write accidentals repeatedly throughout the music (unless other accidentals appear to change it).

Major and Minor Scales

Relative keys: They share the same number of accidentals and the same notes but start on different tones. For example, **A minor** is the relative minor of **C major**.

Enharmonic scales: They have different key signatures yet use the same notes in the same order. For example, **B major** and **C-flat major** are considered enharmonic scales.

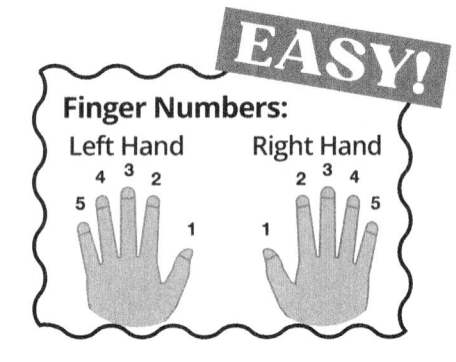

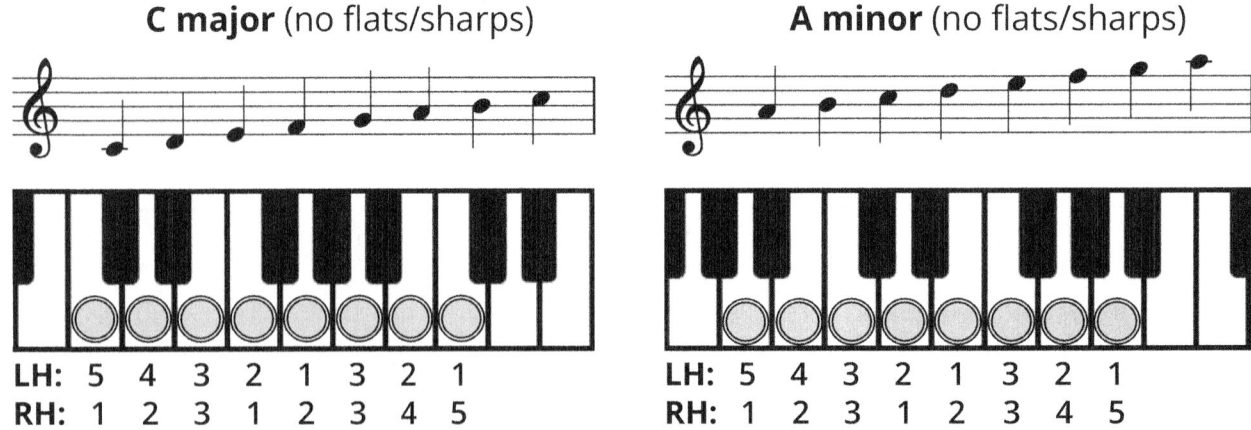

C major and A minor start on different notes but share the same key signature.

G major (one sharp)

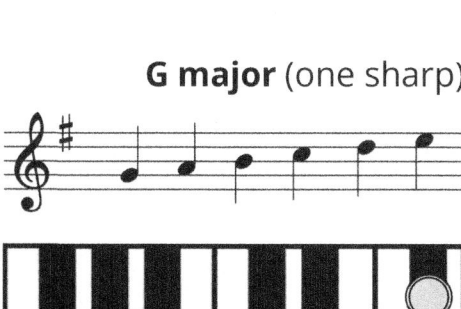

LH: 5 4 3 2 1 3 2 1
RH: 1 2 3 1 2 3 4 5

D major (two sharps)

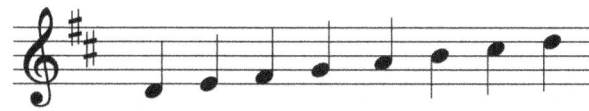
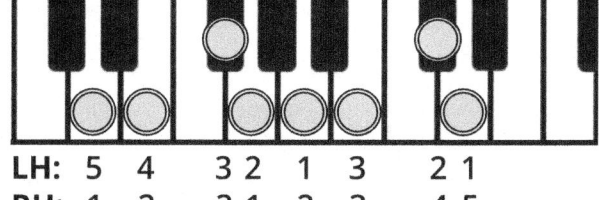

LH: 5 4 3 2 1 3 2 1
RH: 1 2 3 1 2 3 4 5

A major (three sharps)

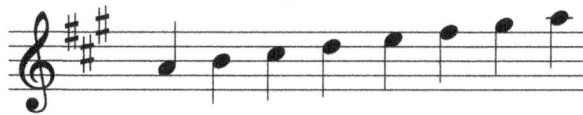
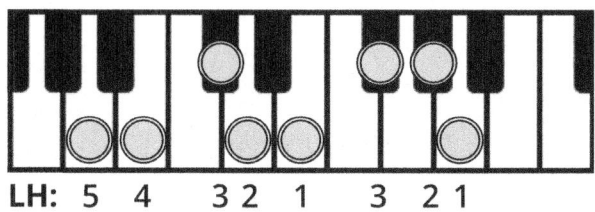

LH: 5 4 3 2 1 3 2 1
RH: 1 2 3 1 2 3 4 5

E major (four sharps)

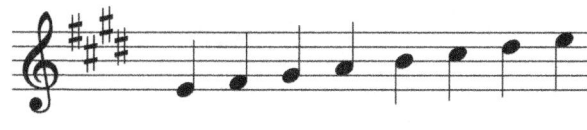
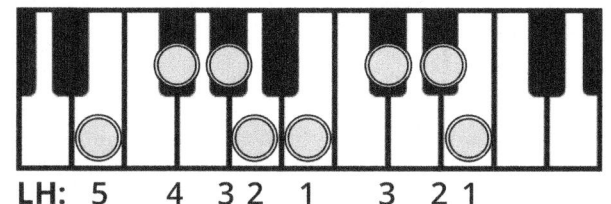

LH: 5 4 3 2 1 3 2 1
RH: 1 2 3 1 2 3 4 5

E minor (one sharp)

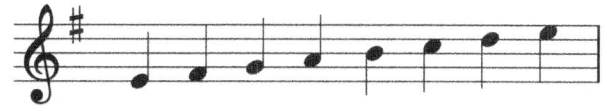
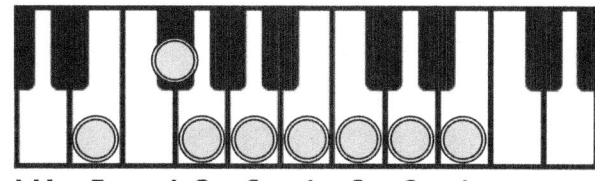

LH: 5 4 3 2 1 3 2 1
RH: 1 2 3 1 2 3 4 5

B minor (two sharps)

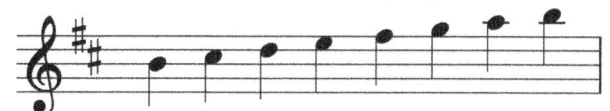
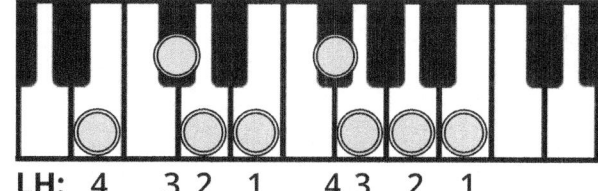

LH: 4 3 2 1 4 3 2 1
RH: 1 2 3 1 2 3 4 5

F# minor (three sharps)

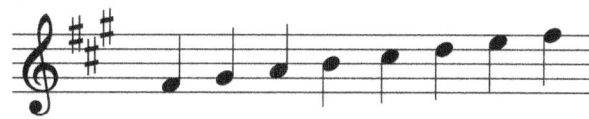
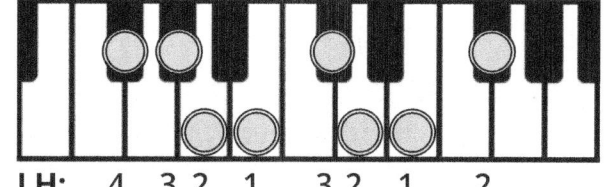

LH: 4 3 2 1 3 2 1 2
RH: 2 3 1 2 3 1 2 3

C# minor (four sharps)

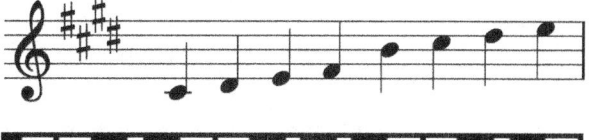
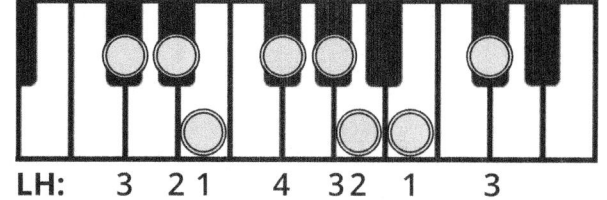

LH: 3 2 1 4 3 2 1 3
RH: 2 3 1 2 3 1 2 3

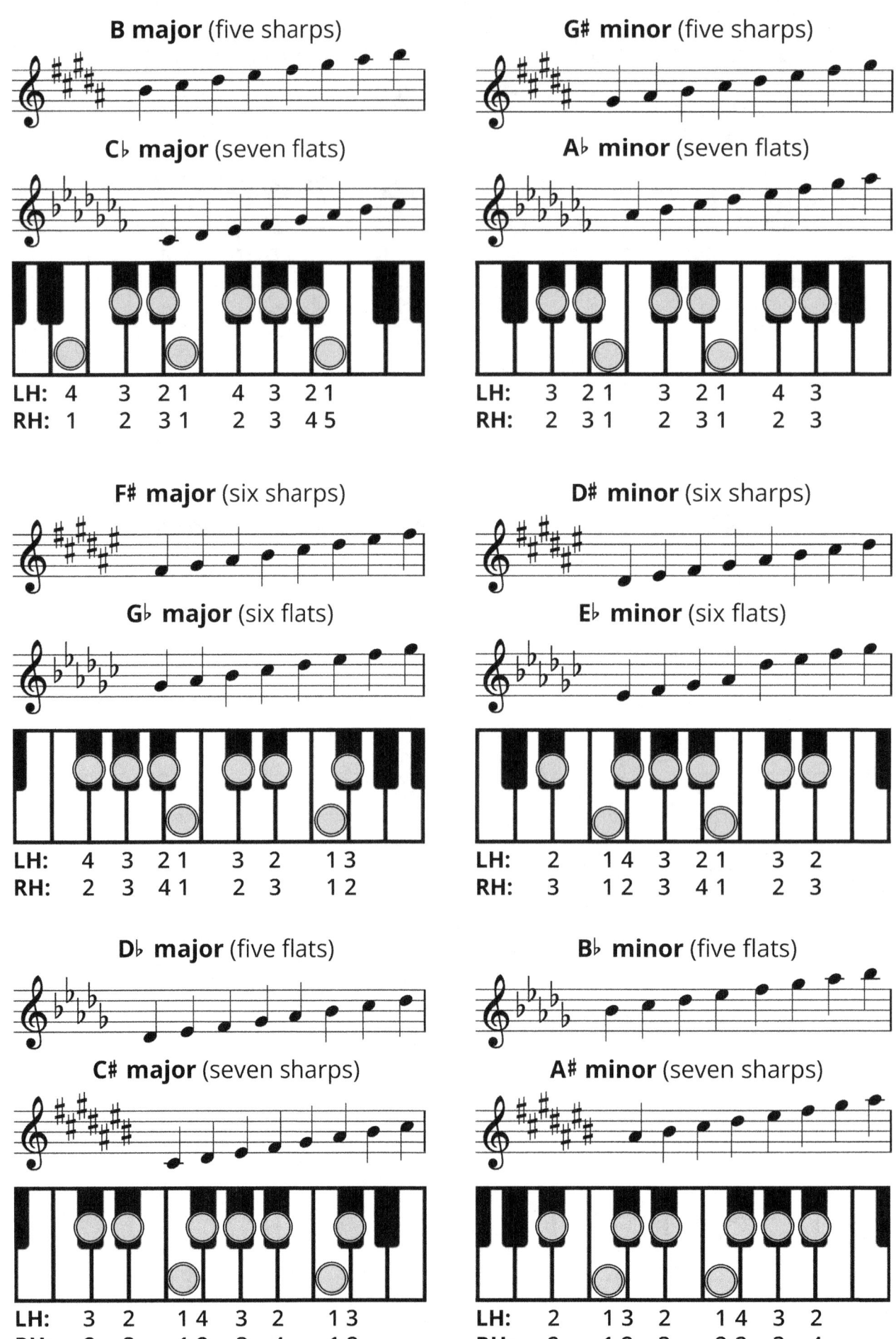

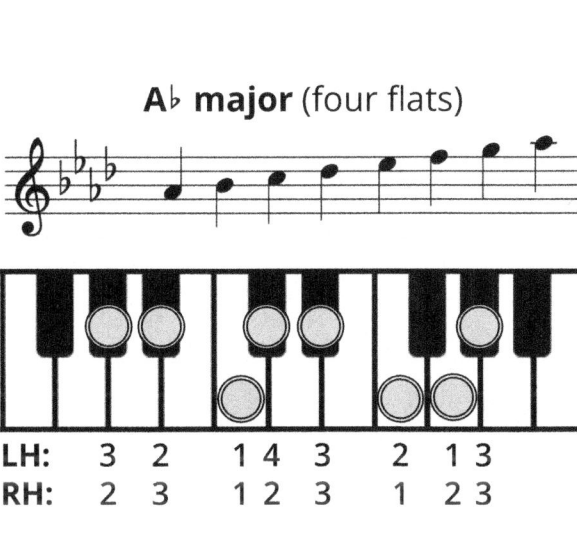

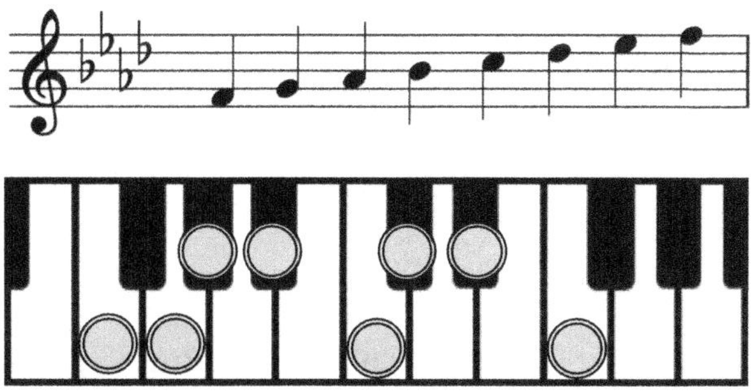

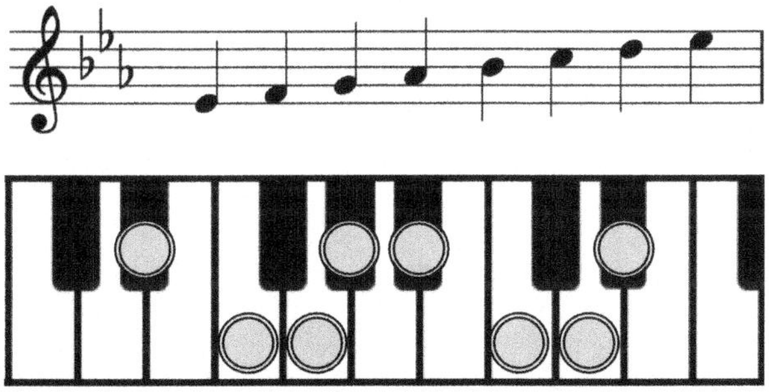

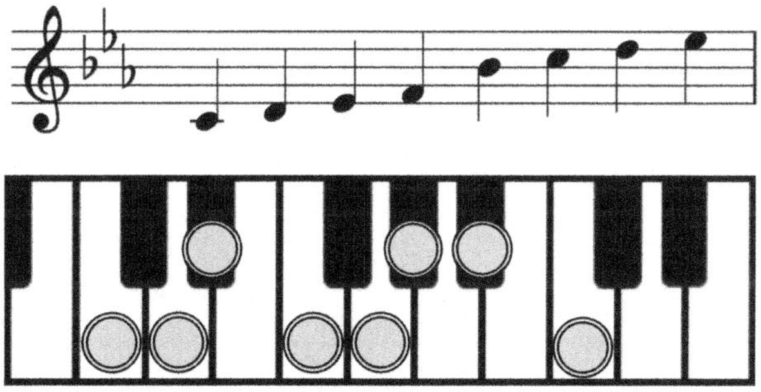

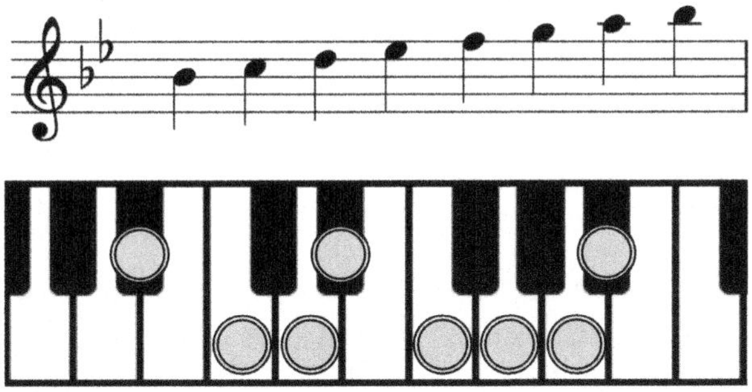

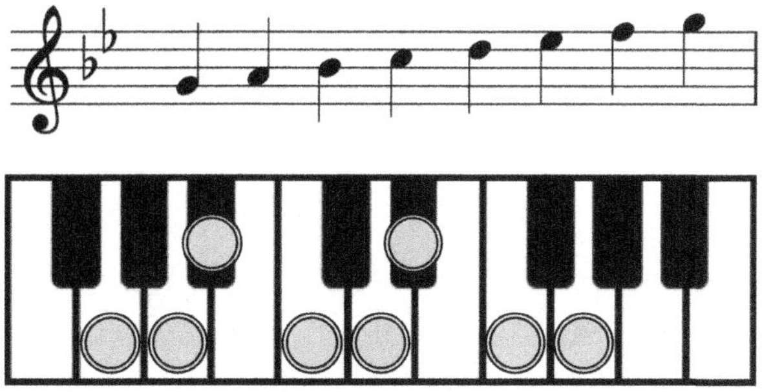

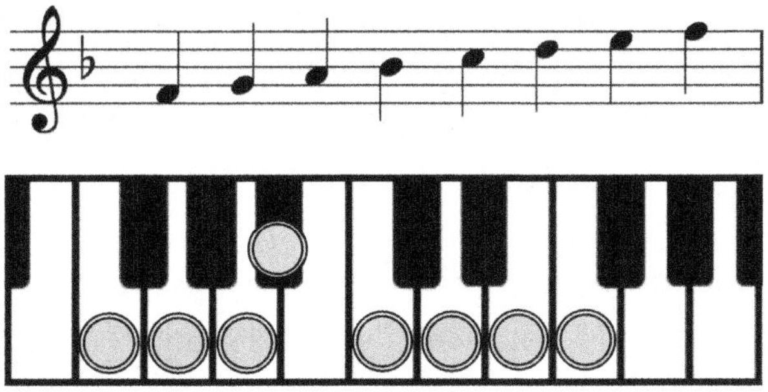

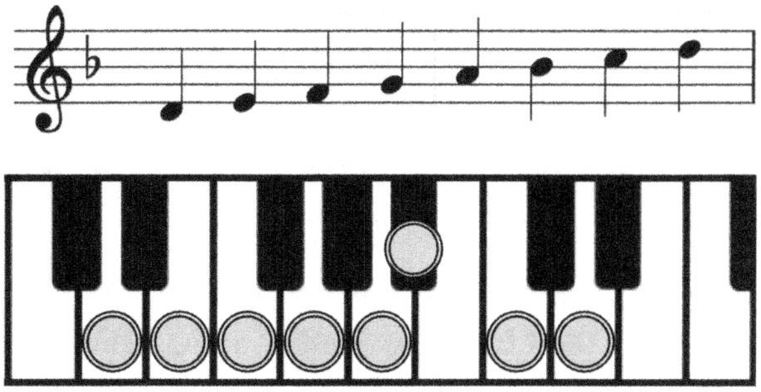

Cirlce of Fifths

The **Circle of Fifths** is a helpful visual tool that shows how all the 15 major and minor keys are related. Every major key has a matching relative minor key that shares the same notes.

- If you move **clockwise**, each step adds one sharp (♯).
- If you move **counterclockwise**, each step adds one flat (♭).
- The Circle represents key signatures up to **seven sharps or flats**.

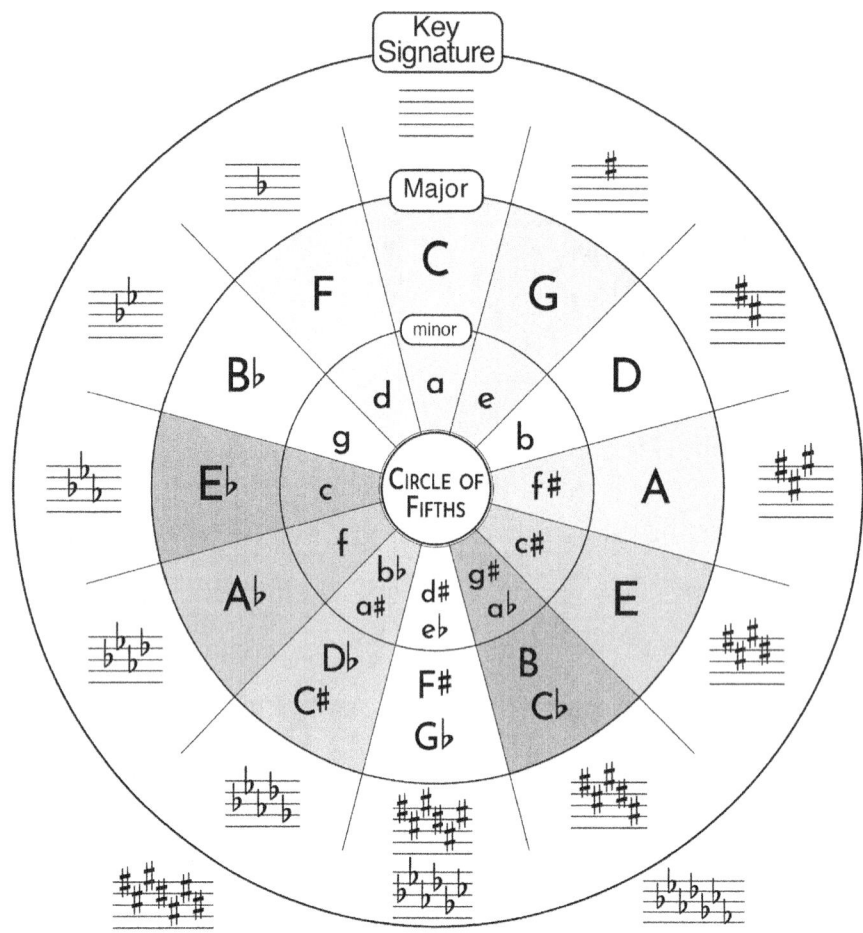

Keys that are in the **same slice of the circle** use the exact same notes, just starting from a different note. For example, **C♯ minor** is the relative minor of **E major**—they use the same notes but begin in different places. Minor scales always start **three half steps (a minor third)** below their relative major.

Keys shown in the **same box** are called **enharmonic scales**. That means they sound exactly the same and use the same notes, but are written differently. For example, **G♯ minor** and **A♭ minor** sound the same, even though their names look different.

Chapter 2
Natural Notes

Instructions with Example

Practice in the Grand Staff

Practice on Keyboard & Staff

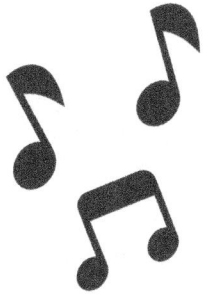

Natural Note Exercises

Two easy steps to complete the exercises:

1. **Clef:** Look at the clef, which tells you what note belongs to each line or space on the staff. In the bass clef, the note **A** is in the lowest space. In the treble clef, the note **A** is one whole step higher.

2. **Name:** Find the note name. Ask yourself: Which line or space is the note on? Then, figure out the name of that note.

EASY!

Notes to remember:
F - G (Clefs)
A - A (Spaces)
Middle C (between Clefs)

The diagram serves as a guide for the exercises:

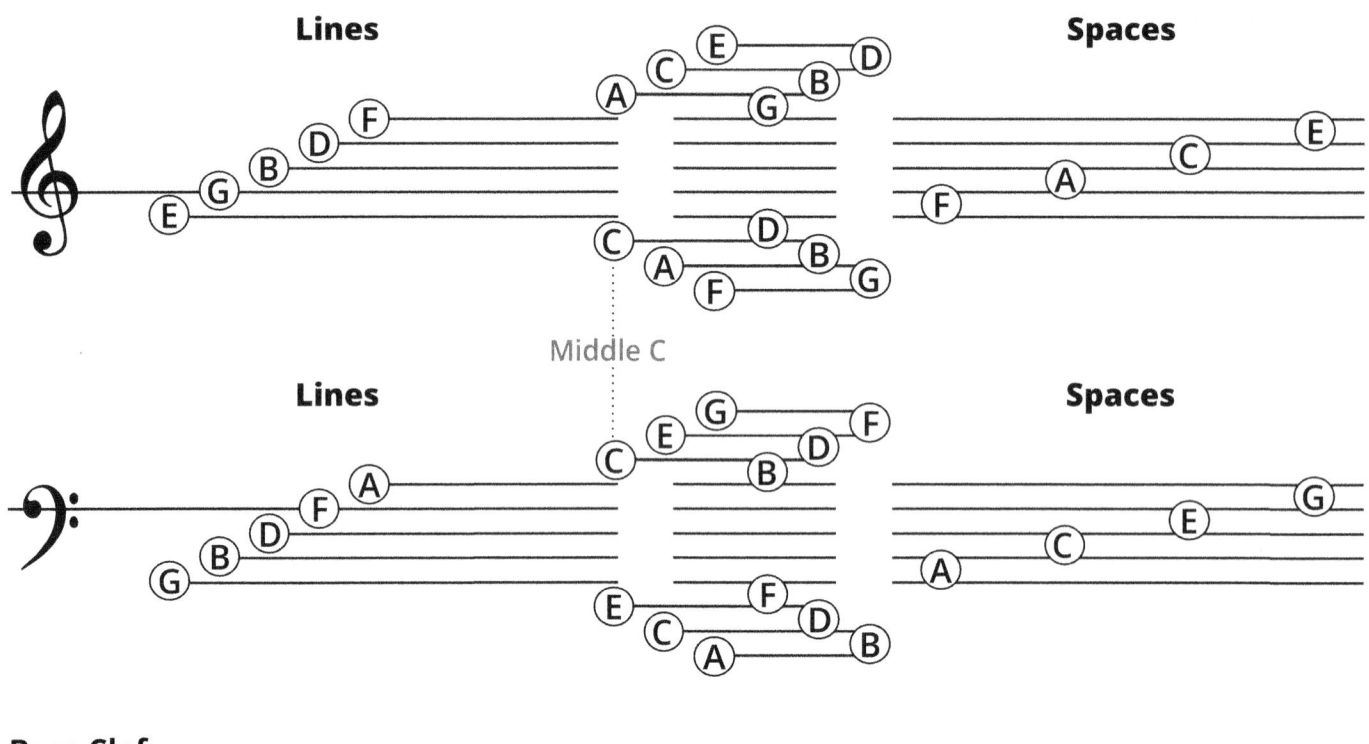

Bass Clef

Example:

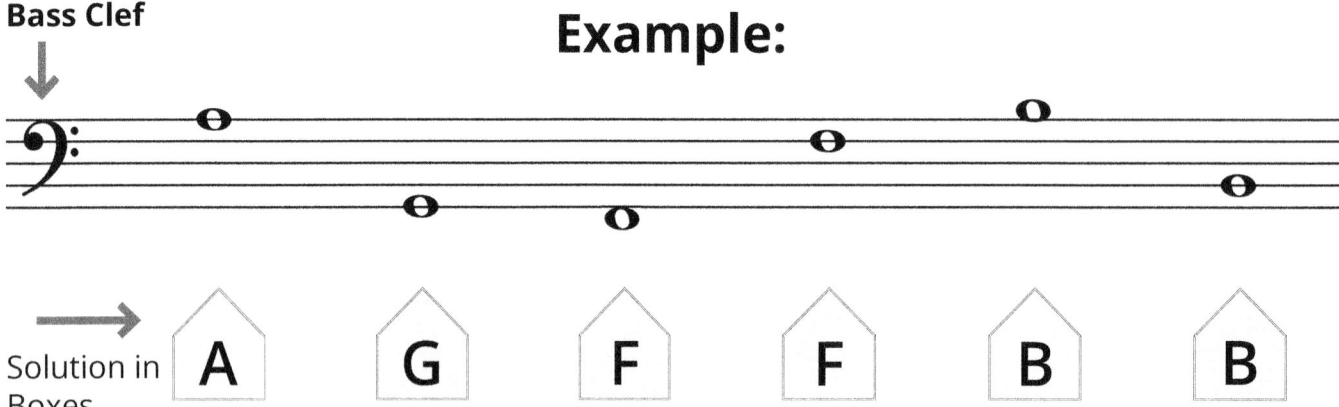

Solution in Boxes: A G F F B B

- 23 -

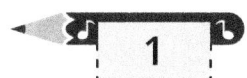

1. Clef   2. Note Name

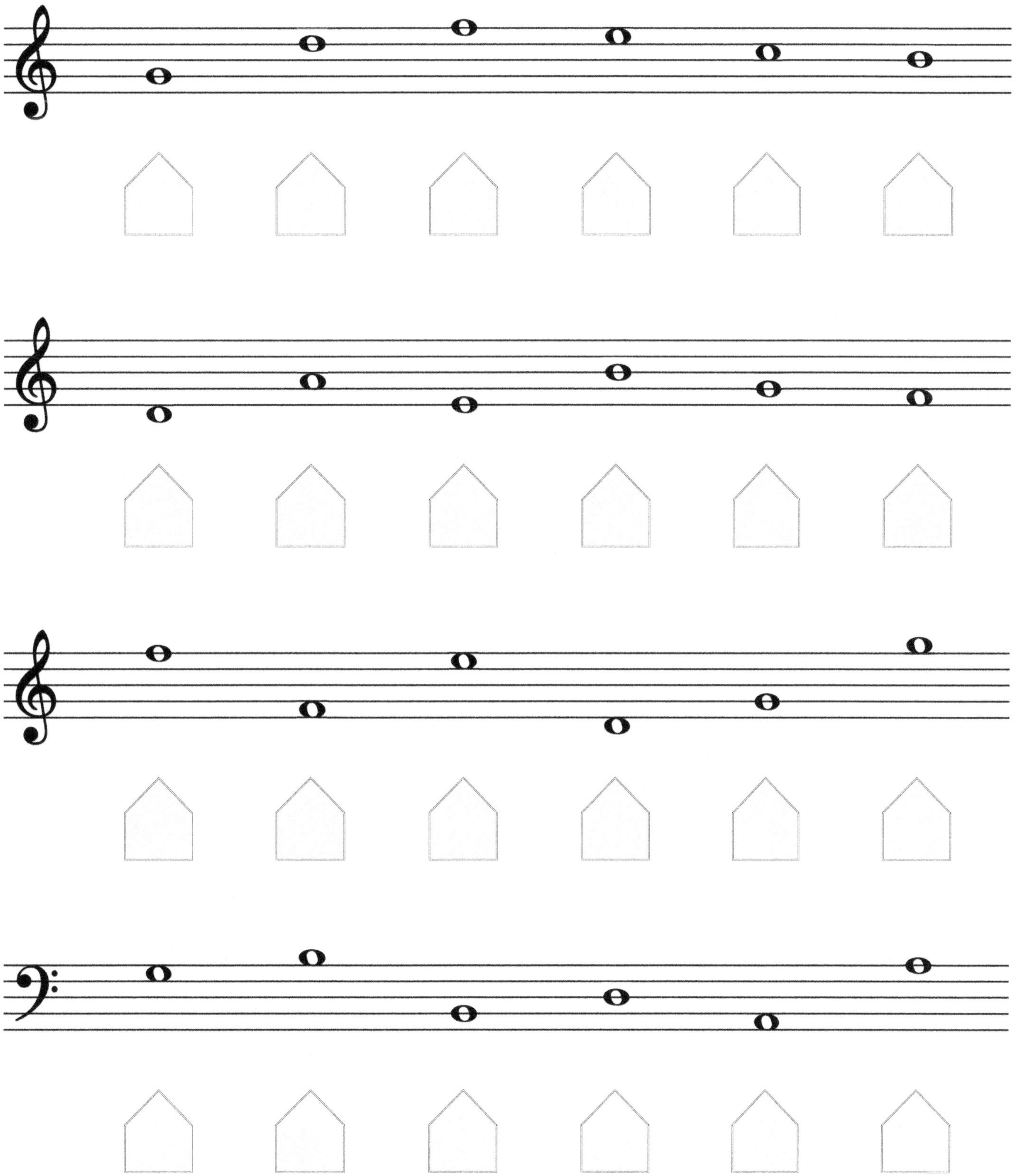

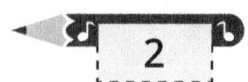

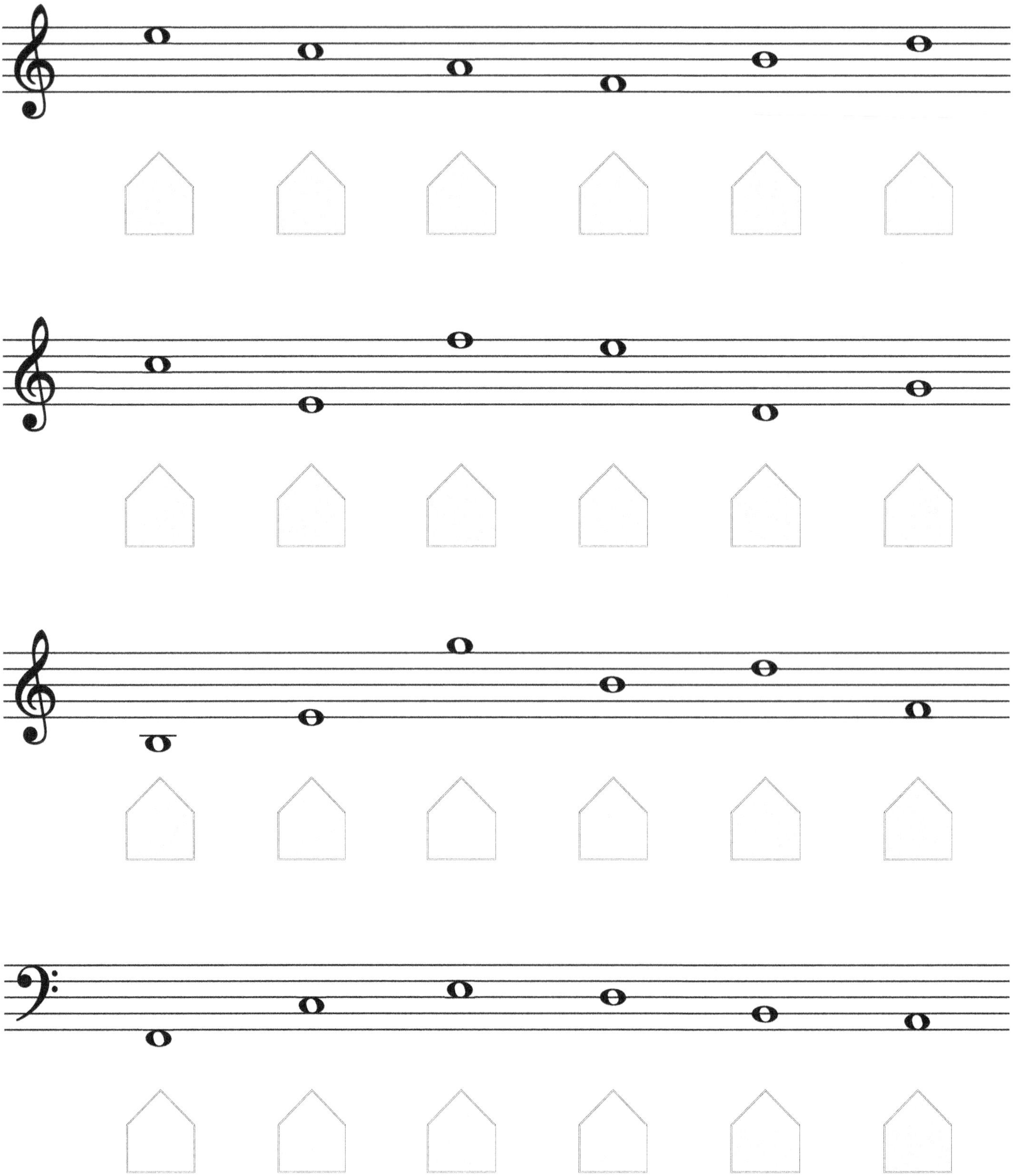

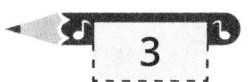

𝄞 1. Clef 𝄞 2. Note Name

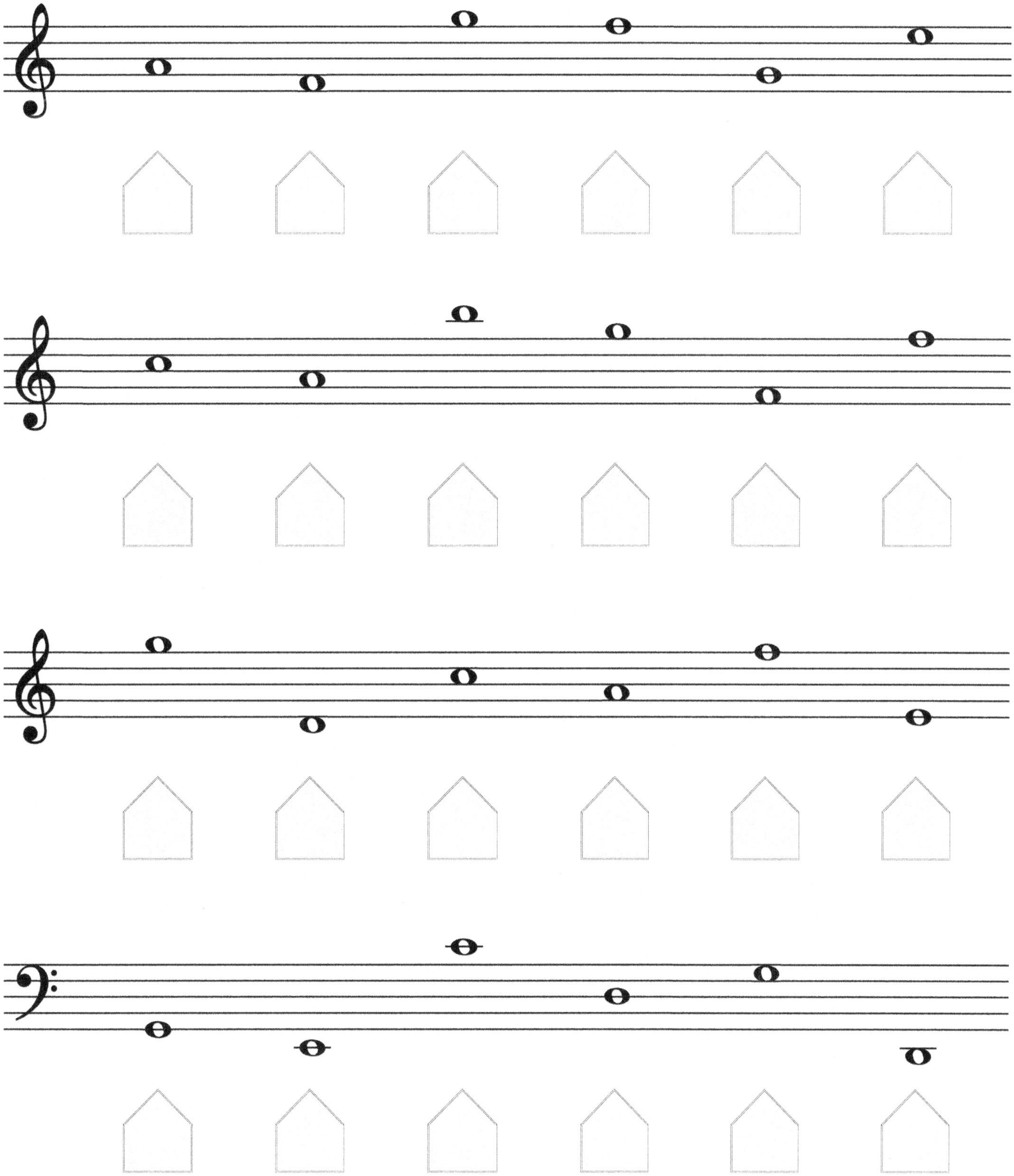

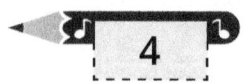

1. Clef 𝄞 2. Note Name

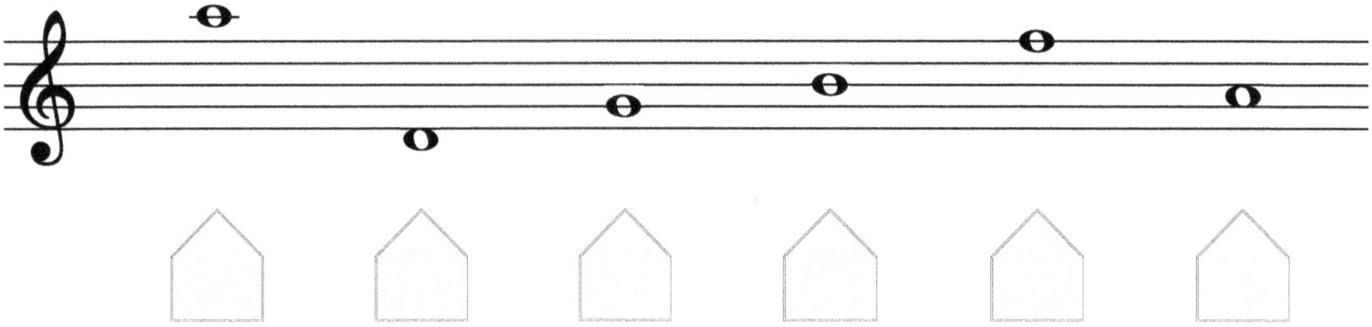

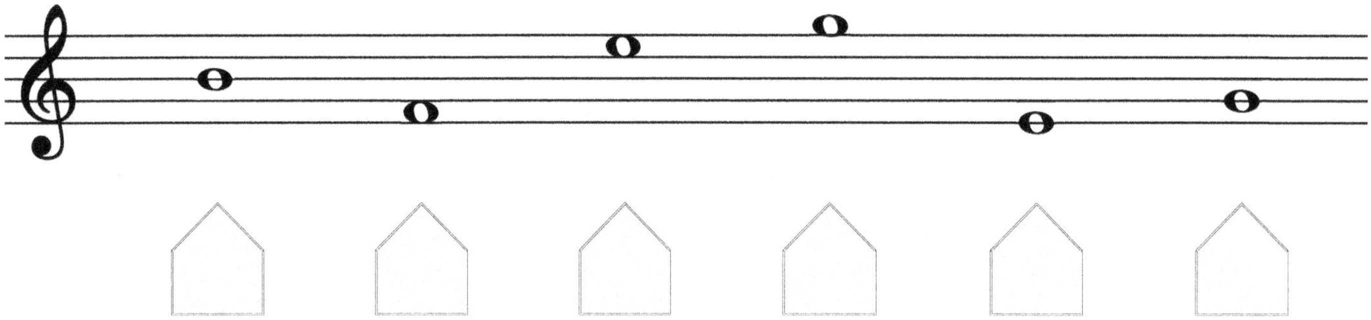

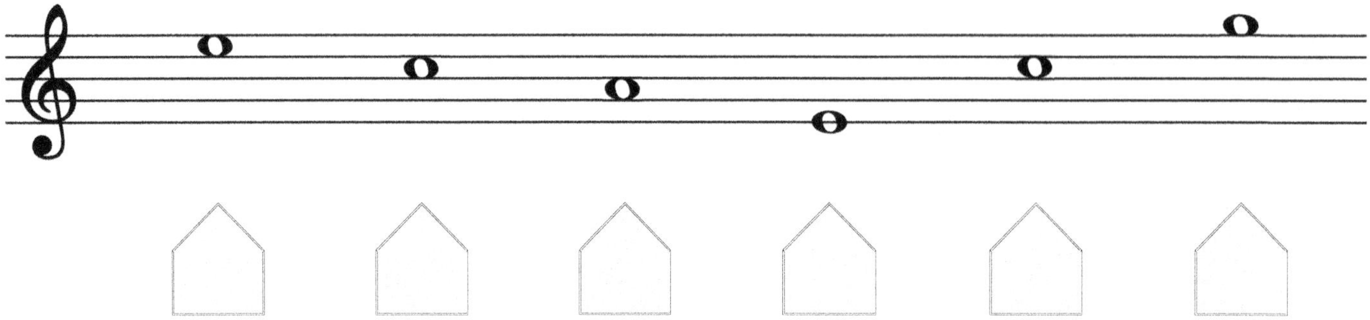

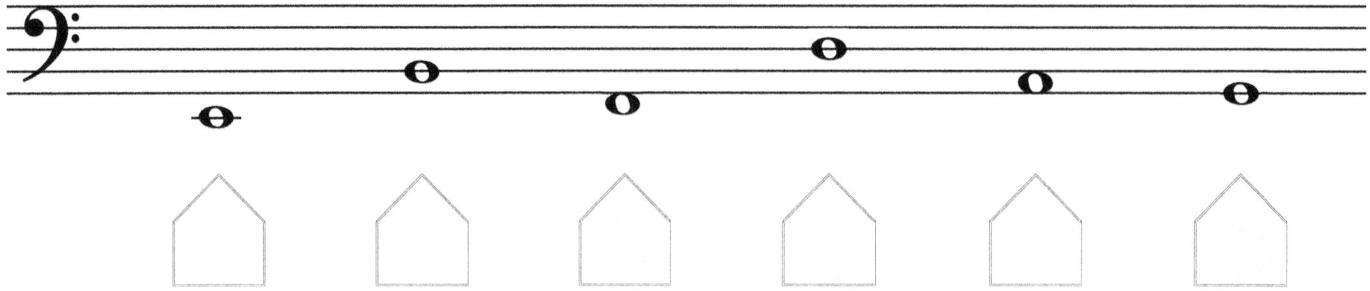

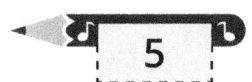

1. Clef
2. Note Name

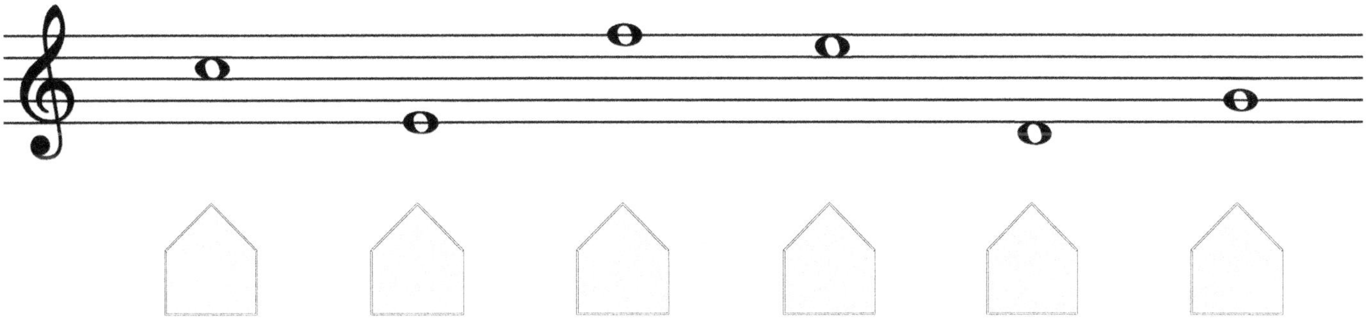

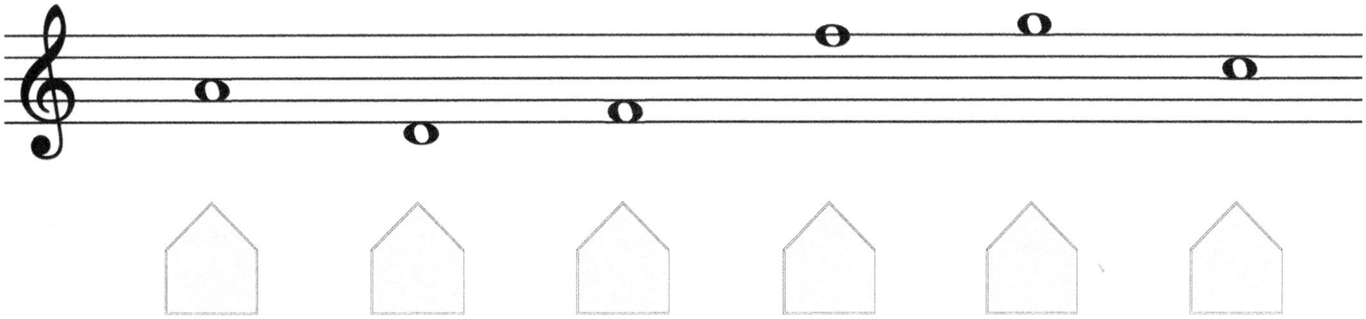

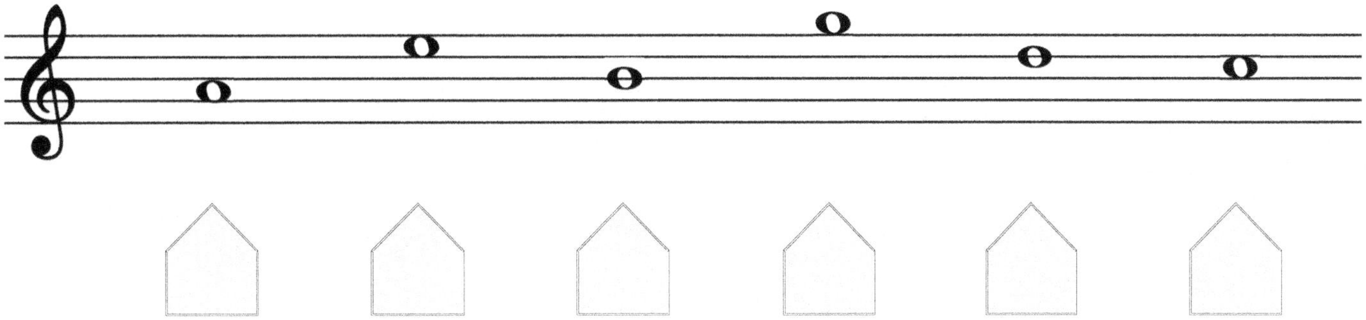

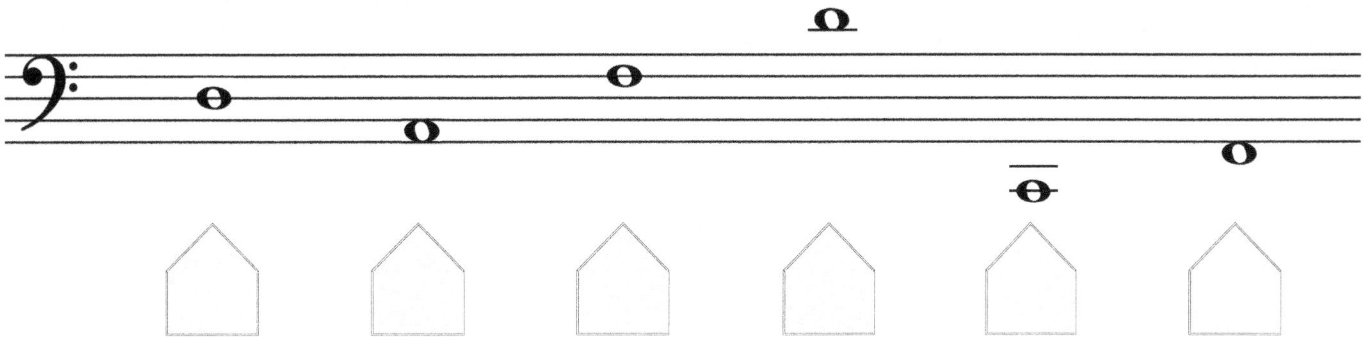

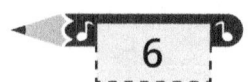

1. Clef 𝄞   2. Note Name

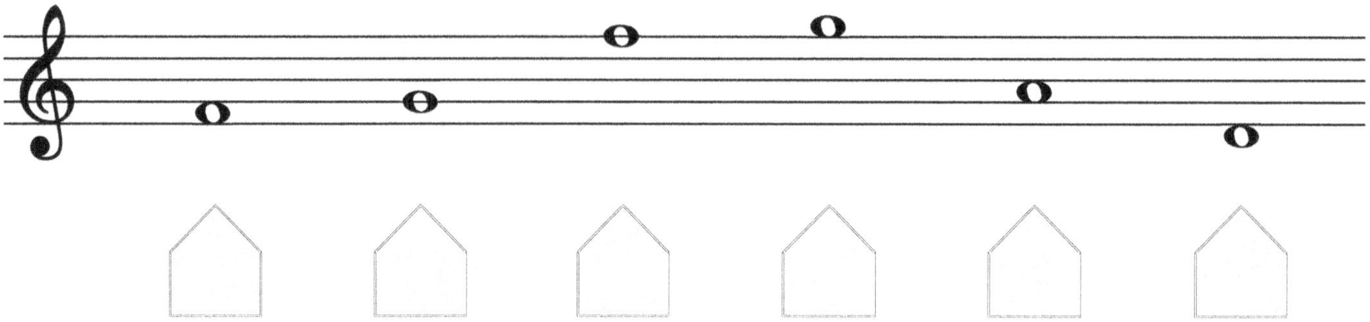

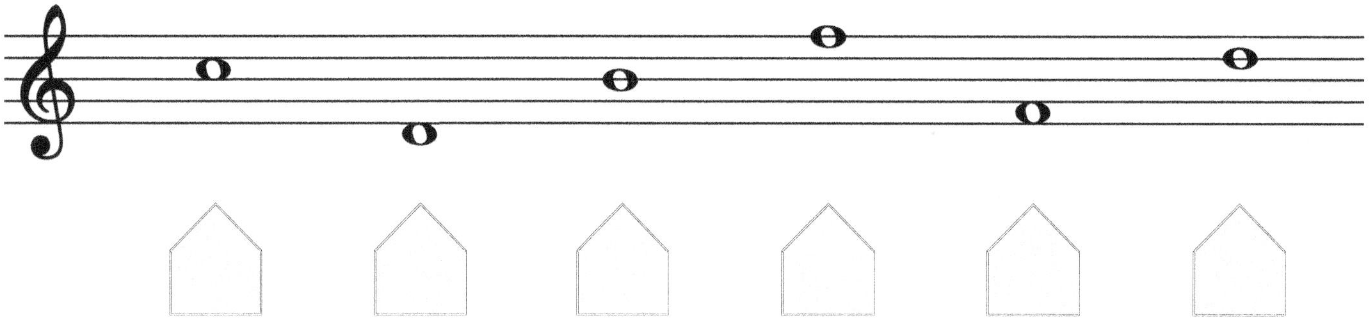

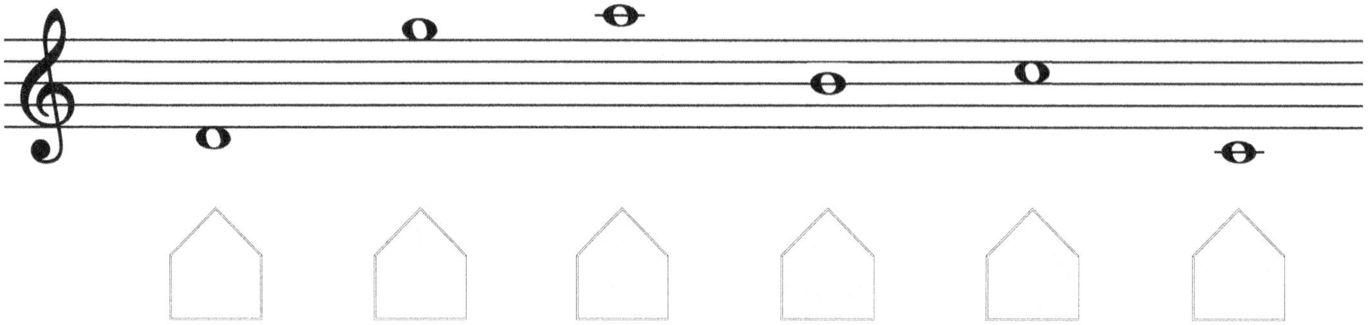

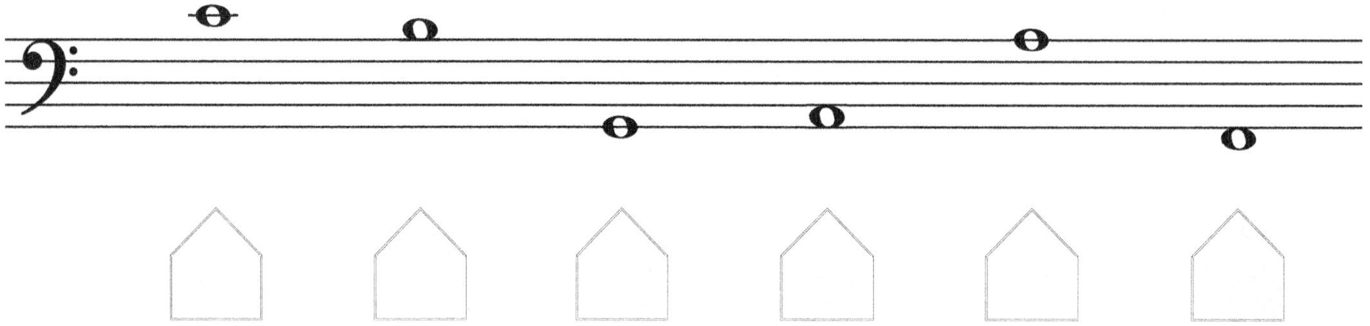

1. Clef
2. Note Name

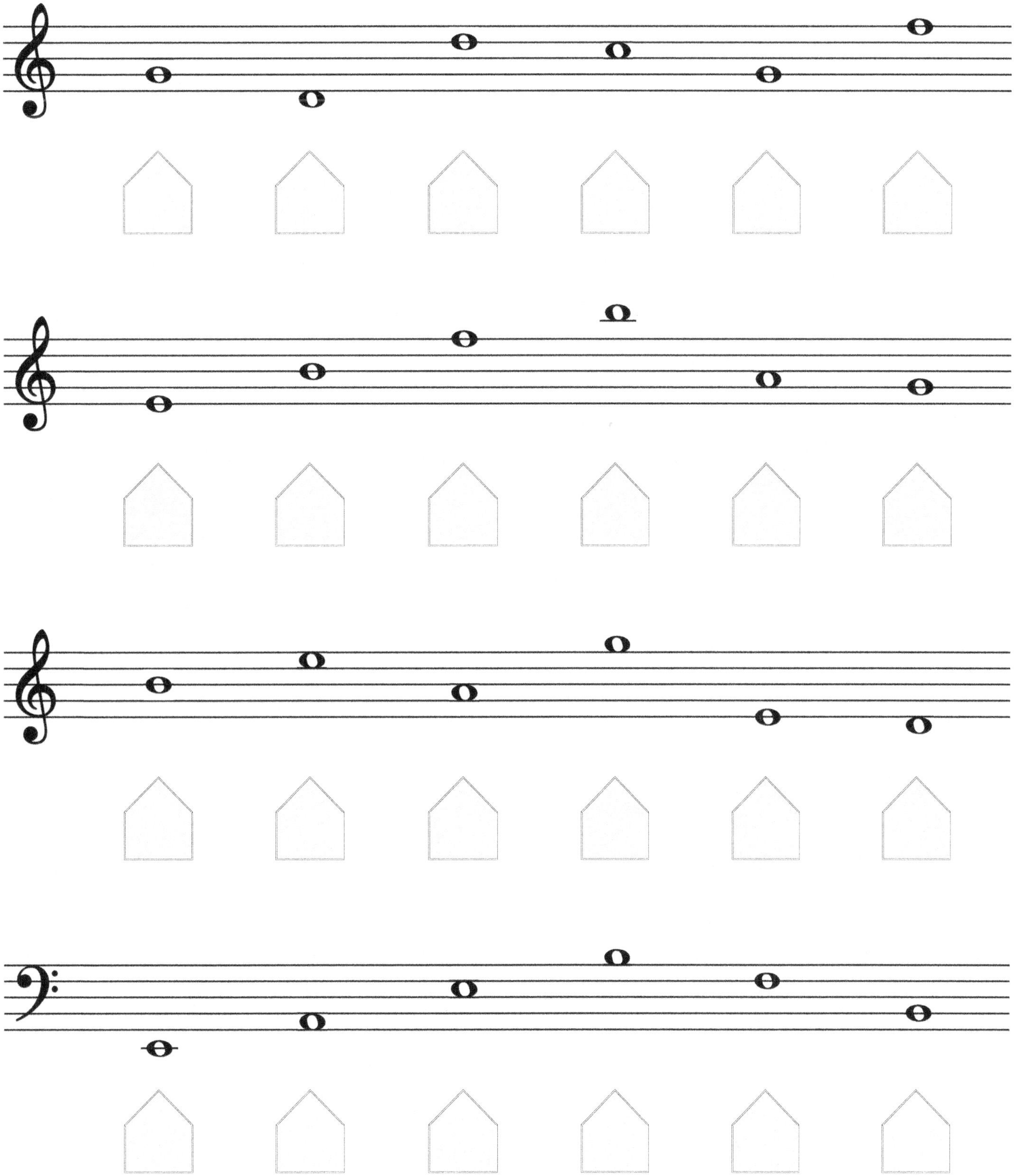

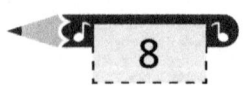

1. Clef 𝄞   2. Note Name 𝅝

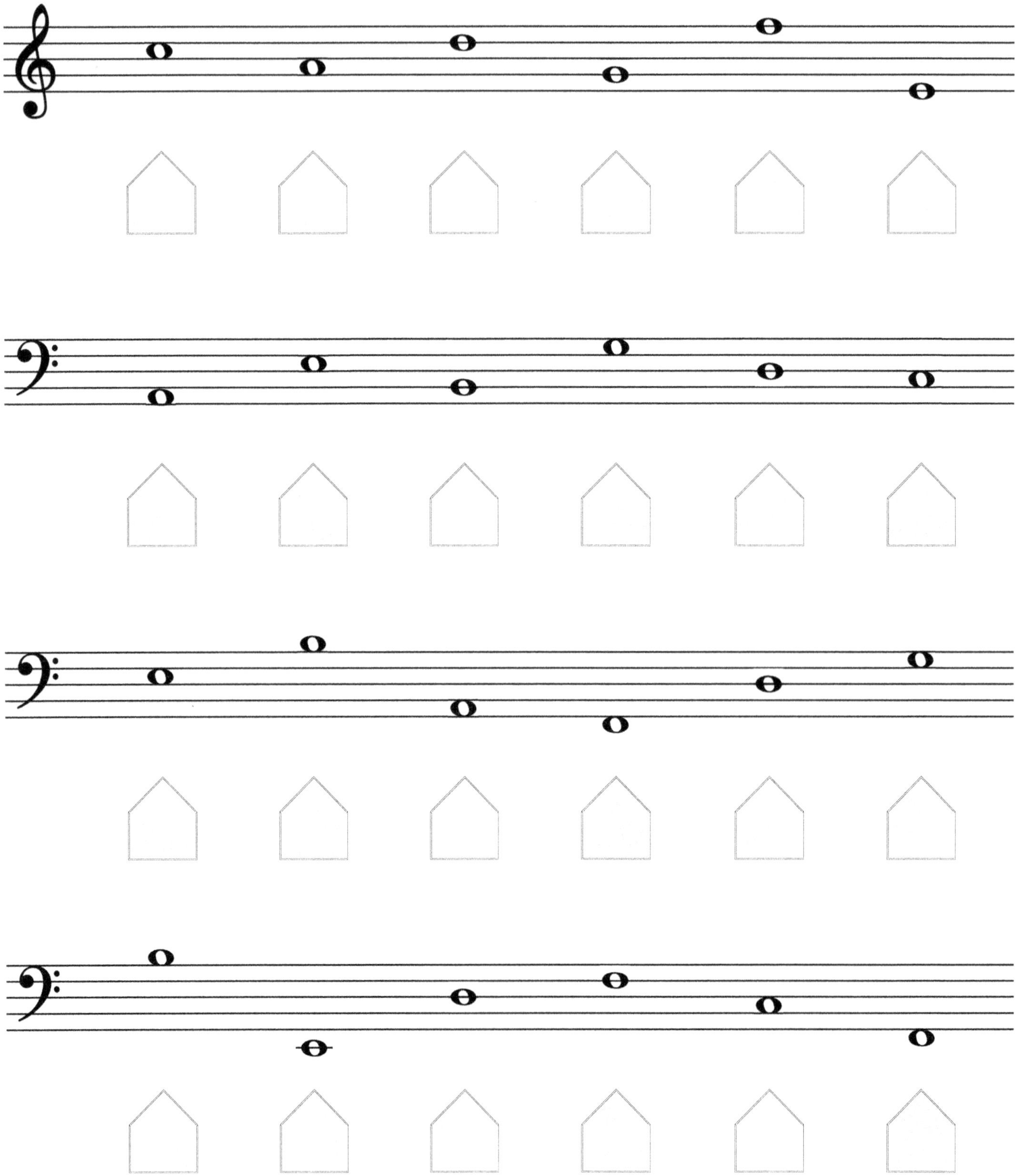

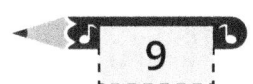

𝄞 1. Clef ═o═ 2. Note Name

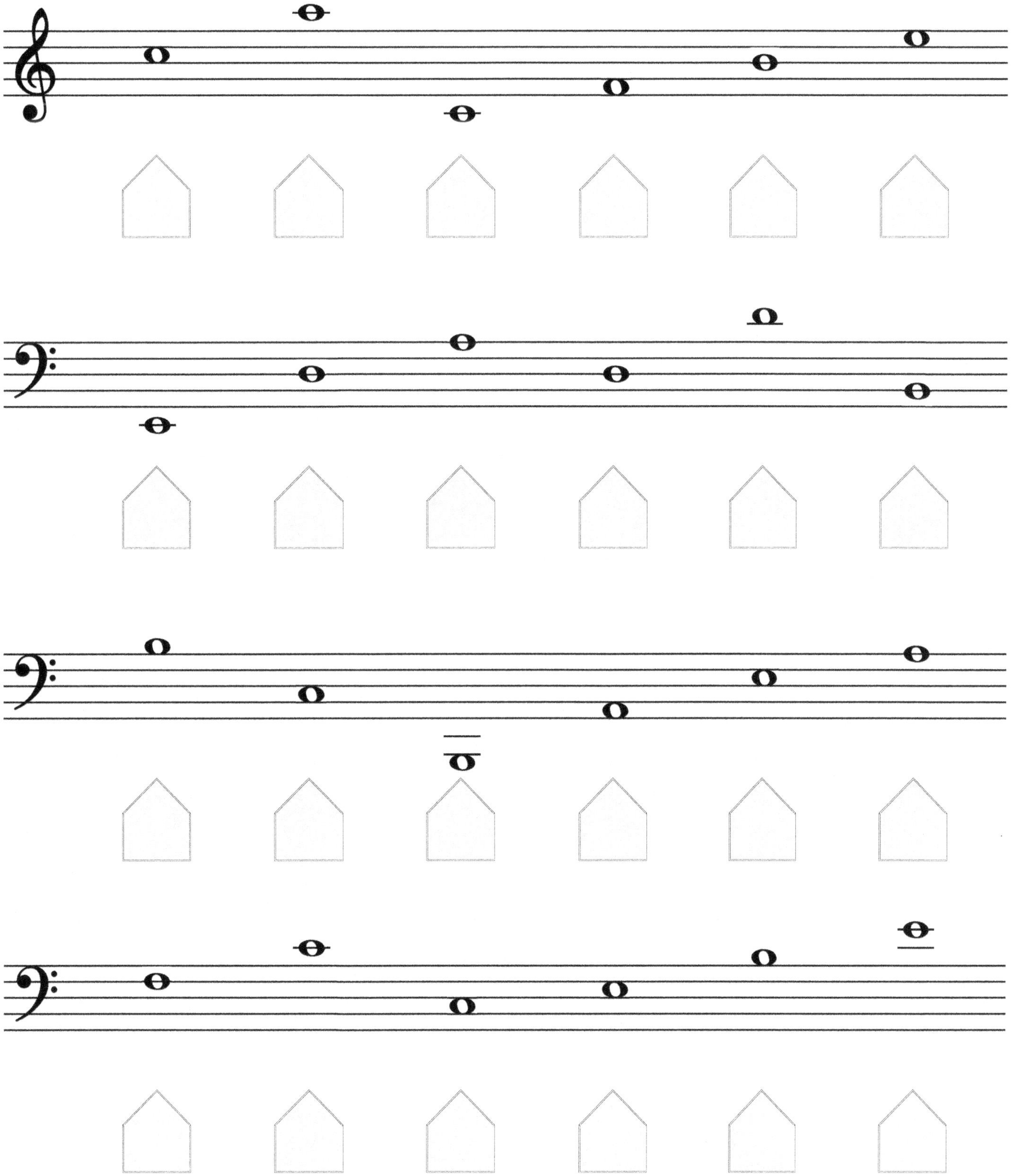

1. Clef 𝄞   2. Note Name

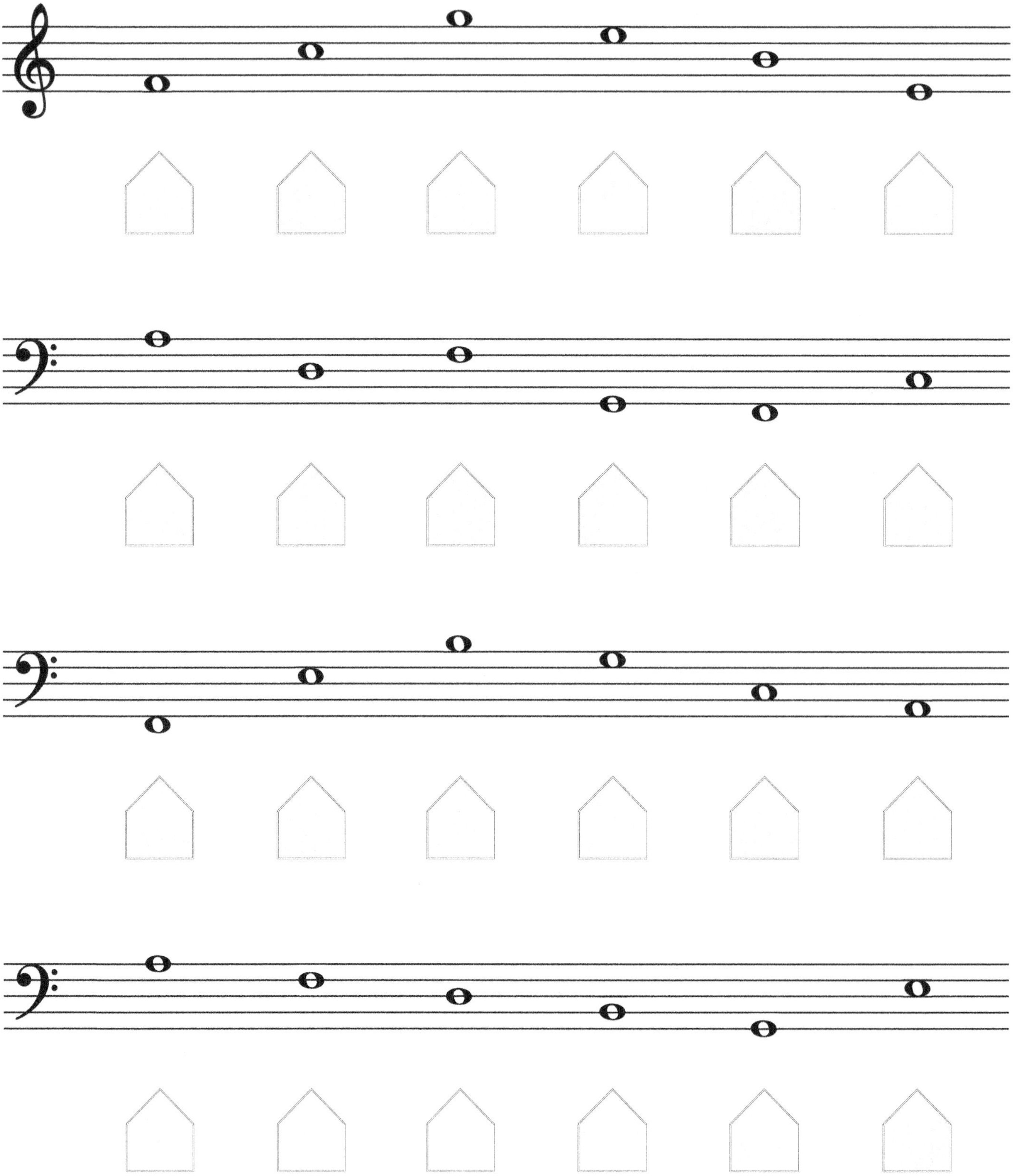

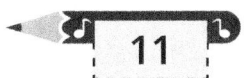

    🎼 1.   𝄞 2.
       Clef   Note Name

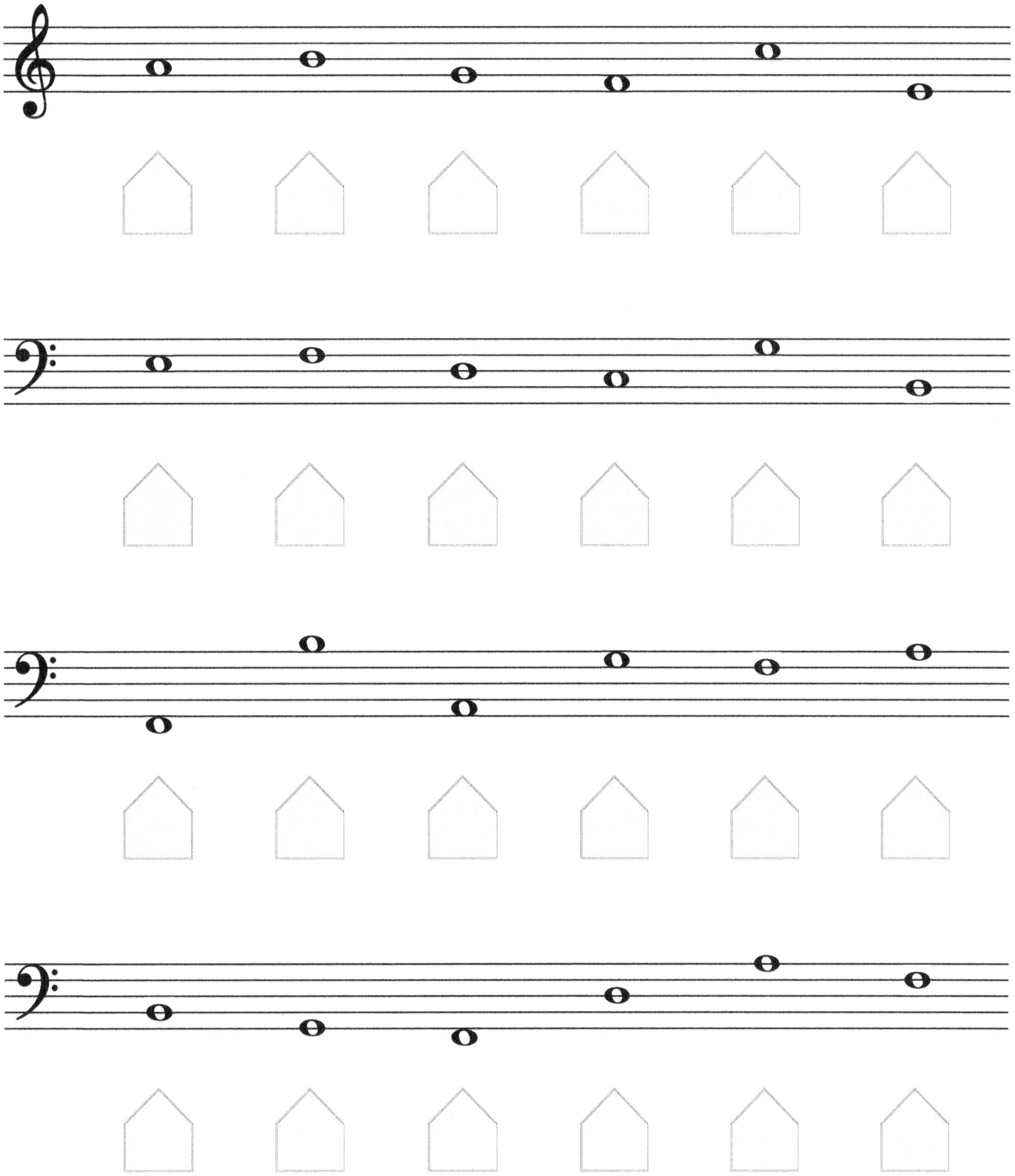

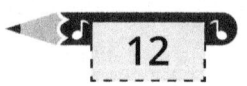

1. Clef
2. Note Name

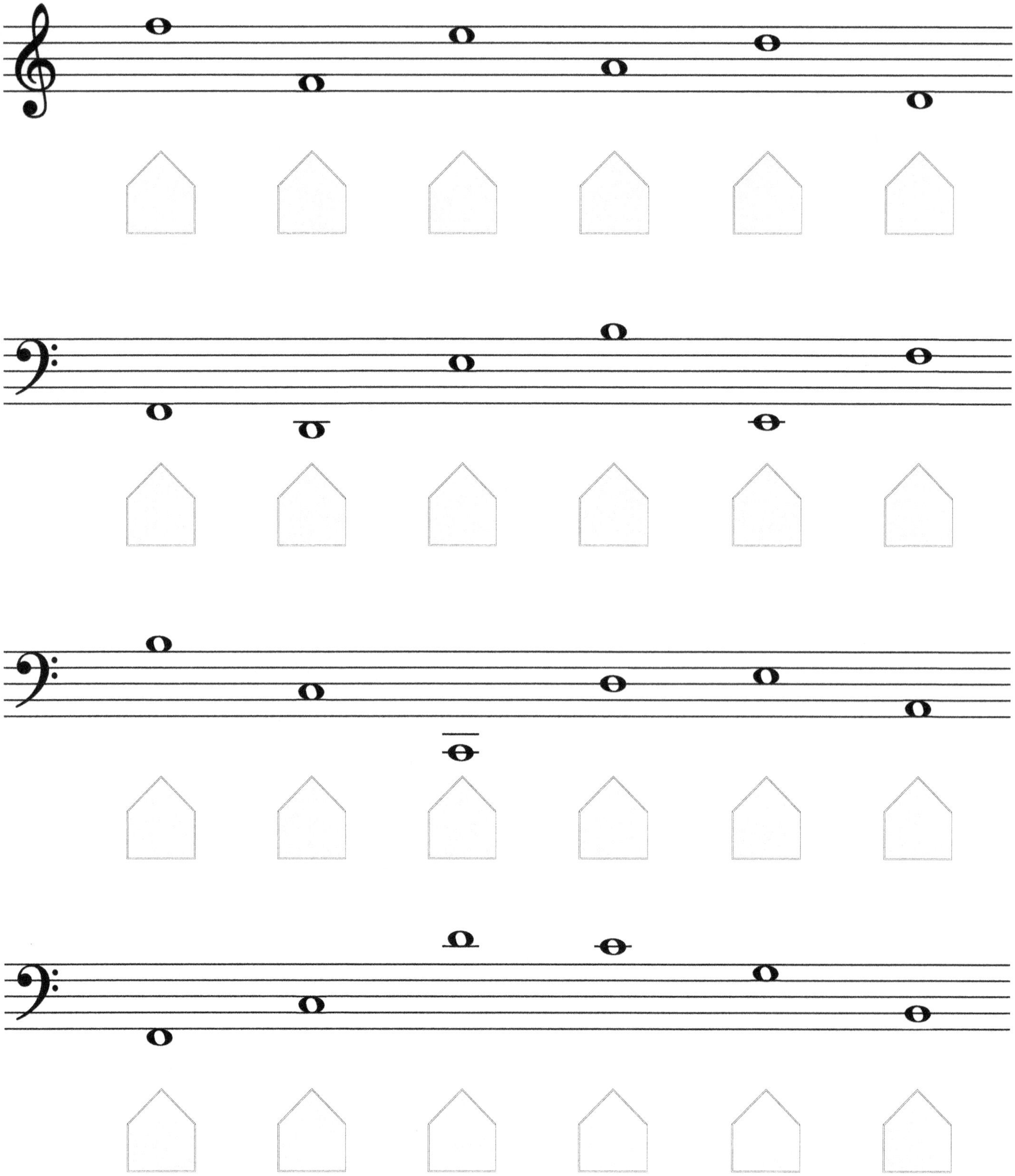

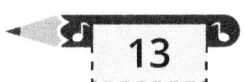

𝄞 1. Clef   𝅝 2. Note Name

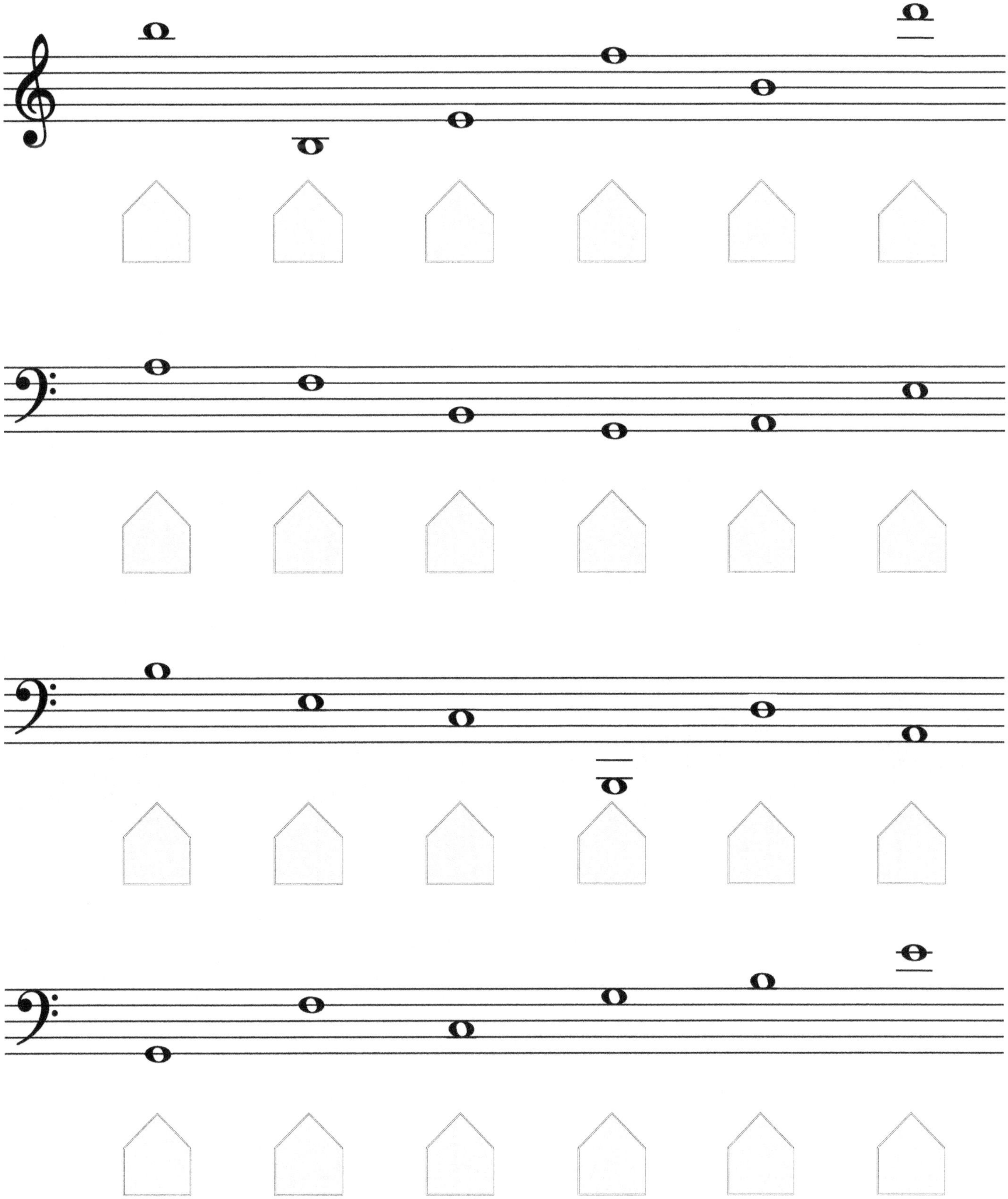

Keyboard Exercises

Three simple steps to complete the exercises:

1. 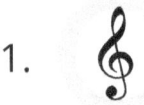 **Clef:** Look at the clef, which tells you what note belongs to each line or space on the staff. In the bass clef, the note **A** is in the lowest space. In the treble clef, the note **A** is one whole step higher.

2. 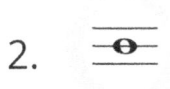 **Name:** Find the note name. Ask yourself: Which line or space is the note on? Then, figure out the name of that note.

3. 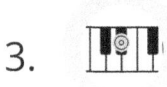 **Keyboard:** Look at the keyboard section and figure out which key goes with the note from the staff. Each keyboard diagram shows a group of **2 or 3 black keys** to help you find your way more easily.

The diagram is a helpful guide for the exercises:

Tip: Use the groups of two and three black keys as landmarks; they make it much easier to find your place on the piano!

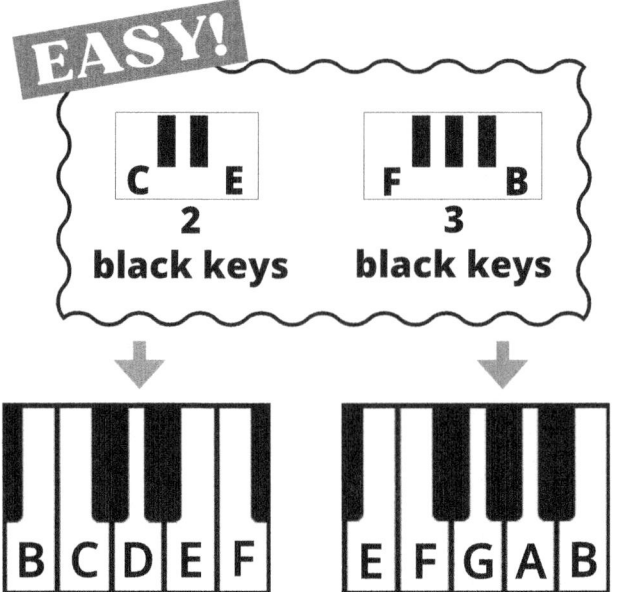

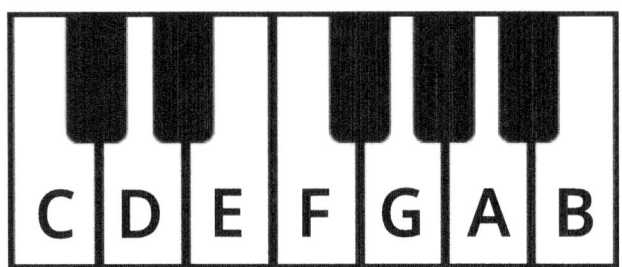

Example:

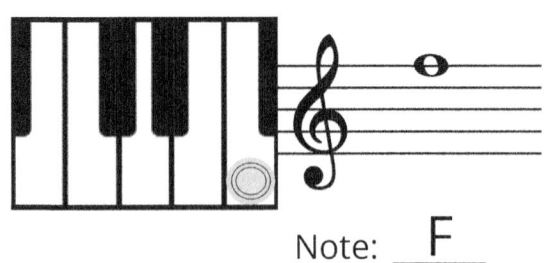

Note: __F__

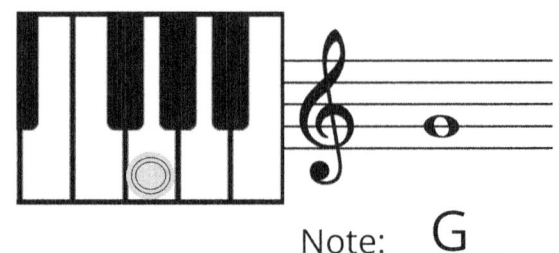

Note: __G__

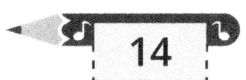

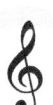 1. Clef 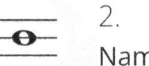 2. Name 3. Keyboard

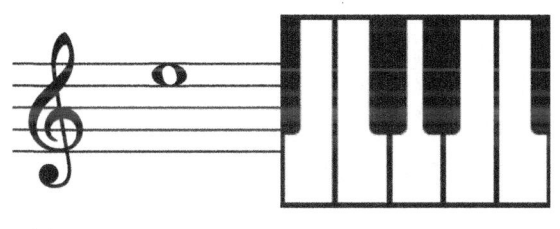

Note: _____

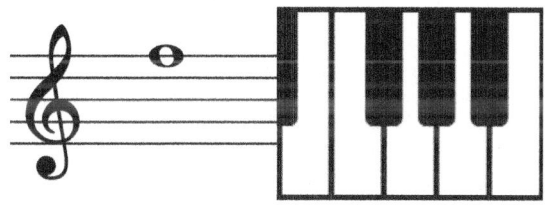

Note: _____

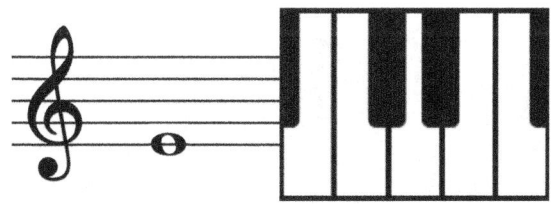

Note: _____

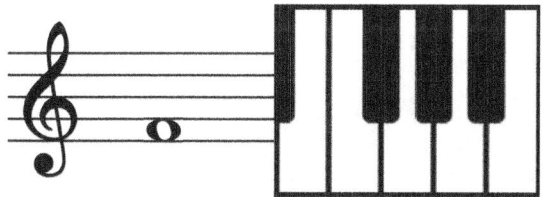

Note: _____

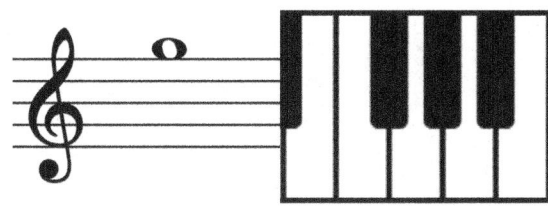

Note: _____

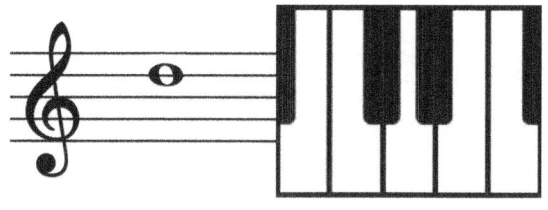

Note: _____

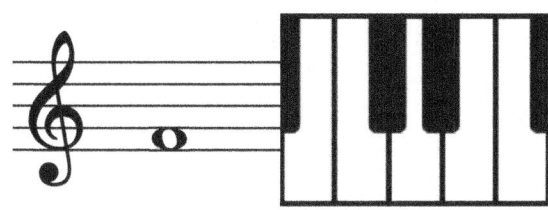

Note: _____

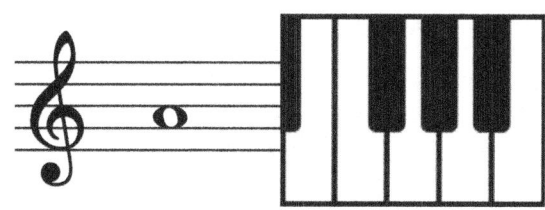

Note: _____

1. Clef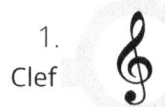
2. Name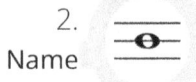
3. Keyboard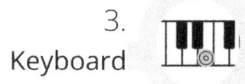

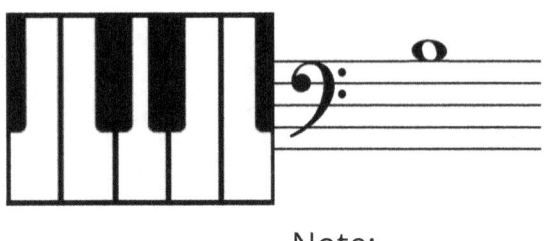

Note: _____

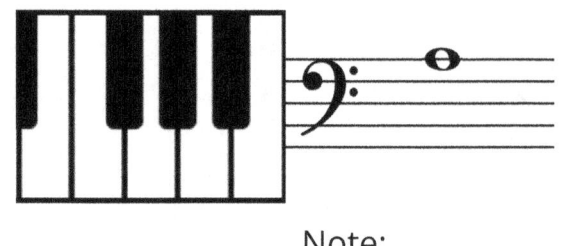

Note: _____

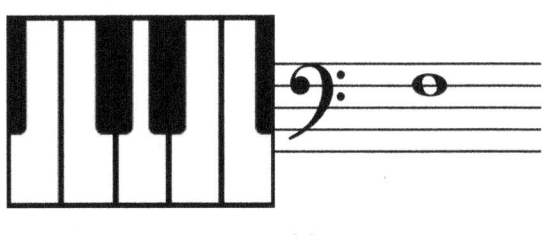

Note: _____

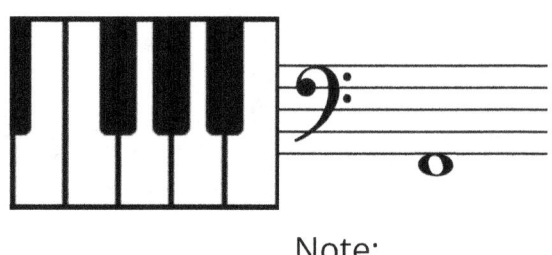

Note: _____

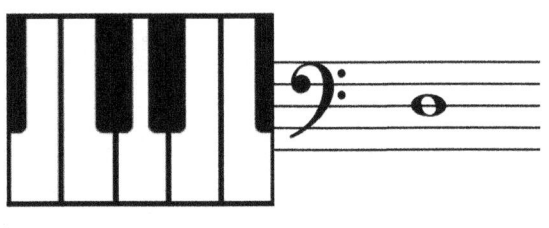

Note: _____

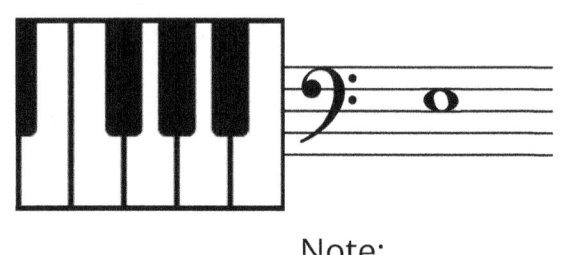

Note: _____

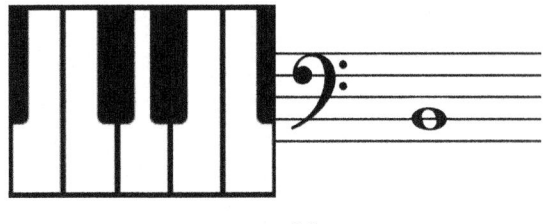

Note: _____

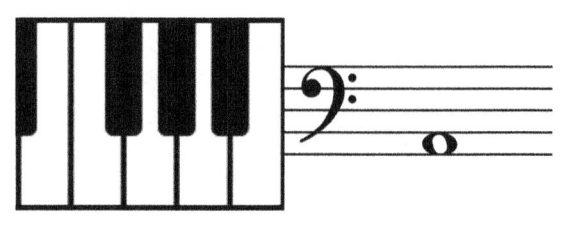

Note: _____

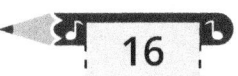

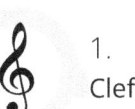 1. Clef 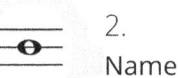 2. Name 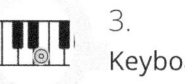 3. Keyboard

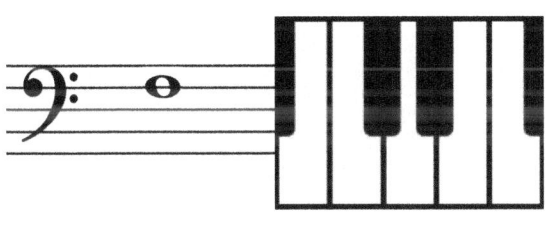

Note: _____

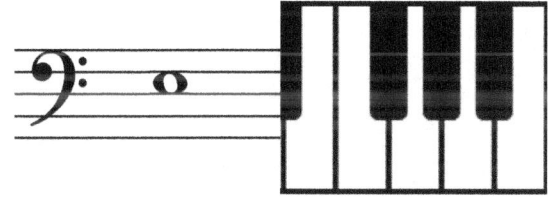

Note: _____

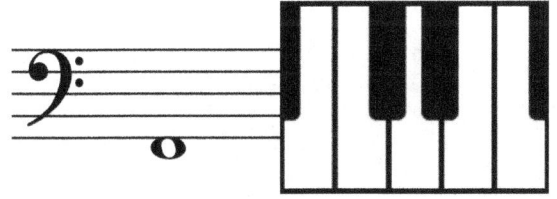

Note: _____

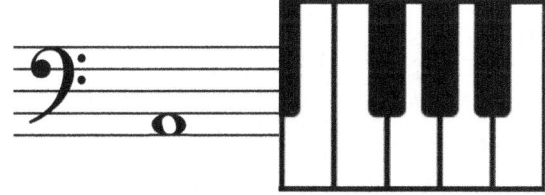

Note: _____

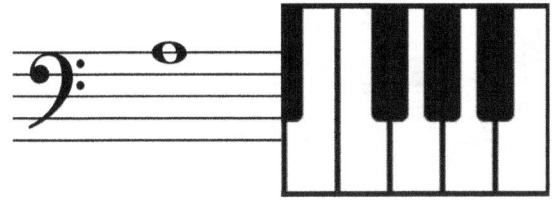

Note: _____

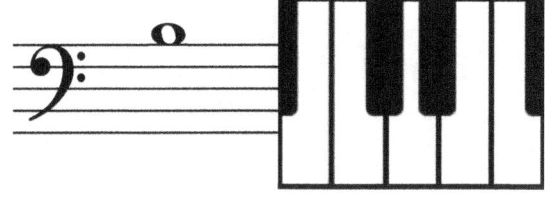

Note: _____

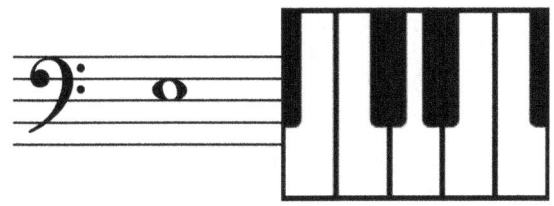

Note: _____

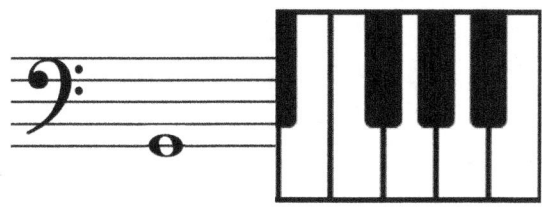

Note: _____

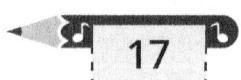

1. Clef 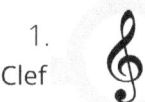 2. Name 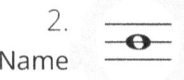 3. Keyboard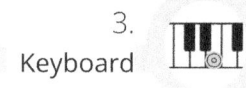

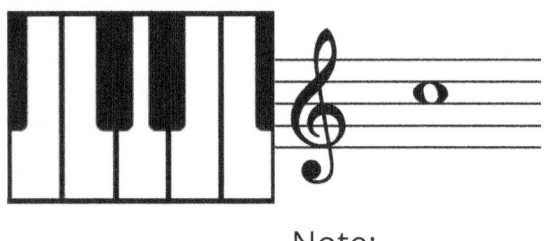
Note: _____

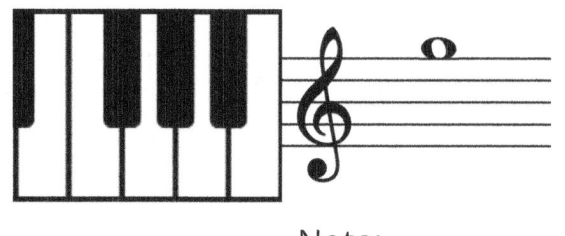
Note: _____

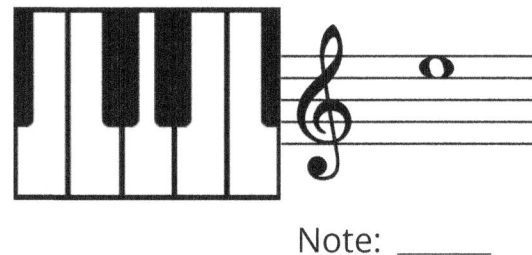
Note: _____

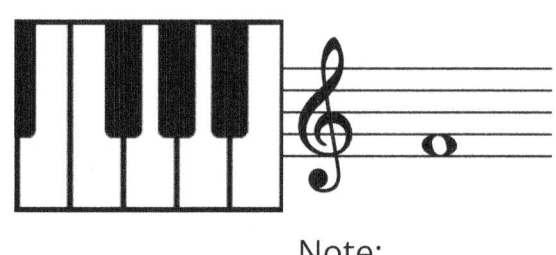
Note: _____

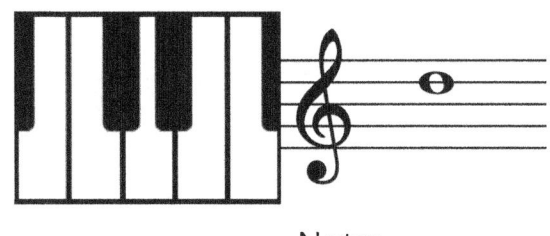
Note: _____

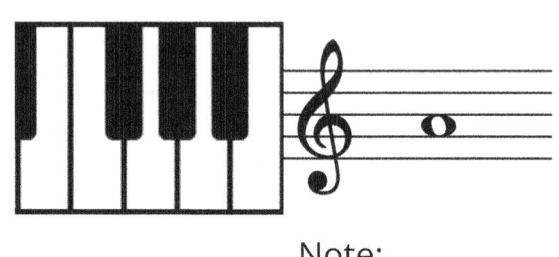
Note: _____

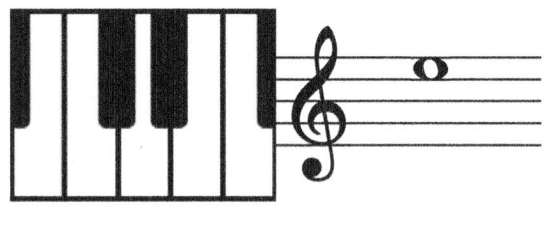
Note: _____

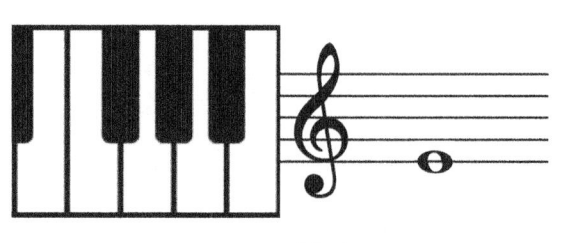
Note: _____

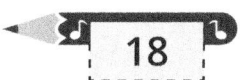

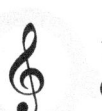 1. Clef   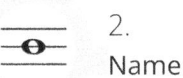 2. Name   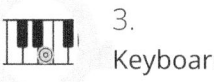 3. Keyboard

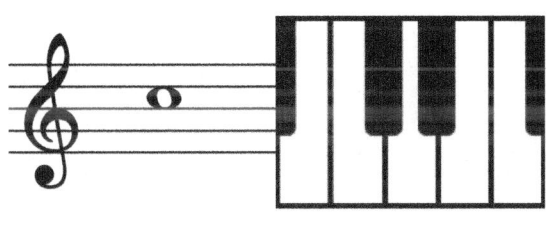

Note: _____

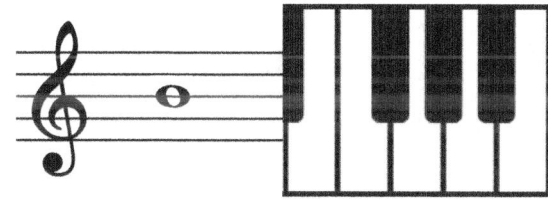

Note: _____

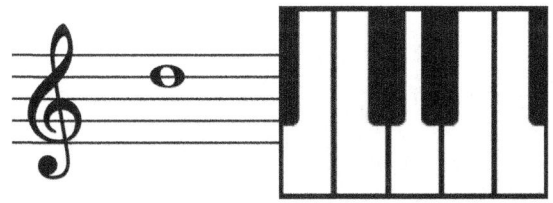

Note: _____

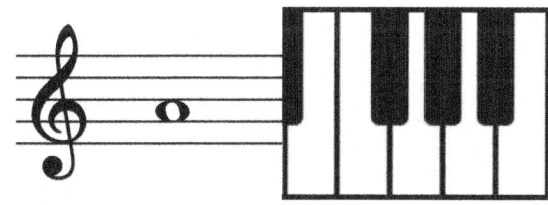

Note: _____

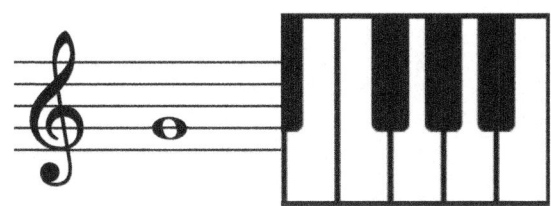

Note: _____

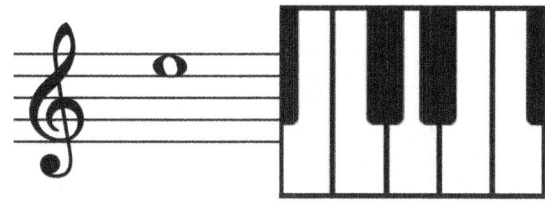

Note: _____

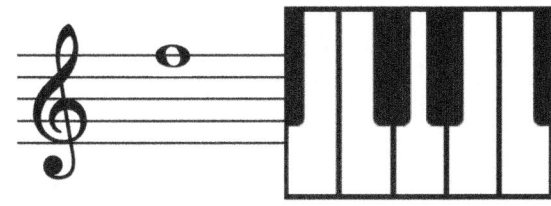

Note: _____

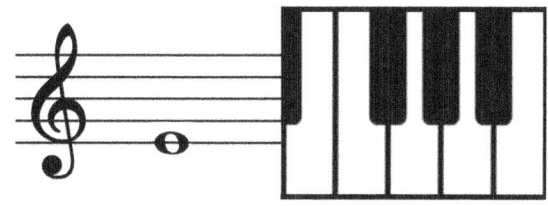

Note: _____

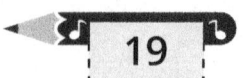

1. Clef 2. Name 3. Keyboard

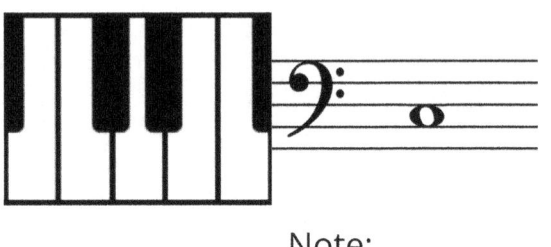

Note: _____

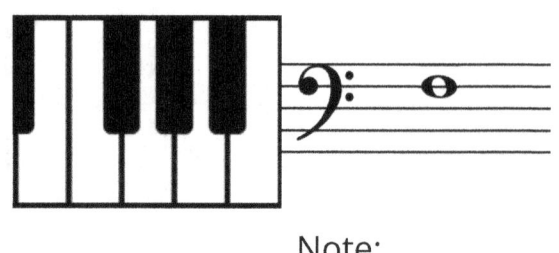

Note: _____

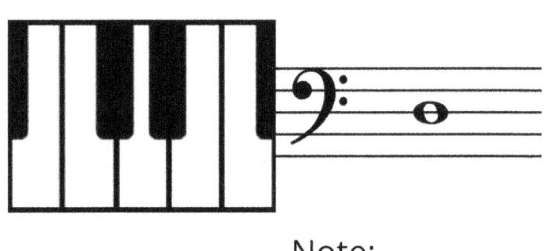

Note: _____

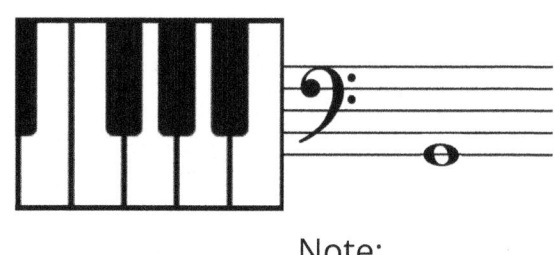

Note: _____

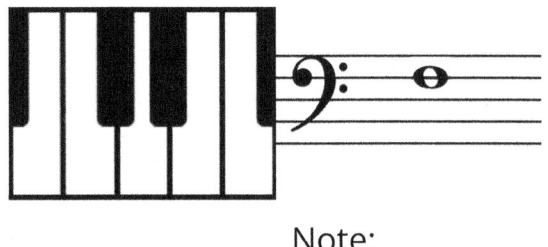

Note: _____

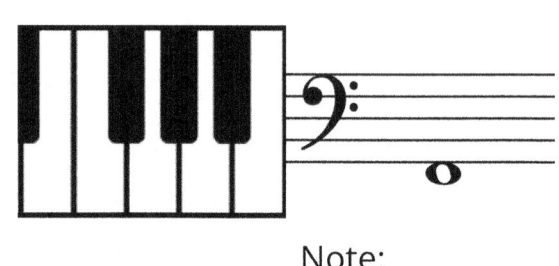

Note: _____

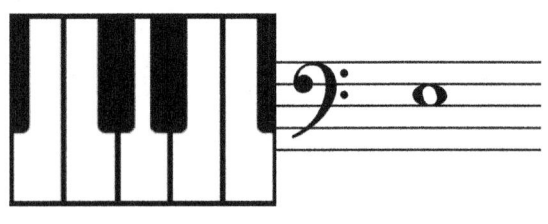

Note: _____

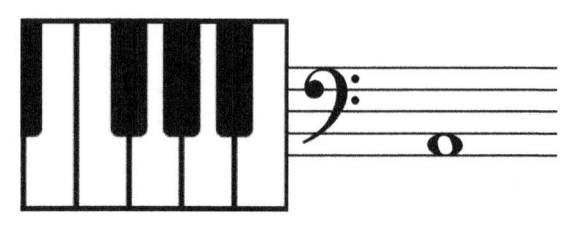

Note: _____

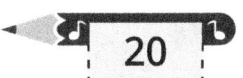

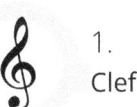 1. Clef 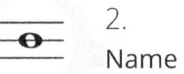 2. Name 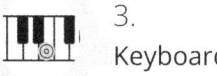 3. Keyboard

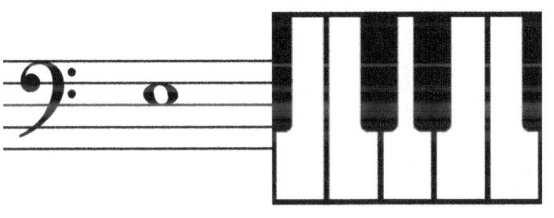

Note: _____

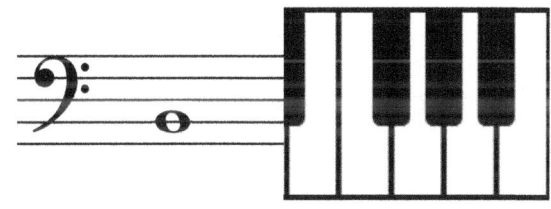

Note: _____

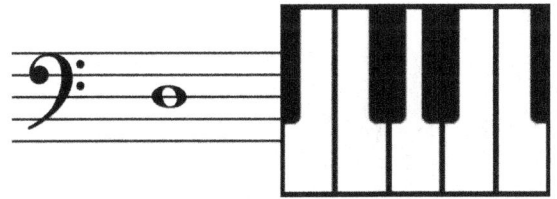

Note: _____

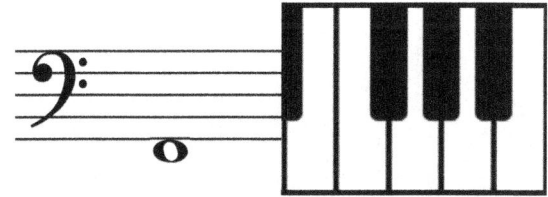

Note: _____

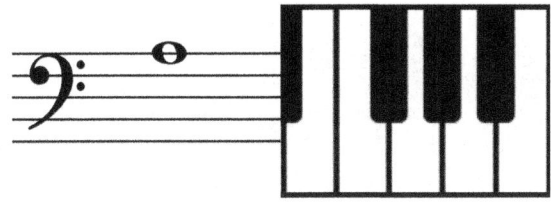

Note: _____

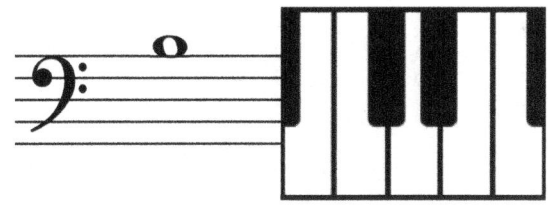

Note: _____

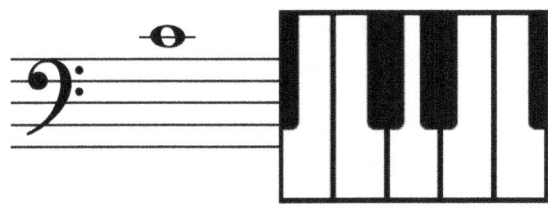

Note: _____

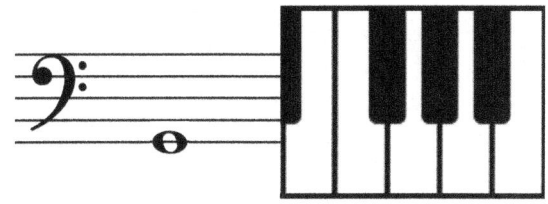

Note: _____

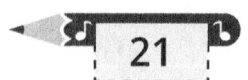

1. Clef 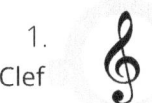   2. Name 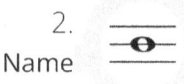   3. Keyboard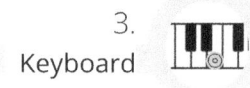

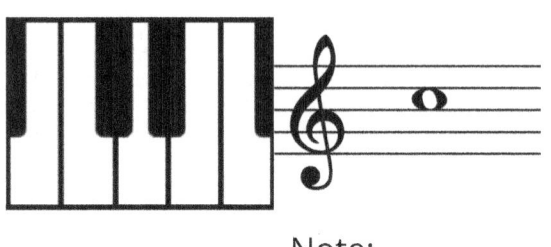

Note: _____

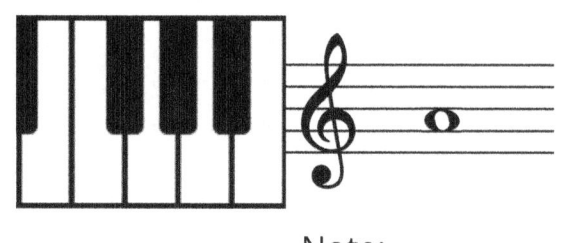

Note: _____

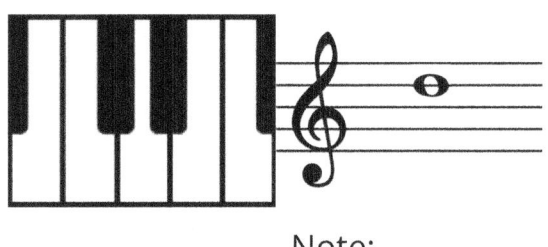

Note: _____

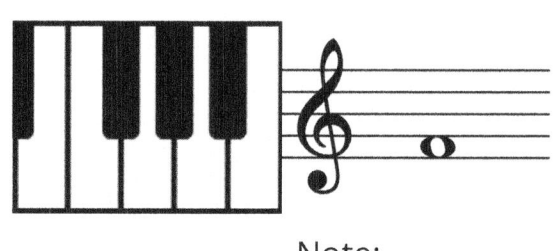

Note: _____

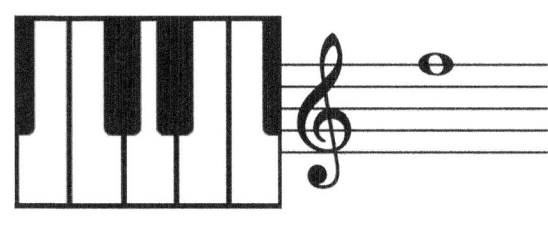

Note: _____

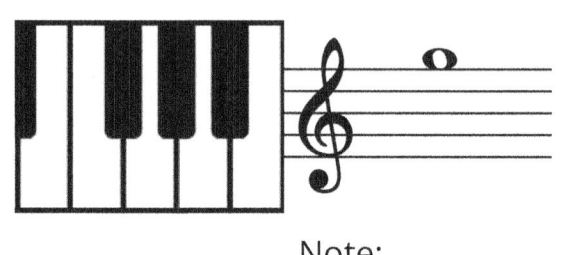

Note: _____

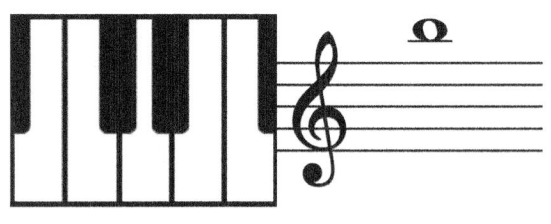

Note: _____

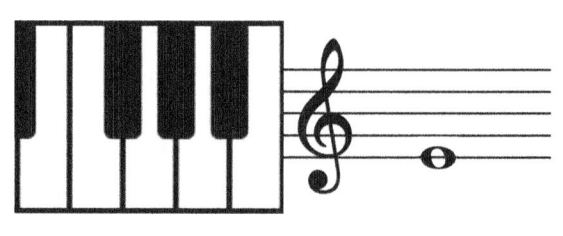

Note: _____

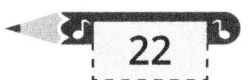

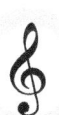 1. Clef 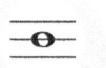 2. Name   3. Keyboard

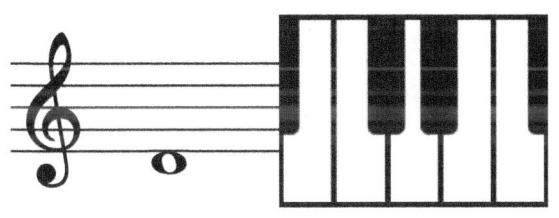

Note: _____

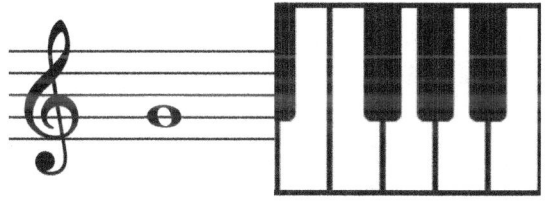

Note: _____

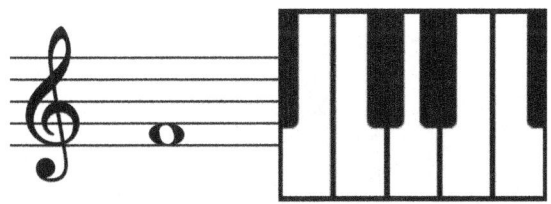

Note: _____

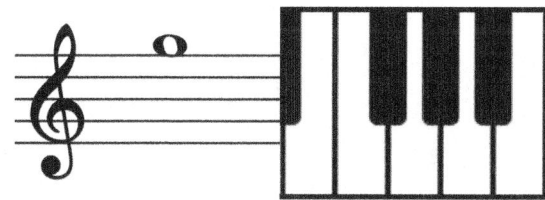

Note: _____

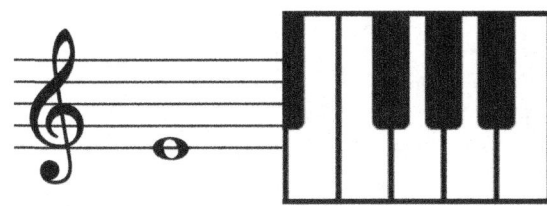

Note: _____

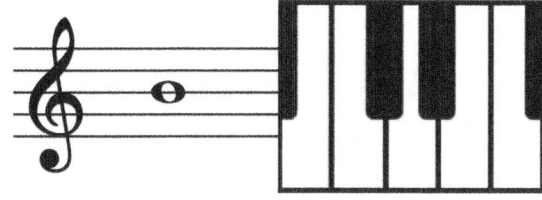

Note: _____

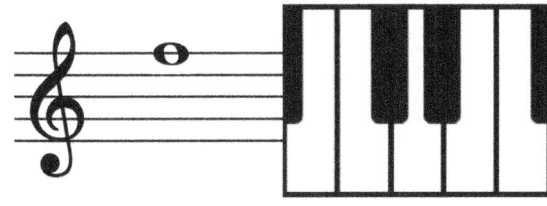

Note: _____

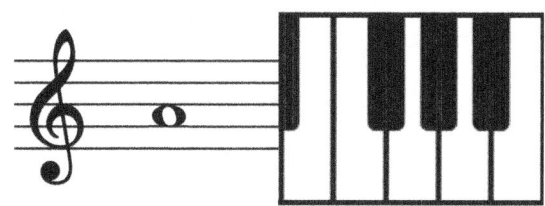

Note: _____

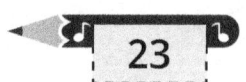

1. Clef 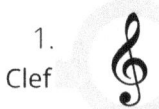 2. Name 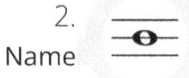 3. Keyboard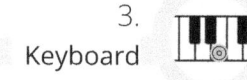

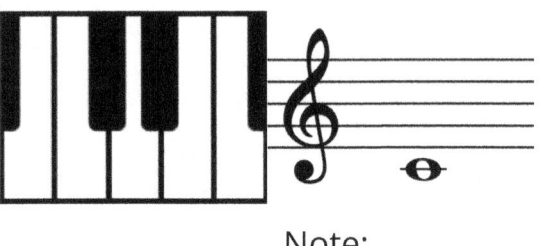

Note: _____

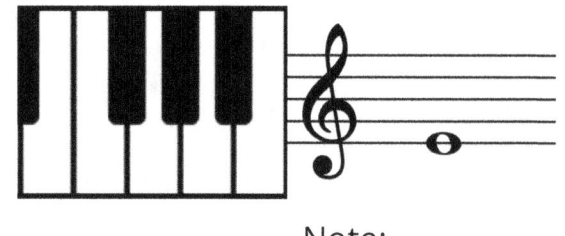

Note: _____

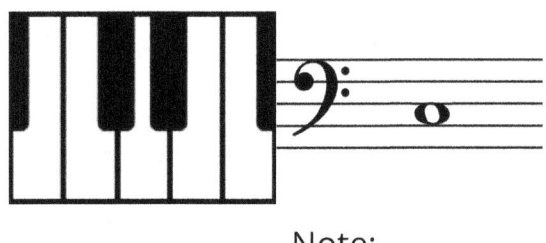

Note: _____

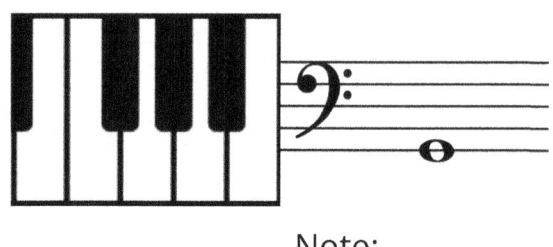

Note: _____

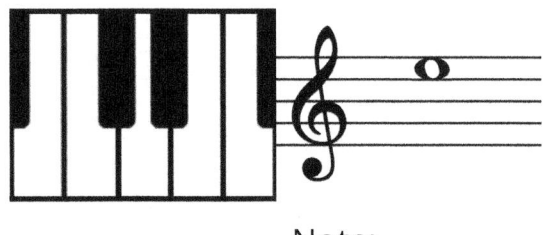

Note: _____

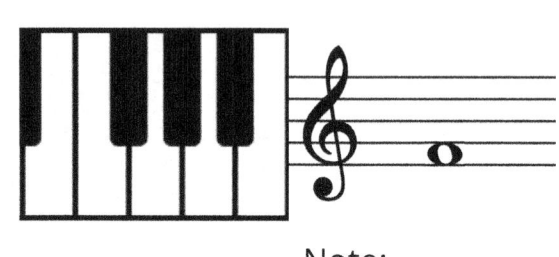

Note: _____

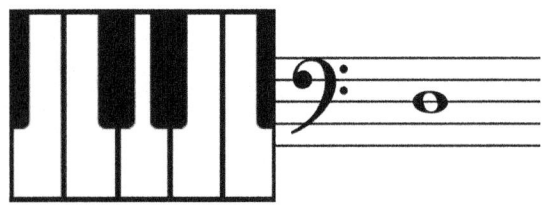

Note: _____

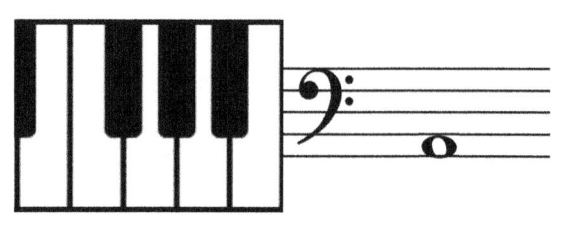

Note: _____

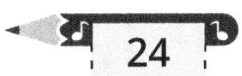

1. Clef   2. Name   3. Keyboard

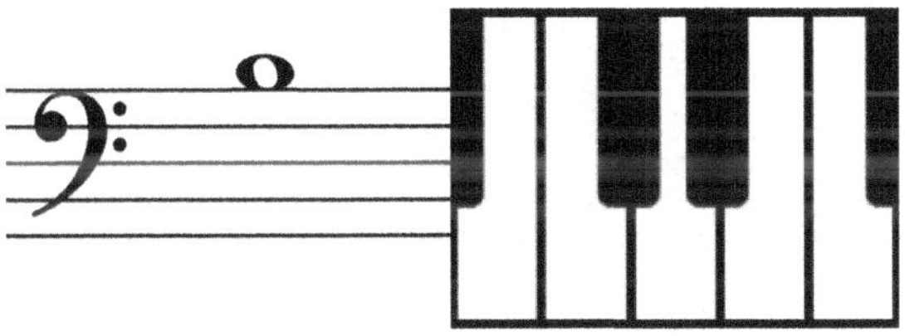

Note: 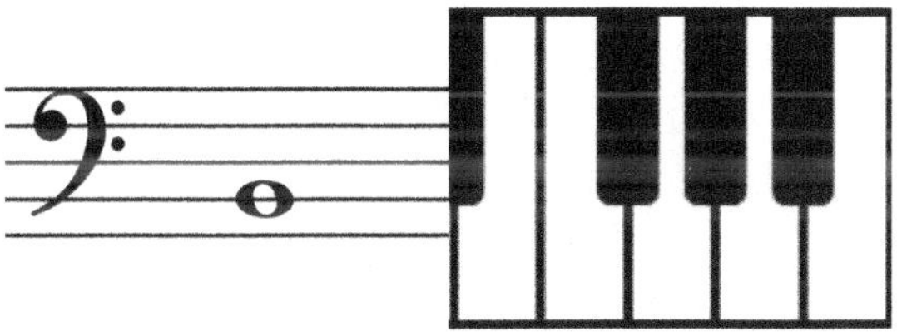 _____   Note: _____

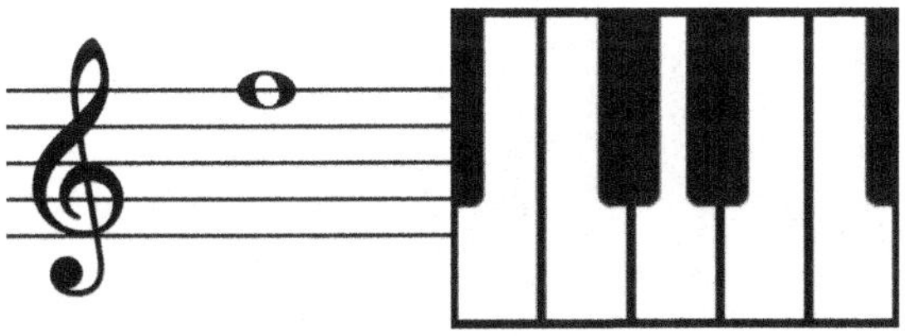

Note: 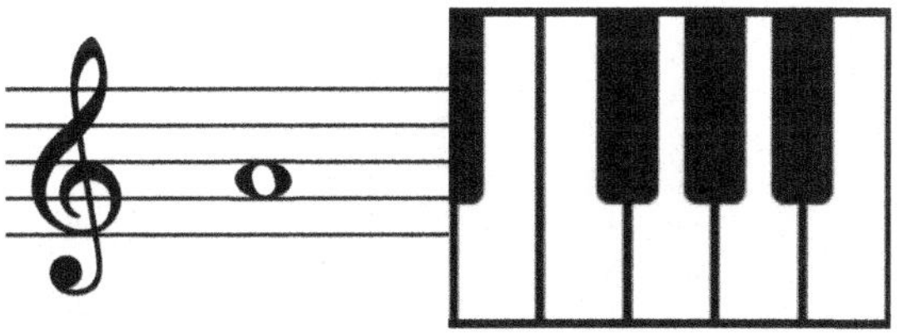 _____   Note: _____

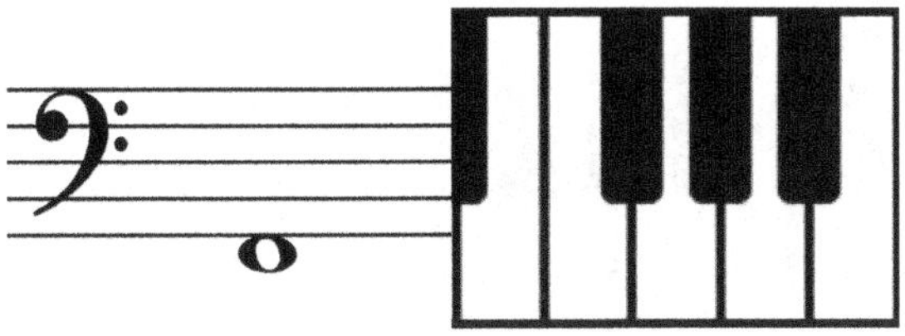

Note: 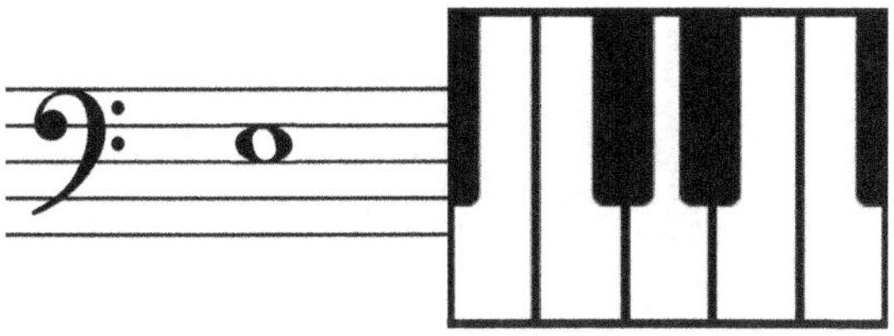 _____   Note: _____

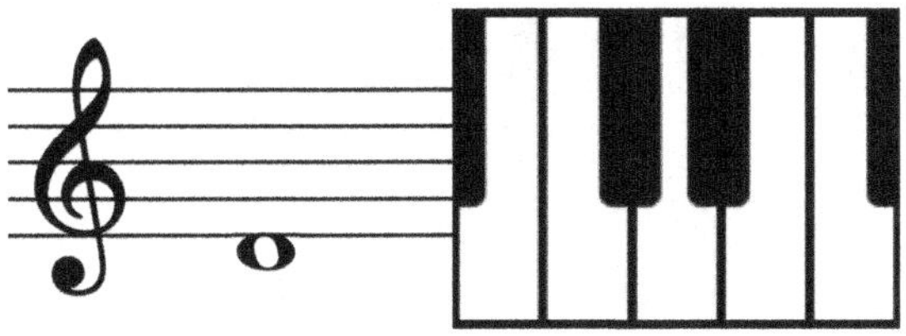

Note: 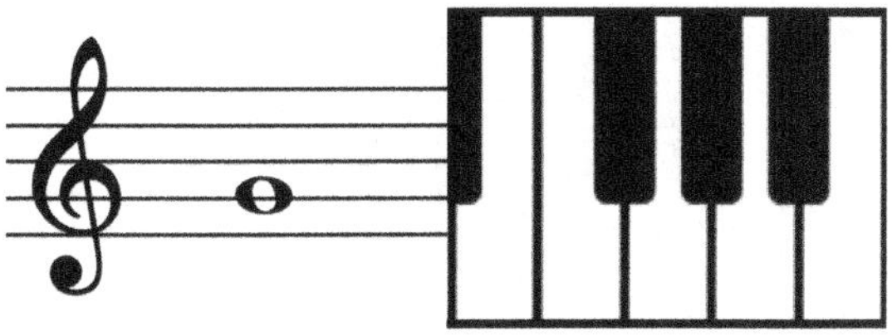 _____   Note: _____

1. Clef 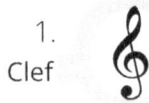   2. Name 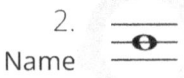   3. Keyboard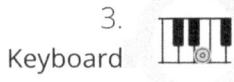

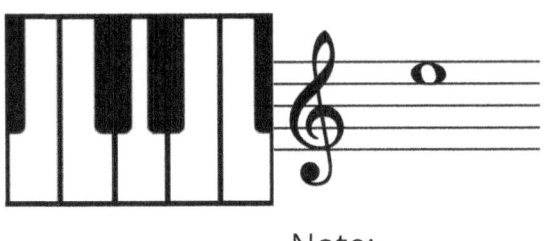

Note: _____

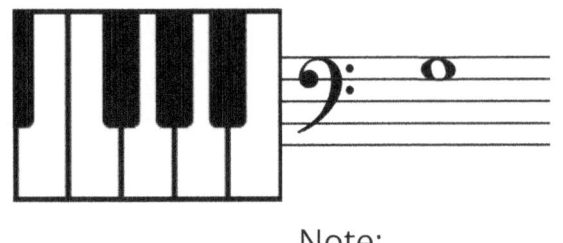

Note: _____

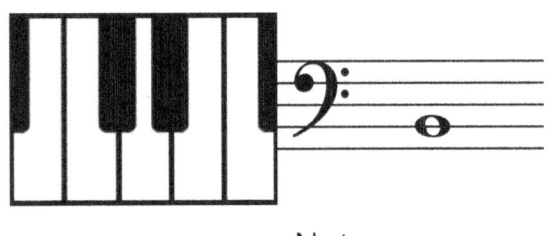

Note: _____

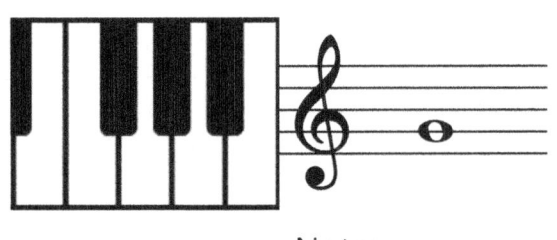

Note: _____

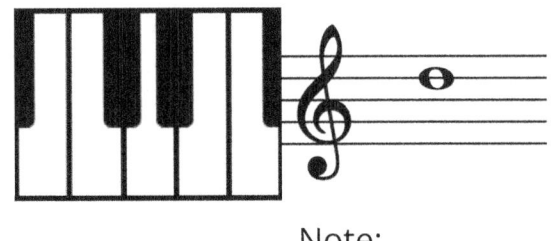

Note: _____

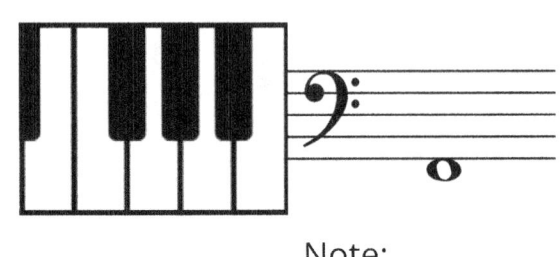

Note: _____

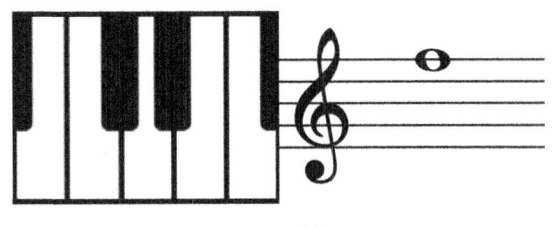

Note: _____

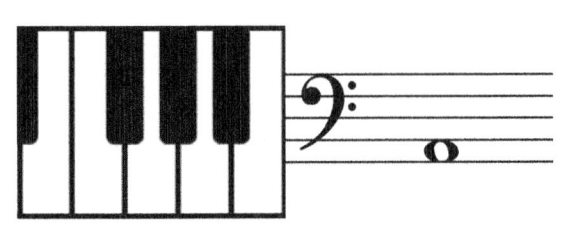

Note: _____

Chapter 3
Accidentals

Instructions with Example

Practice in the Grand Staff

Practice on Keyboard & Staff

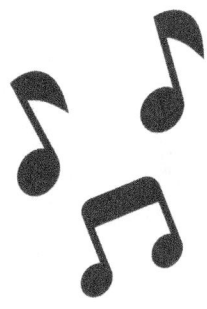

Instructions with Example

Three easy steps to complete the exercises:

1. 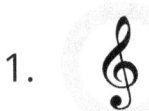 **Clef:** Look at the clef, which tells you what note belongs to each line or space on the staff. In the bass clef, the note **A** is in the lowest space. In the treble clef, the note **A** is one whole step higher.

2. 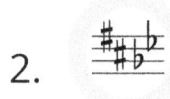 **Accidental:** Look at the accidental. Is it a sharp (♯), flat (♭), or natural (♮) and check how the note changes; use the chart below to see what it turns into. When no accidental is given, the note is in its natural state.

3. 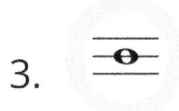 **Name:** Find the note name. Ask yourself: Which line or space is the note on? Then, figure out the name of that note.

The diagram is a helpful guide for the exercises:

Natural Notes	Sharp-Notes ♯	Flat-Notes ♭
C	C♯	C♭
D	D♯	D♭
E	E♯	E♭
F	F♯	F♭
G	G♯	G♭
A	A♯	A♭
B	B♯	B♭

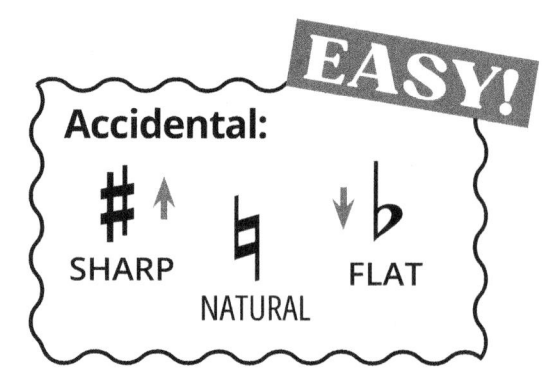

Example:

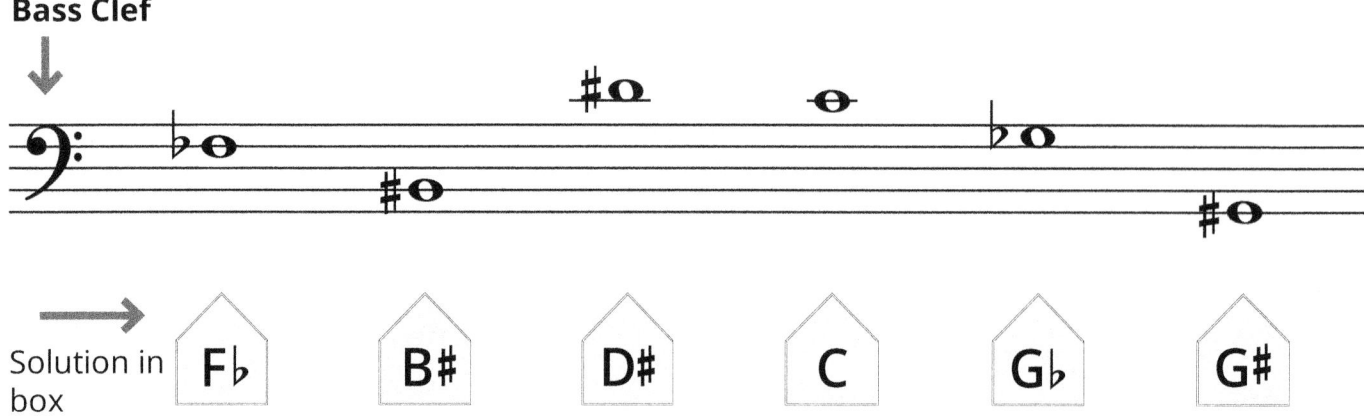

Solution in box → F♭ B♯ D♯ C G♭ G♯

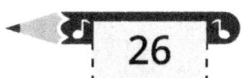

1. Clef 2. Accidental 3. Name

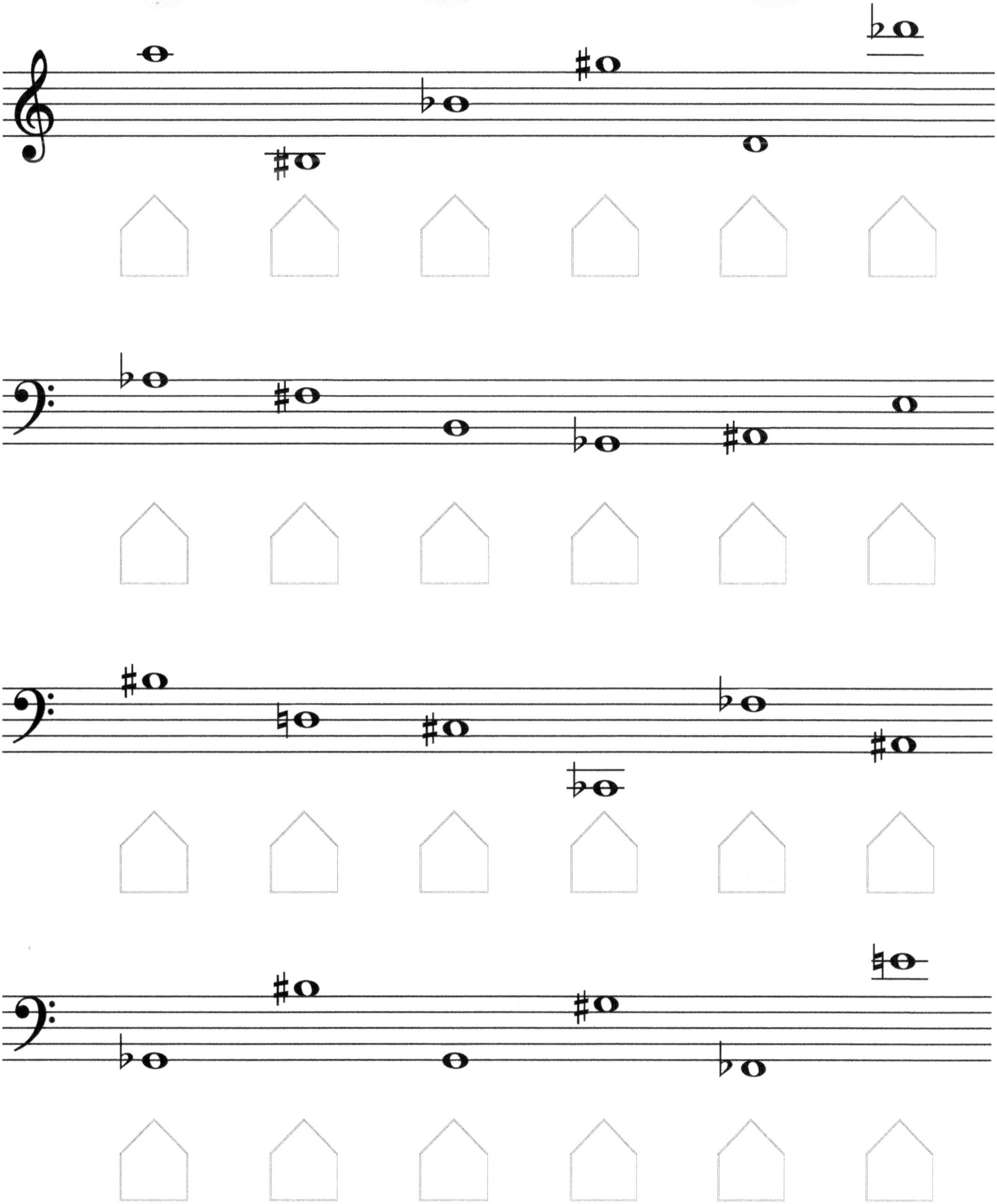

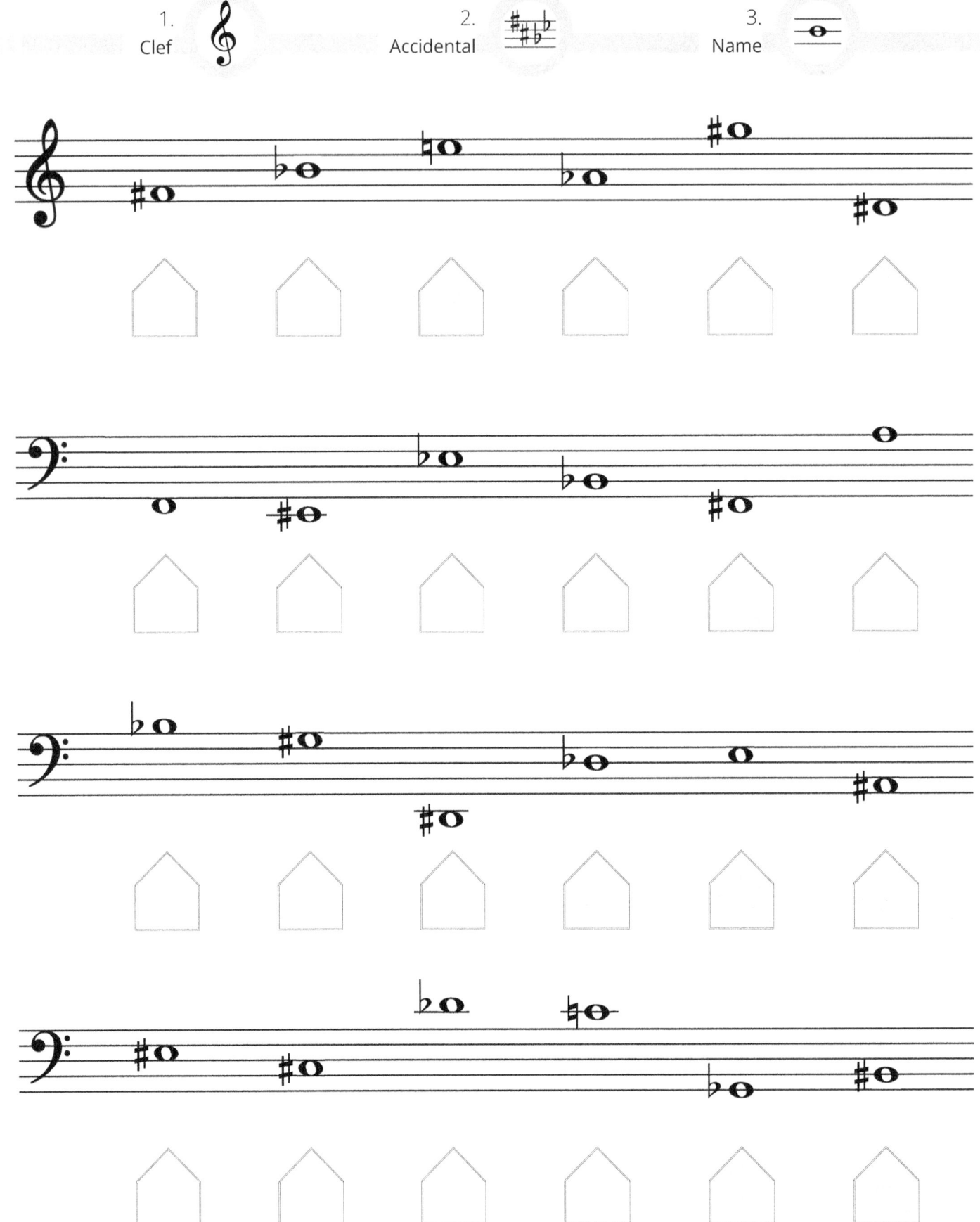

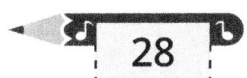

1. Clef 2. Accidental 3. Name

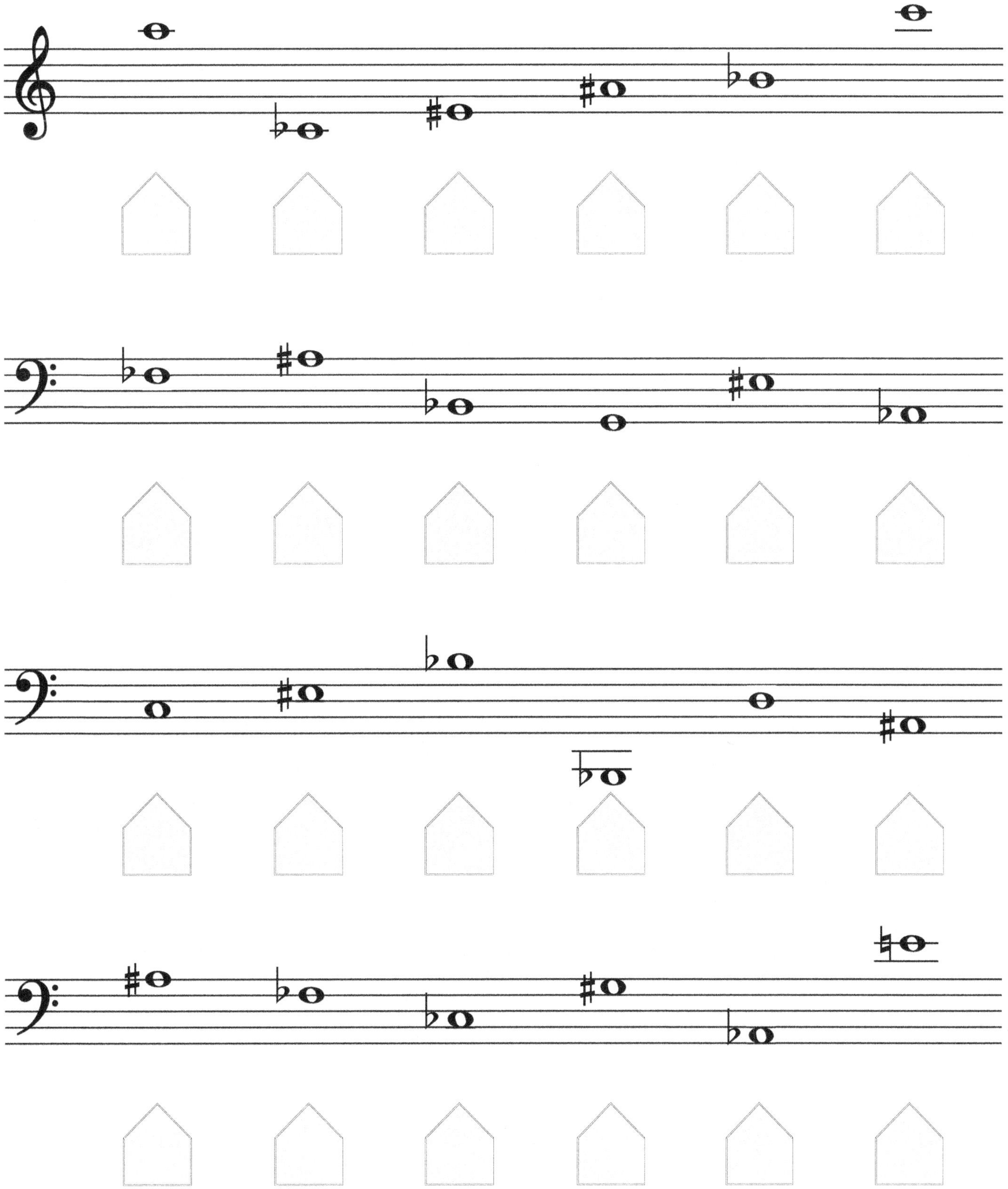

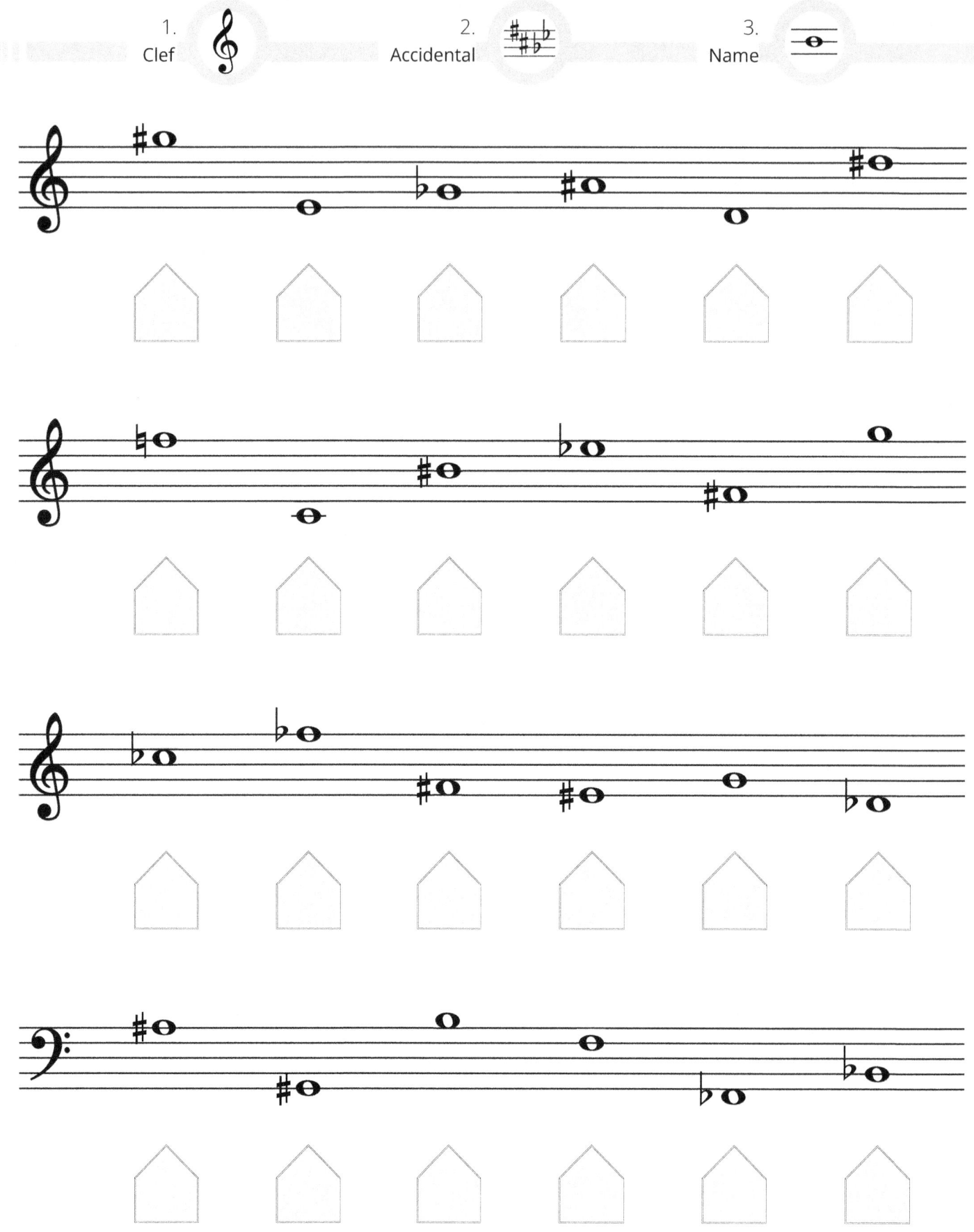

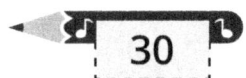

1. Clef
2. Accidental
3. Name

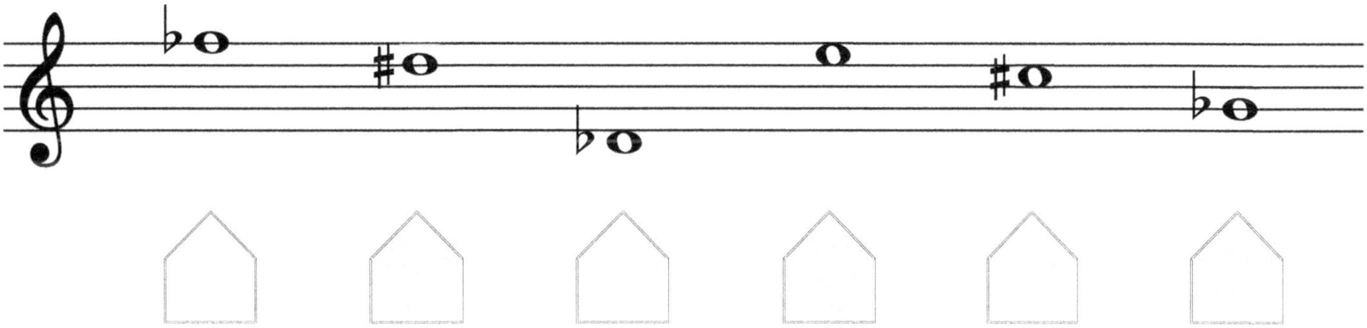

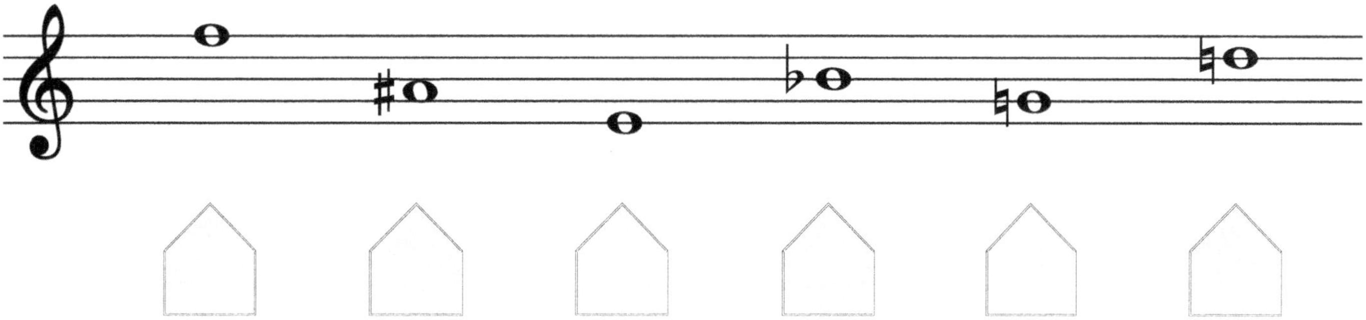

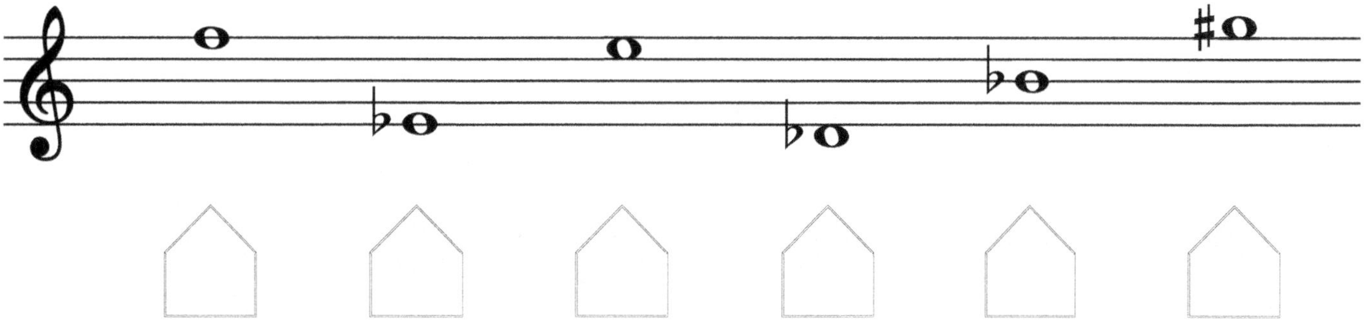

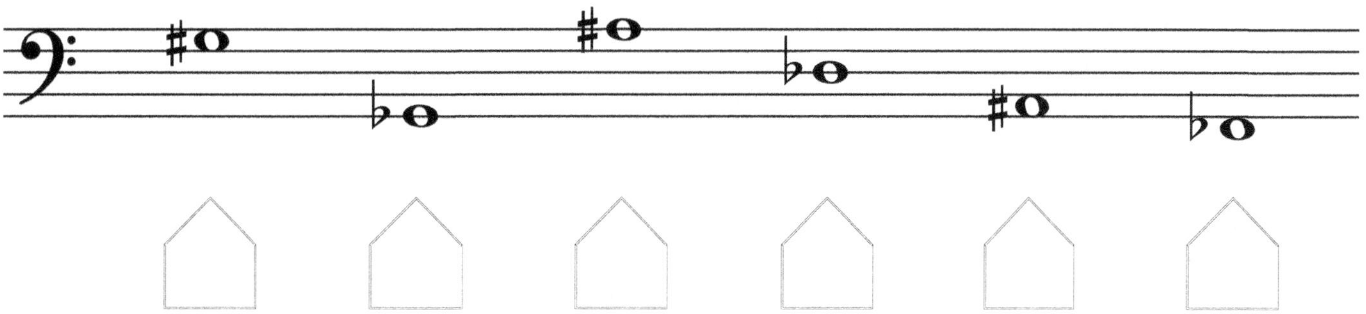

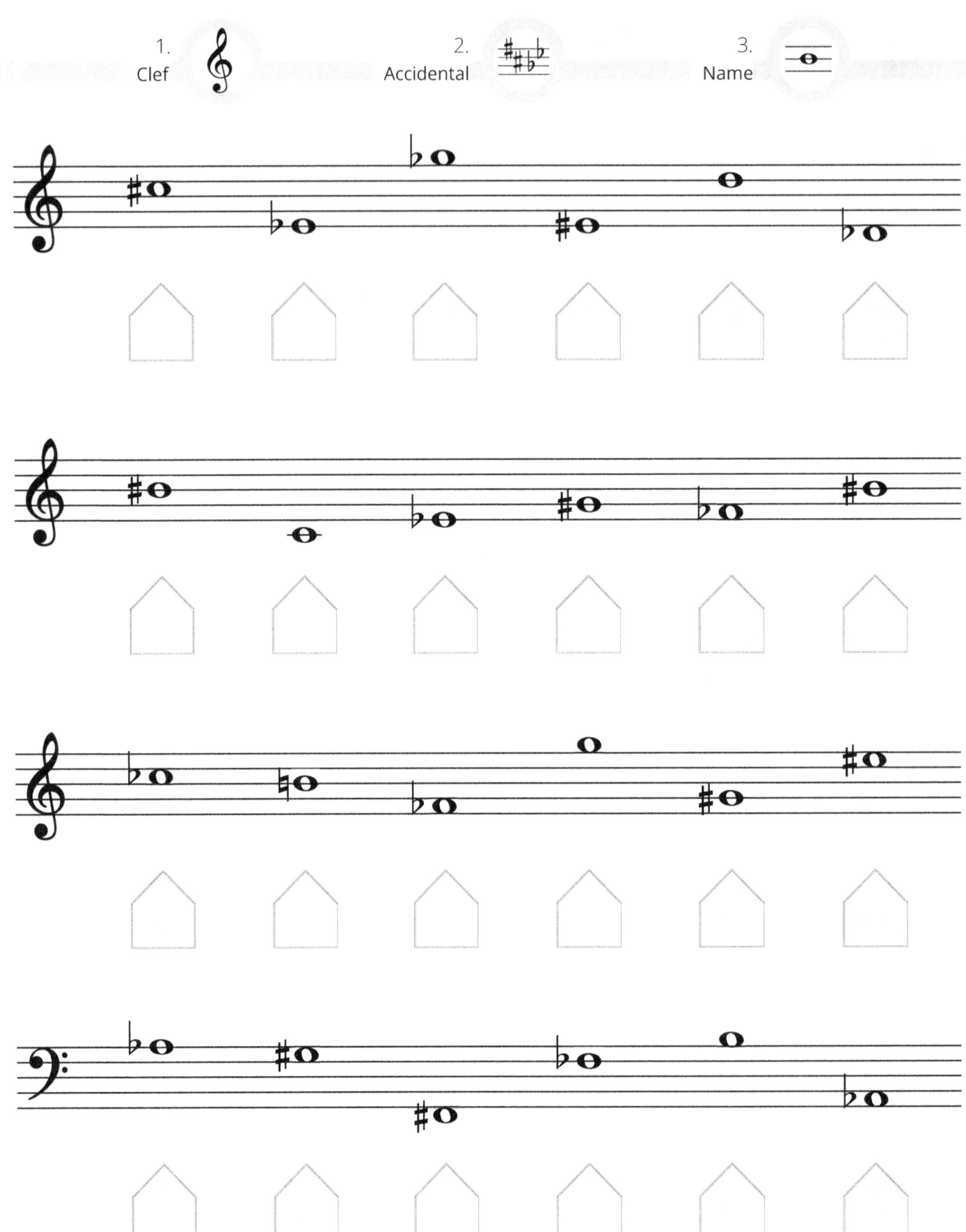

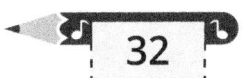

1. Clef
2. Accidental
3. Name

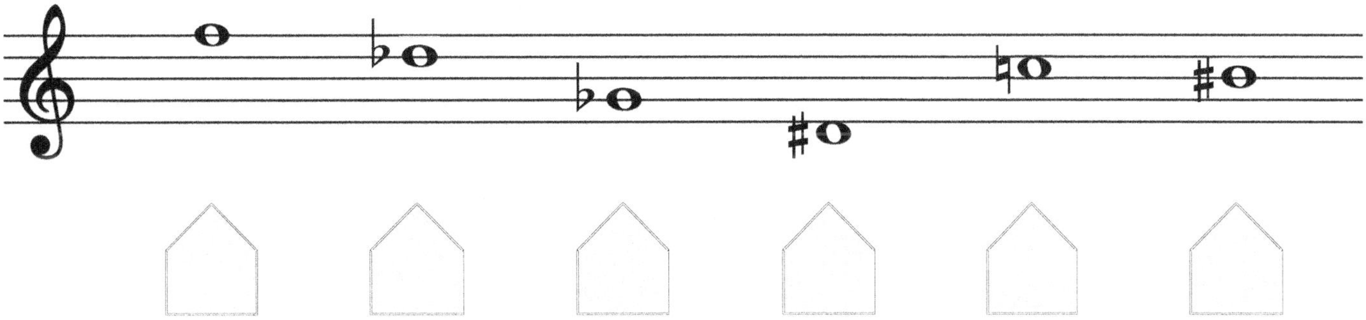

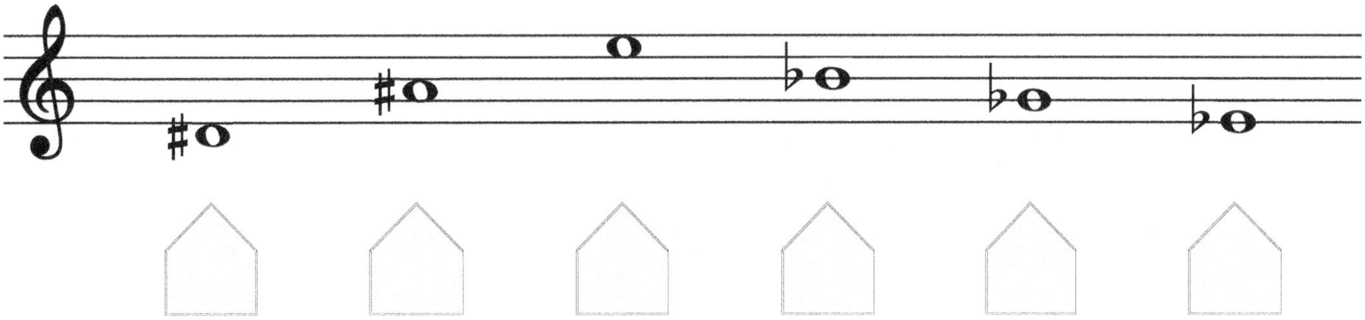

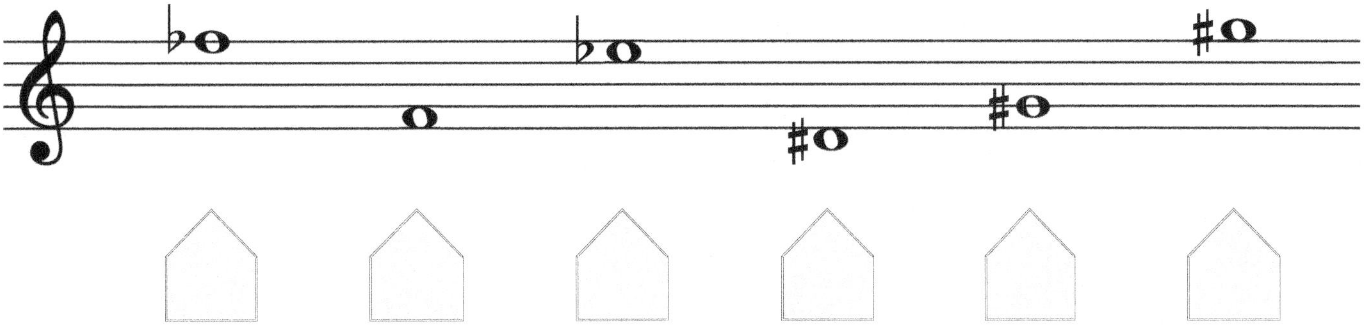

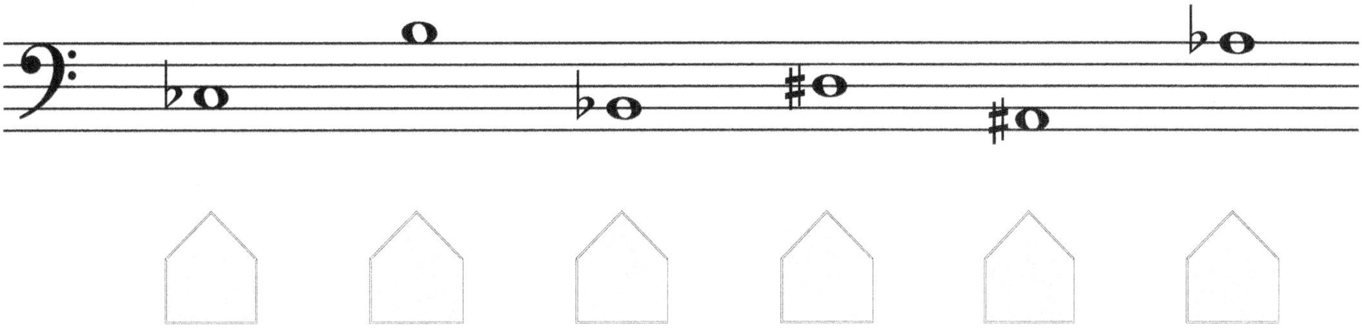

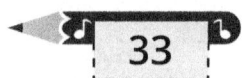

1. Clef   2. Accidental   3. Name

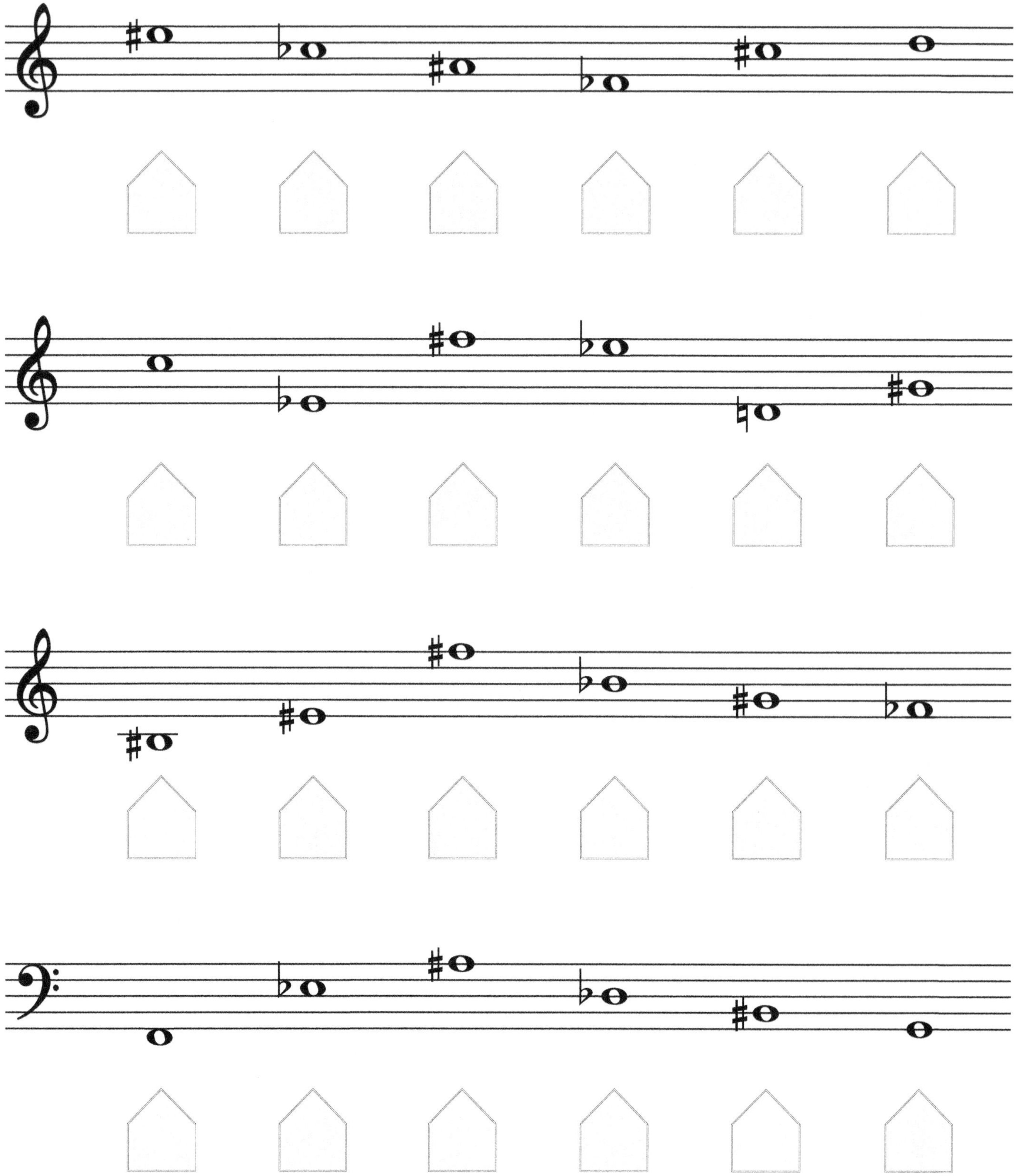

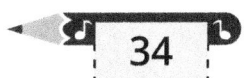

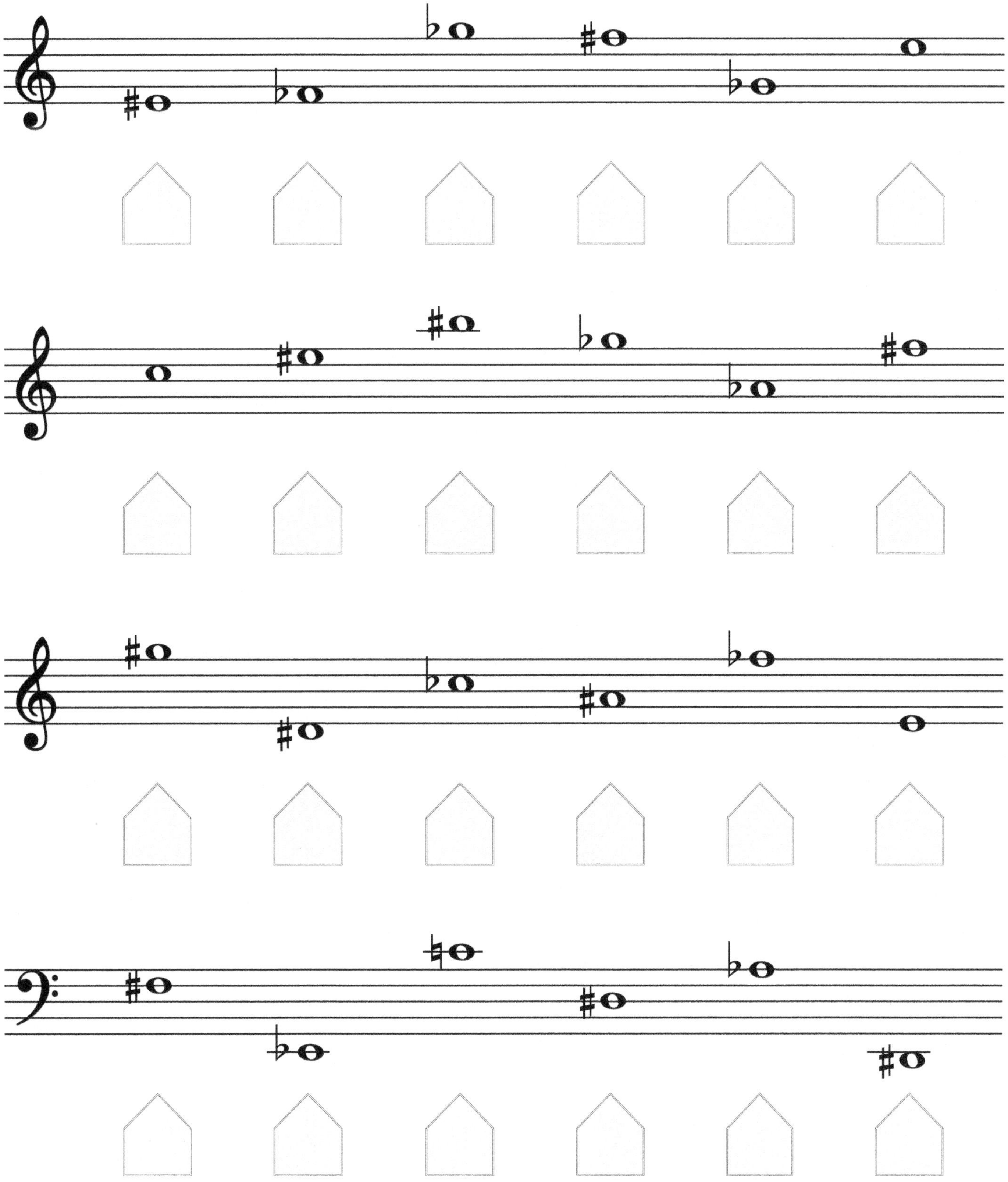

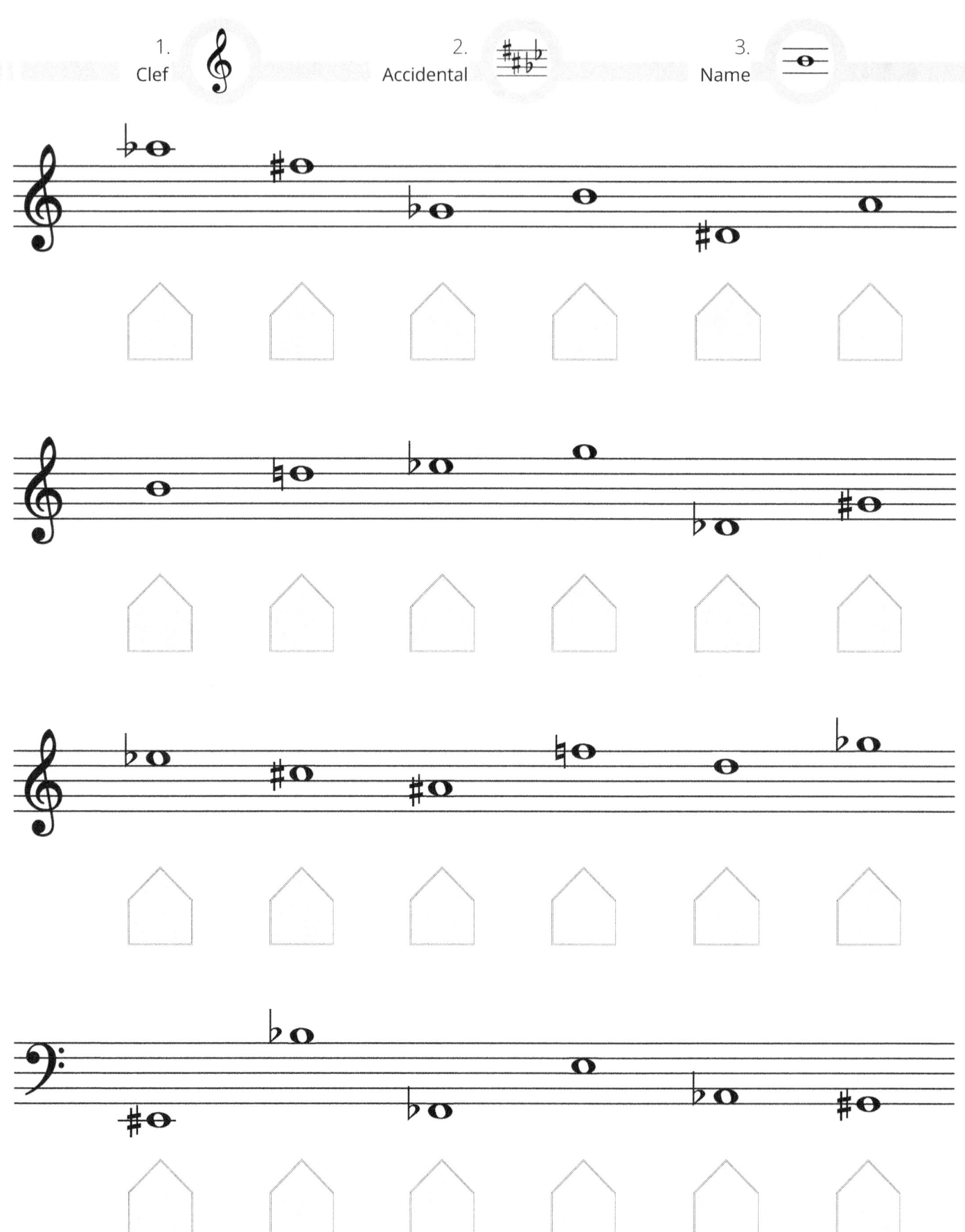

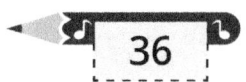

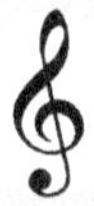

1. Clef   2. Accidental   3. Name

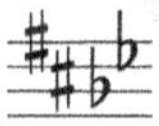

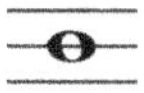

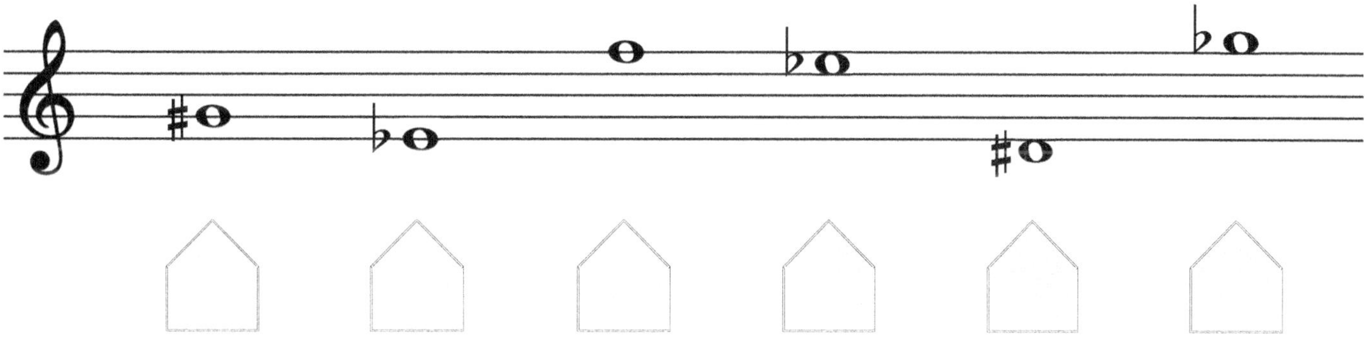

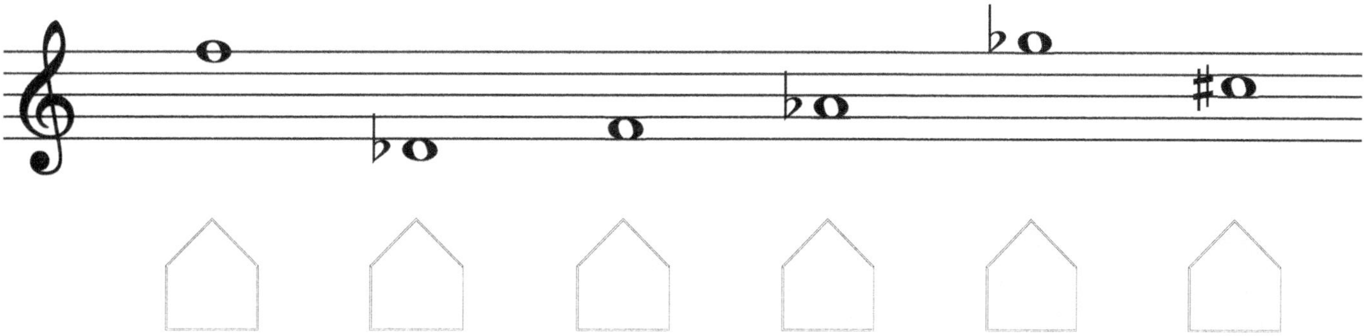

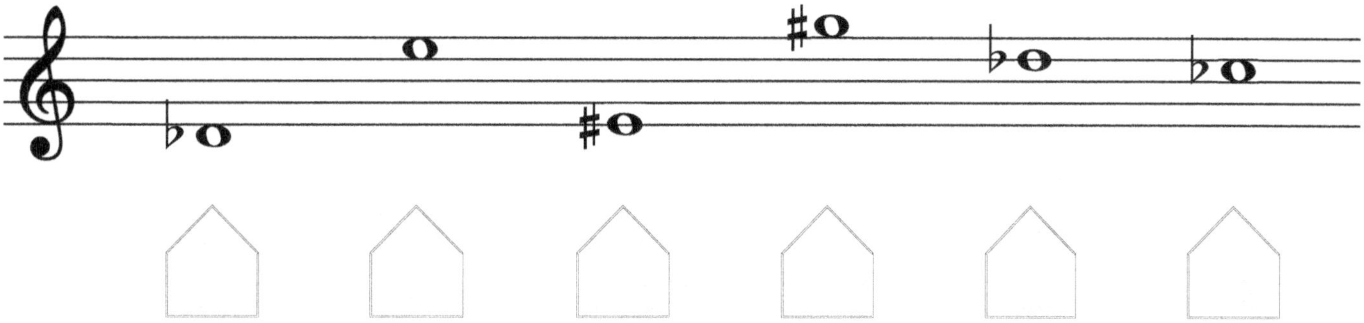

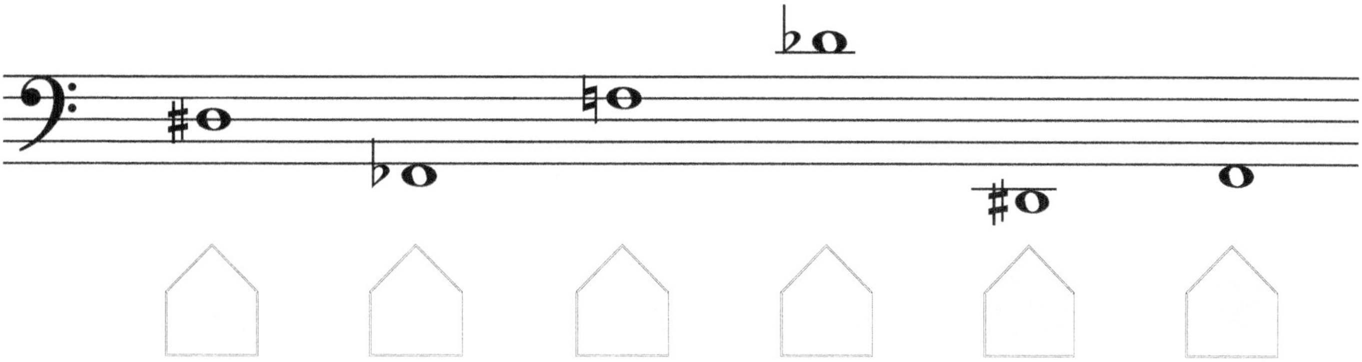

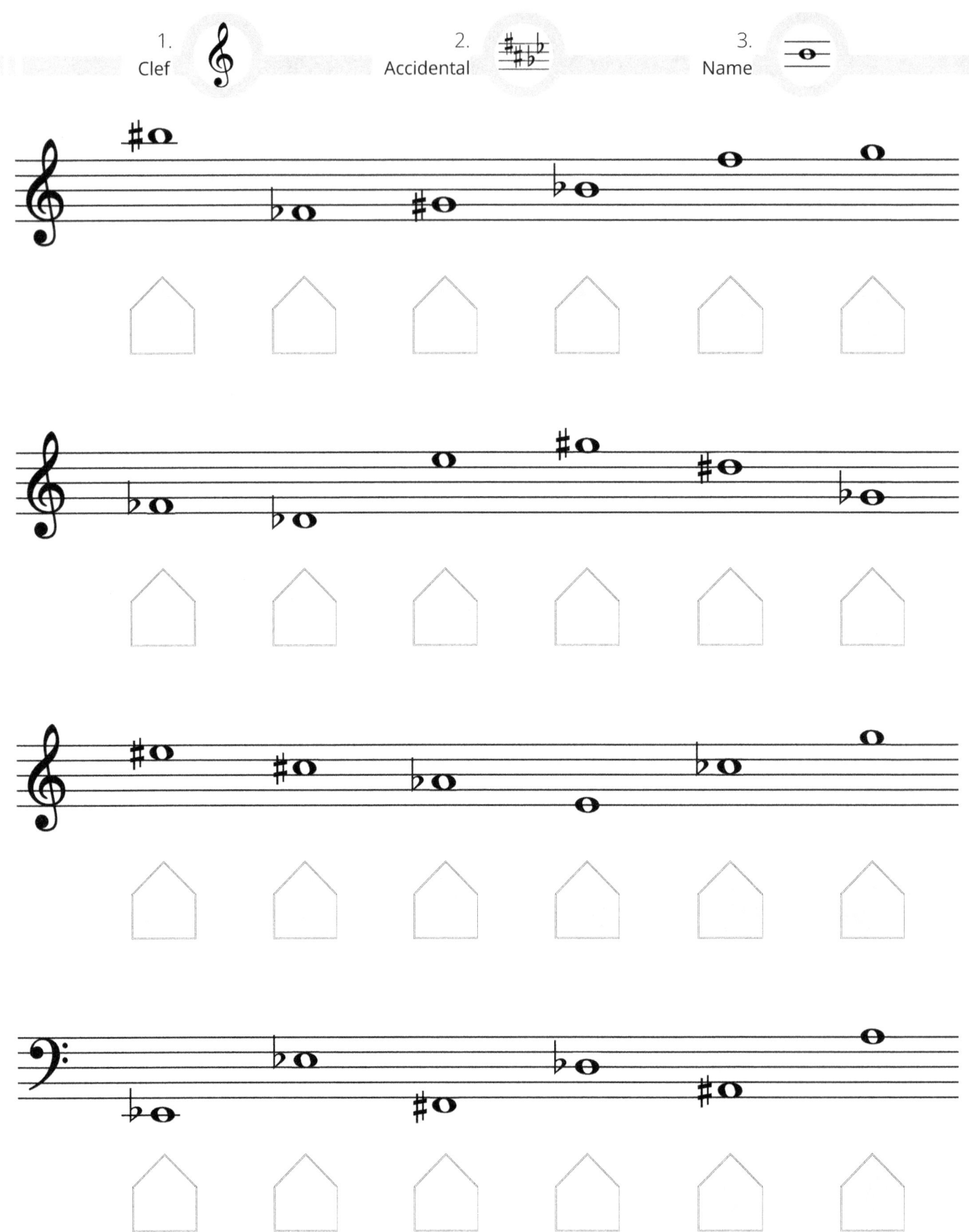

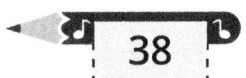

1. Clef 2. Accidental 3. Name

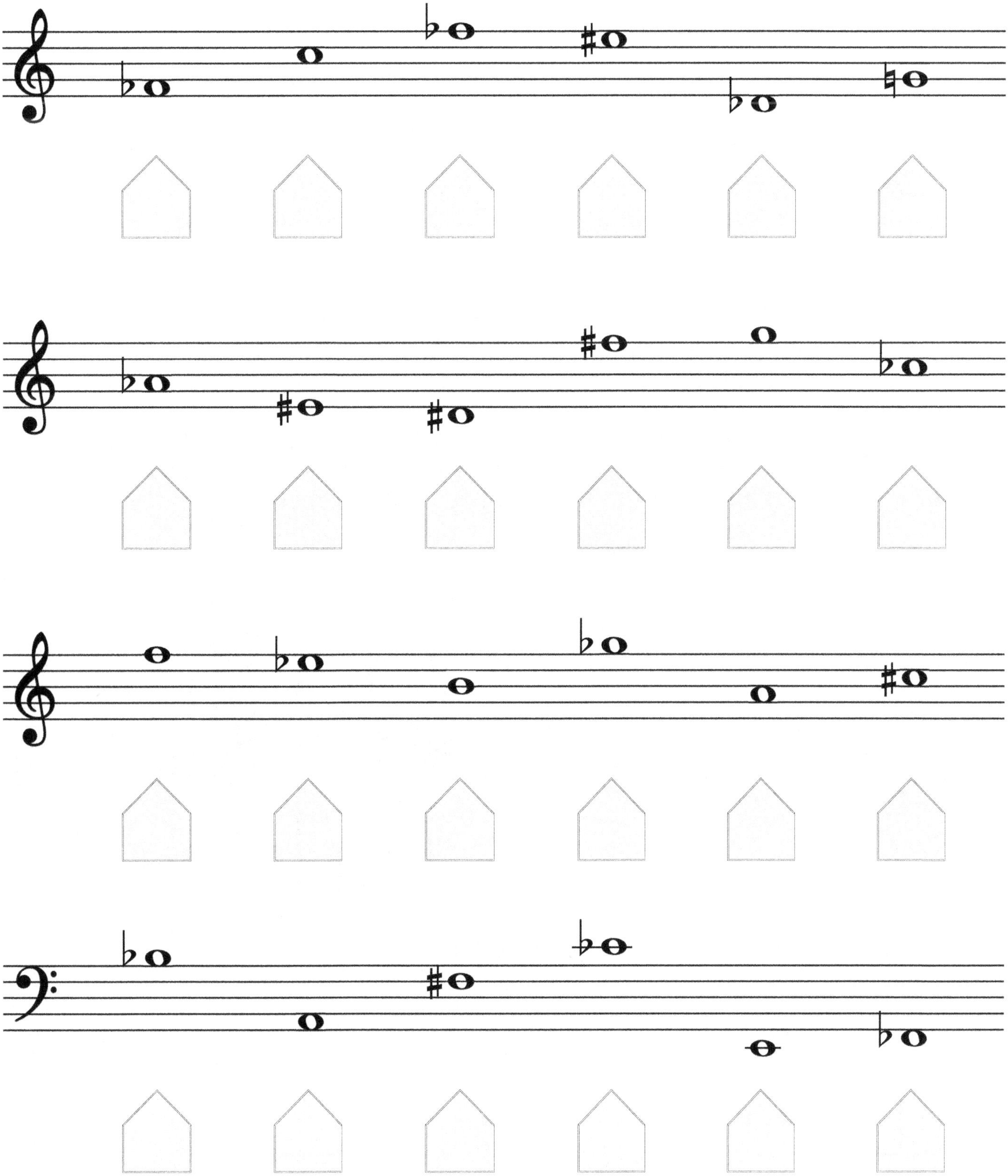

Keyboard Exercises

Four simple steps to complete the exercises:

1. 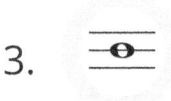 **Clef:** **Look at the clef**, which tells you what note belongs to each line or space on the staff. In the bass clef, the note **A** is in the lowest space. In the treble clef, the note **A** is one whole step higher.

2. 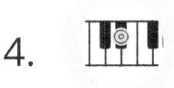 **Accidental:** Look at the accidental. Is it a sharp (#), flat (♭), or natural (♮) and check how the note changes; use the chart below to see what it turns into. When no accidental is given, the note is in its natural state.

3. **Name: Find the note name.** Ask yourself: Which line or space is the note on? Then, figure out the name of that note.

4. **Keyboard: Look at the keyboard section** and figure out which key goes with the note from the staff. Each keyboard diagram shows a group of **2 or 3 black keys** to help you find your way more easily.

The diagrams serve as an aid for the exercises:

Natural Notes	Sharp-Notes #	Flat-Notes ♭
C	C#	C♭
D	D#	D♭
E	E#	E♭
F	F#	F♭
G	G#	G♭
A	A#	A♭
B	B#	B♭

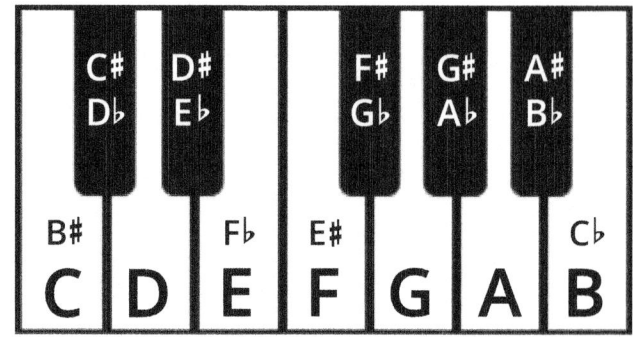

Example:

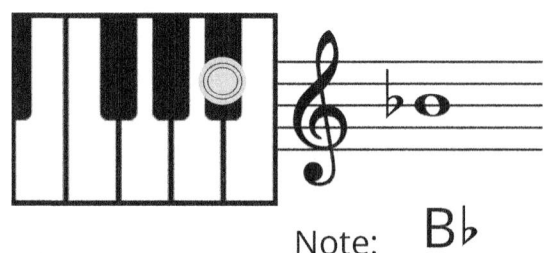

Note: **B♭**

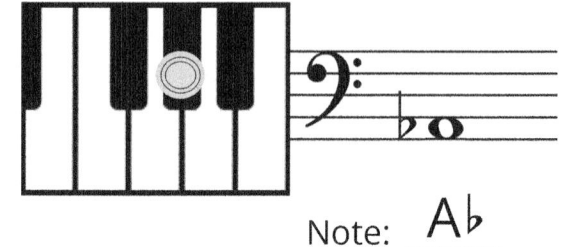

Note: **A♭**

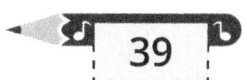

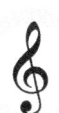 1. Clef 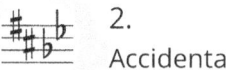 2. Accidental 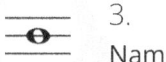 3. Name 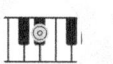 4. Keyboard

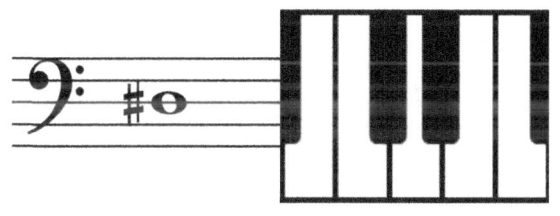

Note: _____

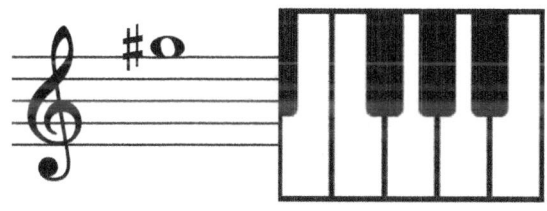

Note: _____

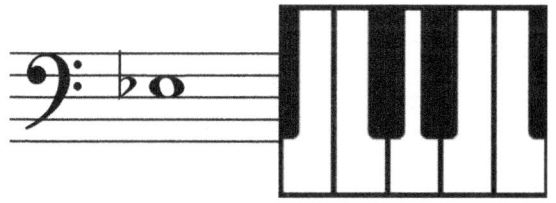

Note: _____

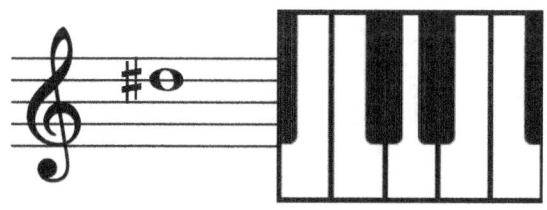

Note: _____

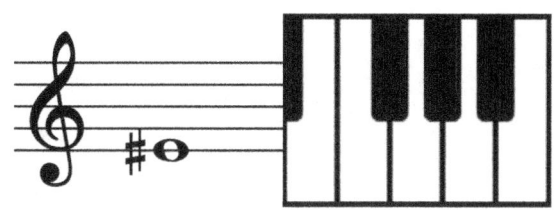

Note: _____

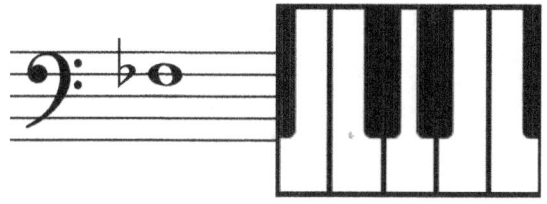

Note: _____

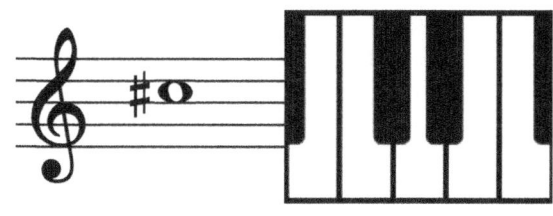

Note: _____

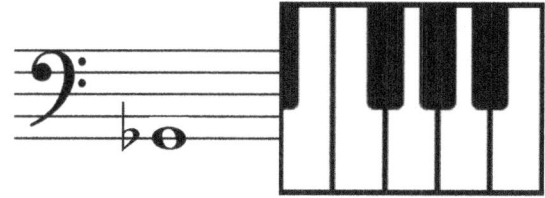

Note: _____

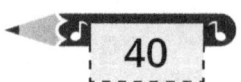

1. Clef 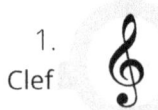 2. Accidental 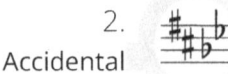 3. Name 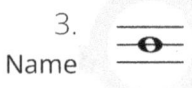 4. Keyboard

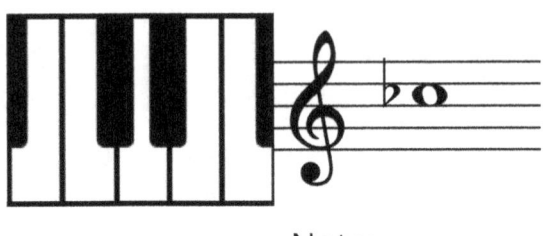

Note: _____

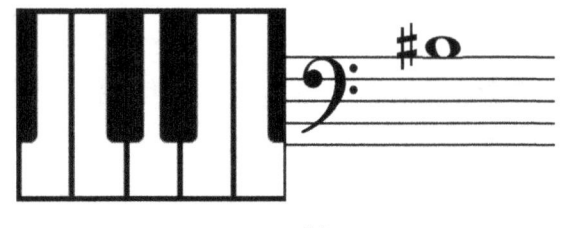

Note: _____

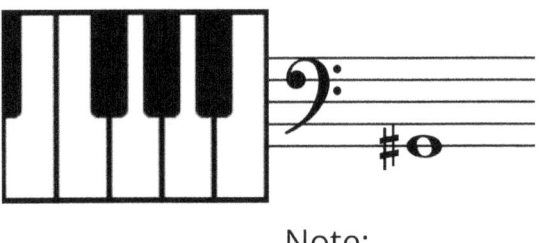

Note: _____

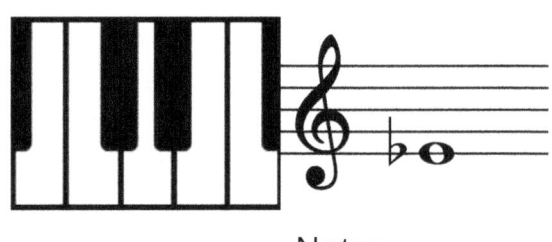

Note: _____

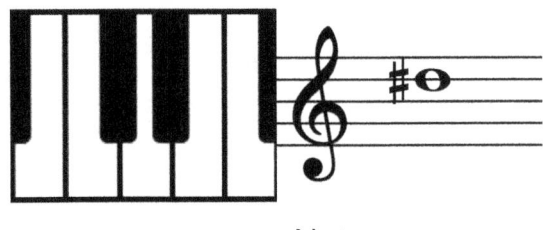

Note: _____

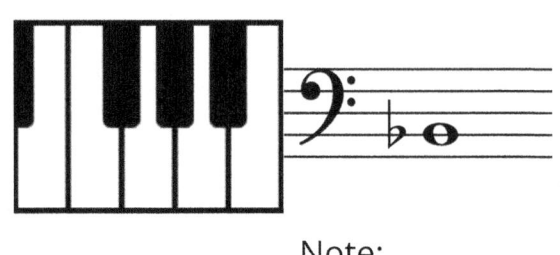

Note: _____

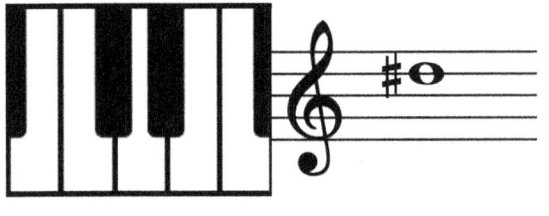

Note: _____

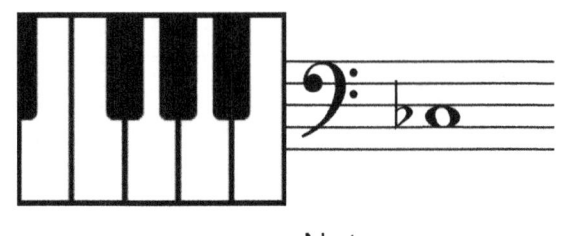

Note: _____

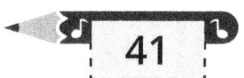

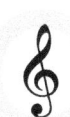 1. Clef 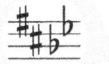 2. Accidental 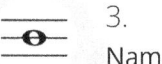 3. Name   4. Keyboard

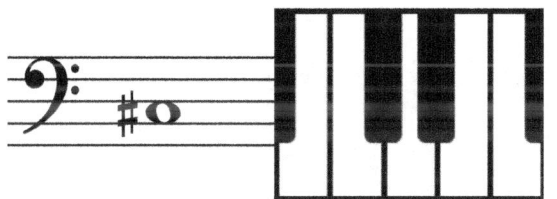

Note: _____

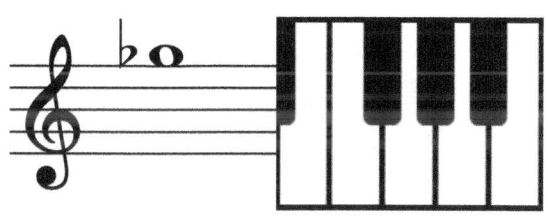

Note: _____

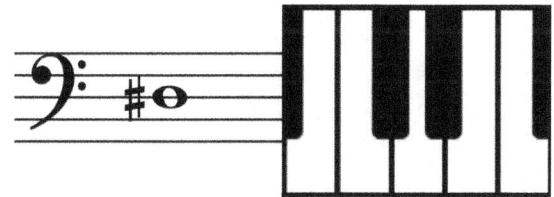

Note: _____

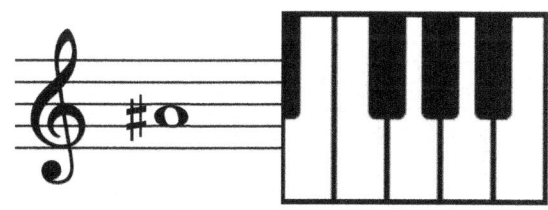

Note: _____

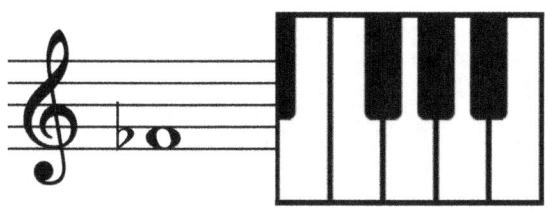

Note: _____

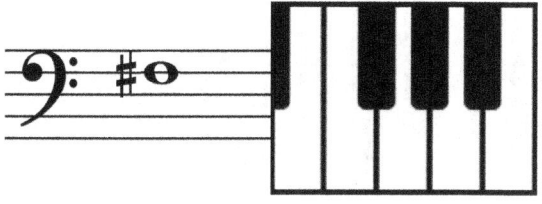

Note: _____

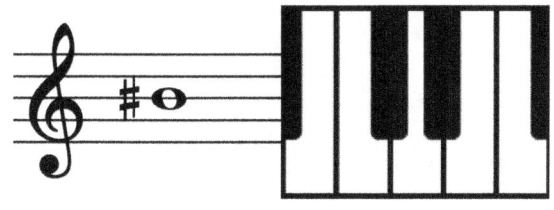

Note: _____

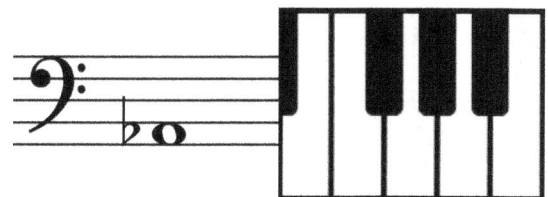

Note: _____

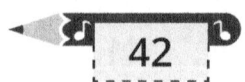

1. Clef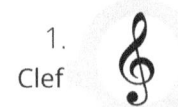
2. Accidental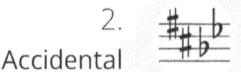
3. Name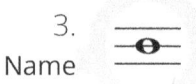
4. Keyboard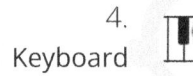

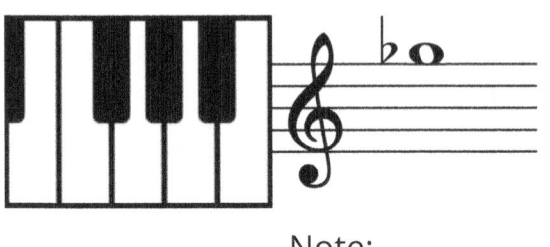
Note: _____

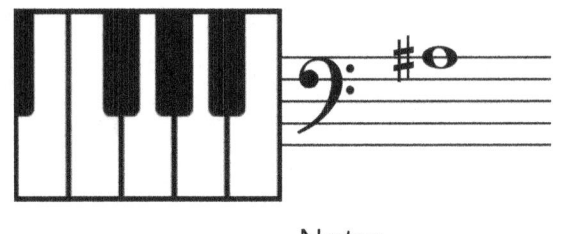
Note: _____

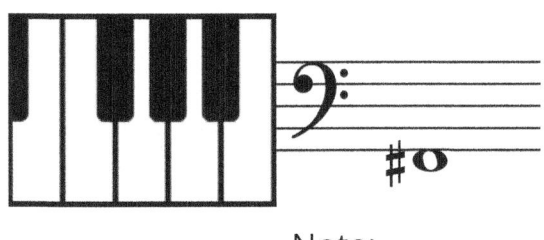
Note: _____

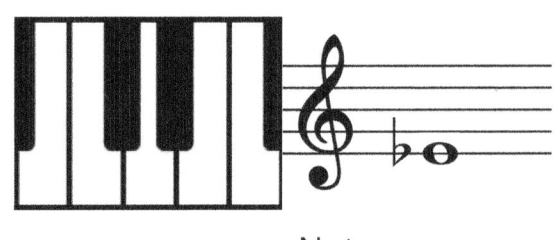
Note: _____

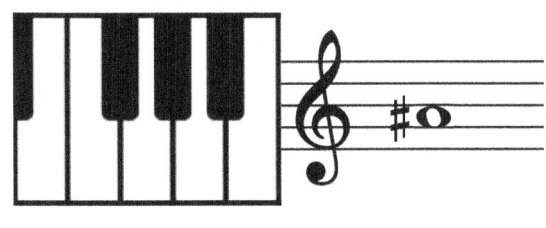
Note: _____

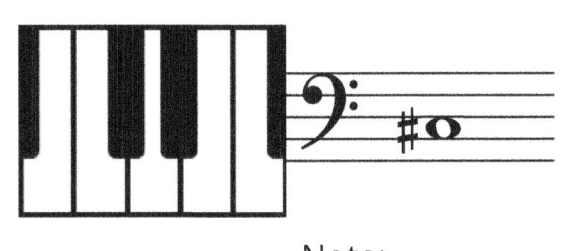
Note: _____

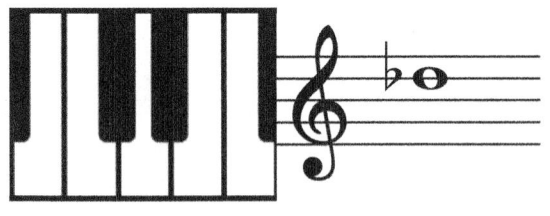
Note: _____

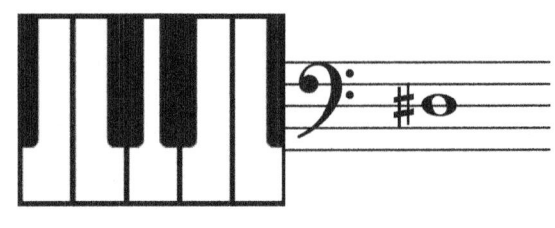
Note: _____

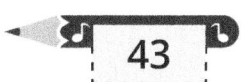

 1. Clef   2. Accidental 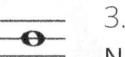 3. Name  4. Keyboard

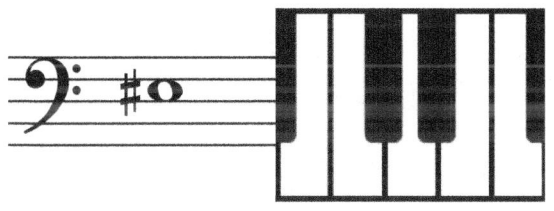

Note: _____

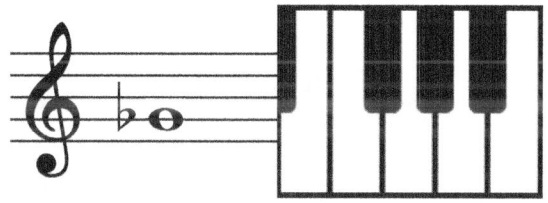

Note: _____

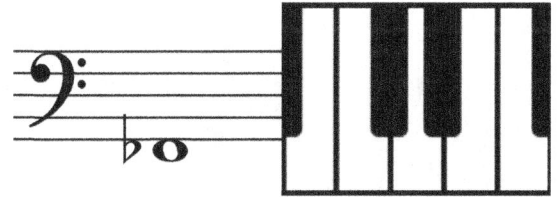

Note: _____

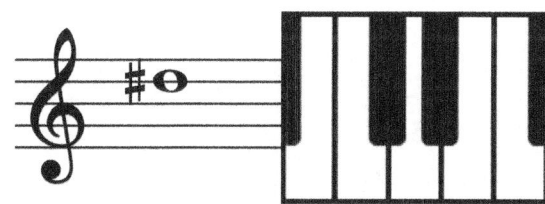

Note: _____

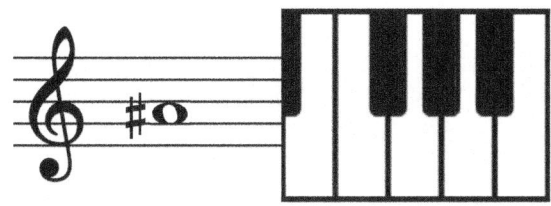

Note: _____

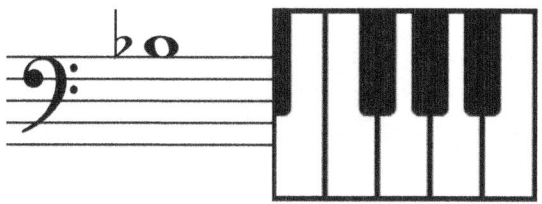

Note: _____

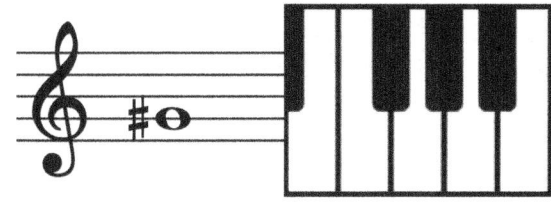

Note: _____

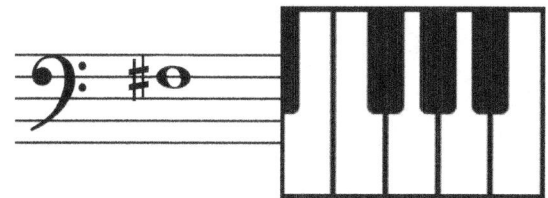

Note: _____

1. Clef 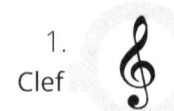　2. Accidental 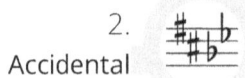　3. Name 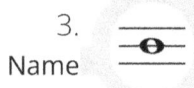　4. Keyboard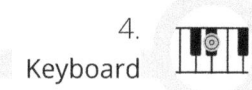

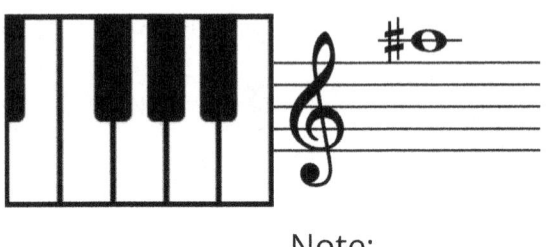
Note: _____

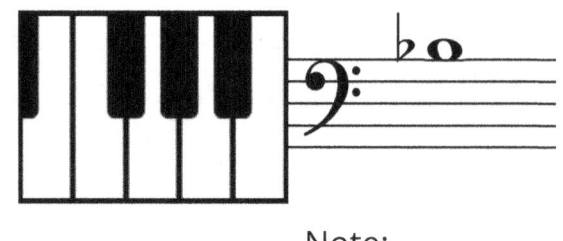
Note: _____

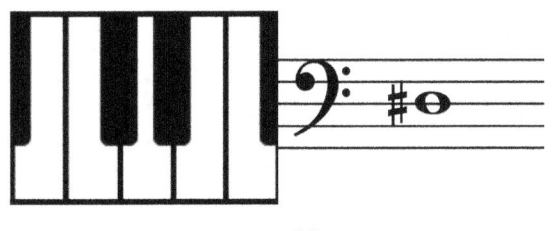
Note: _____

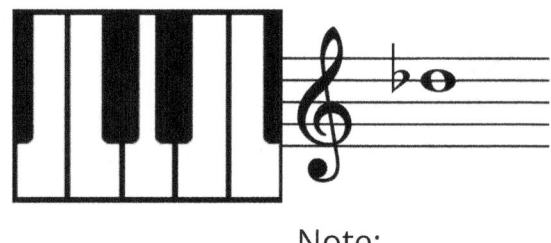
Note: _____

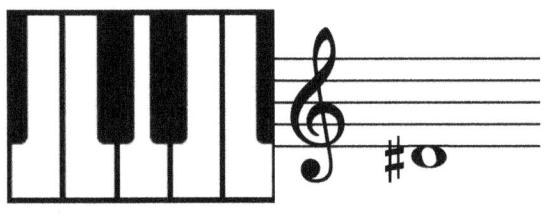
Note: _____

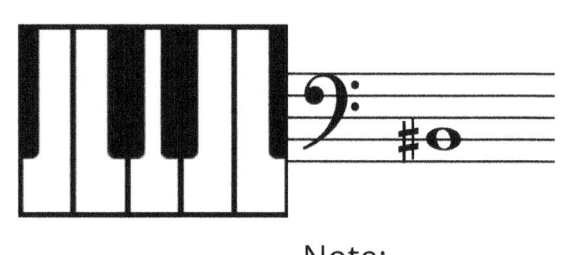
Note: _____

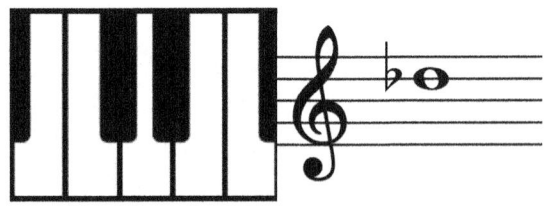
Note: _____

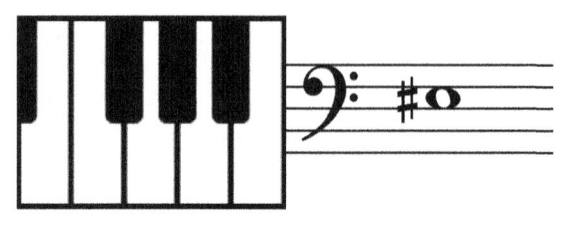
Note: _____

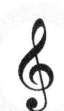 1. Clef   2. Accidental   3. Name   4. Keyboard

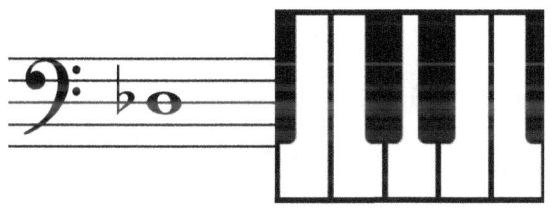

Note: _____

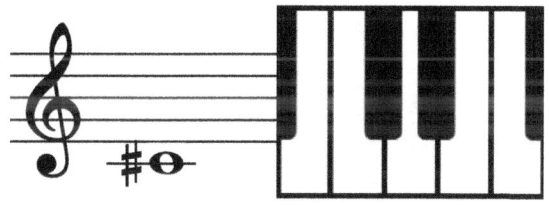

Note: _____

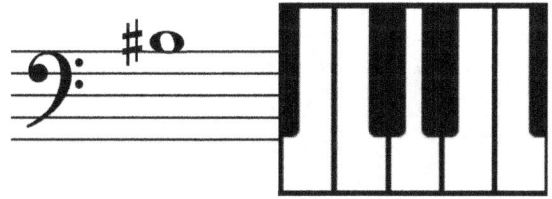

Note: _____

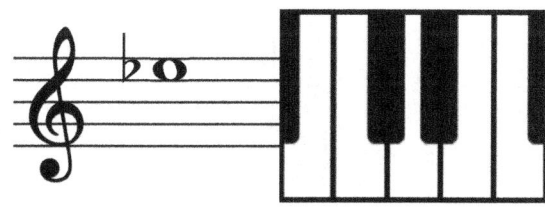

Note: _____

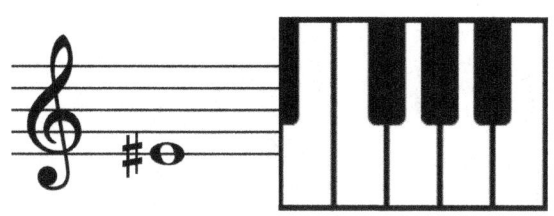

Note: _____

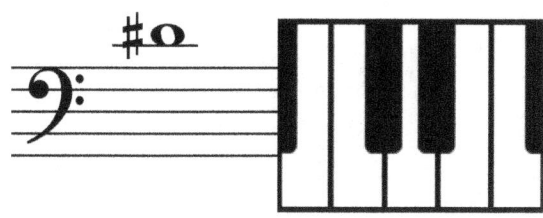

Note: _____

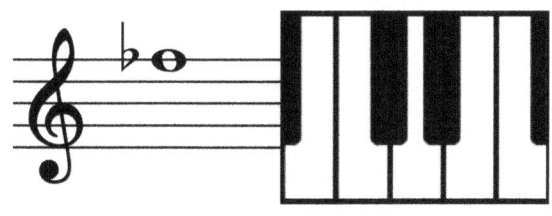

Note: _____

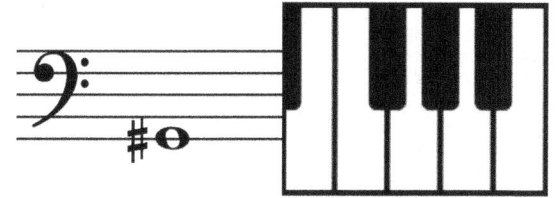

Note: _____

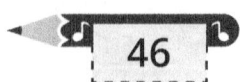

1. Clef 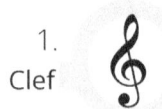　　2. Accidental 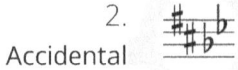　　3. Name 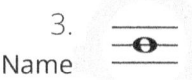　　4. Keyboard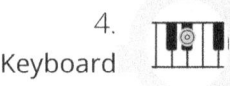

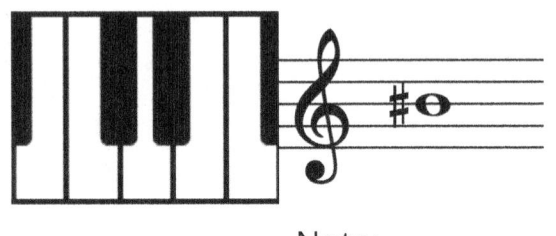
Note: _____

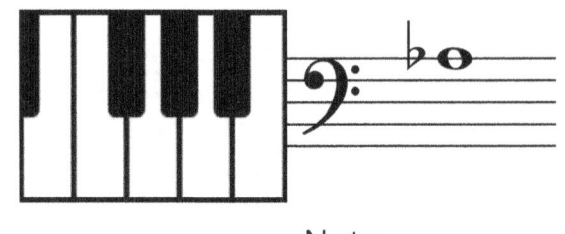
Note: _____

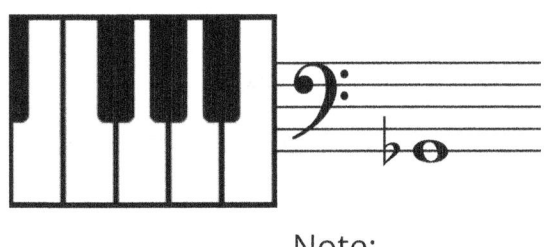
Note: _____

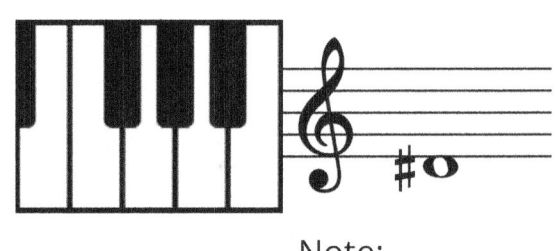
Note: _____

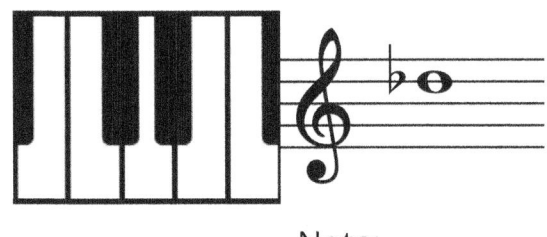
Note: _____

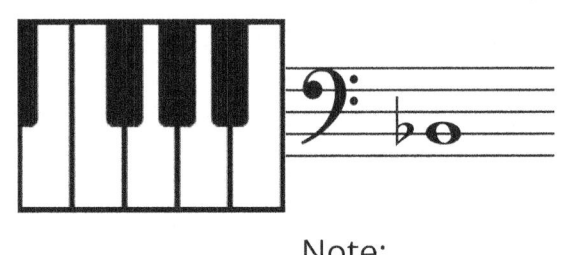
Note: _____

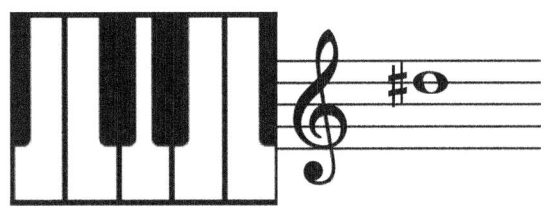
Note: _____

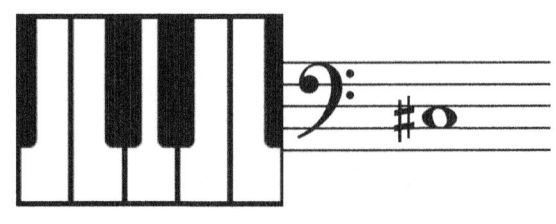
Note: _____

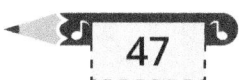

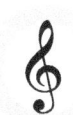 1. Clef 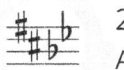 2. Accidental 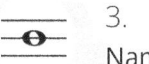 3. Name 4. Keyboard

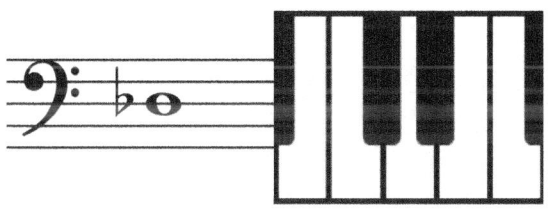

Note: _____

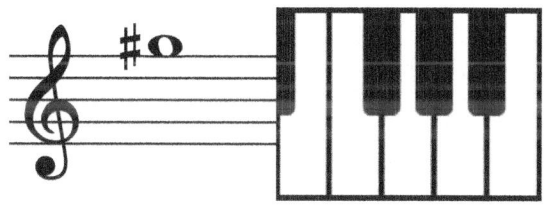

Note: _____

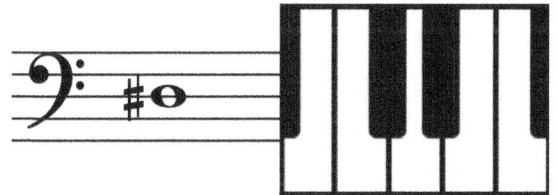

Note: _____

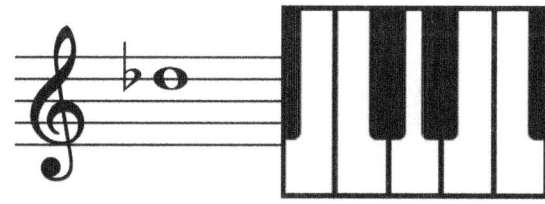

Note: _____

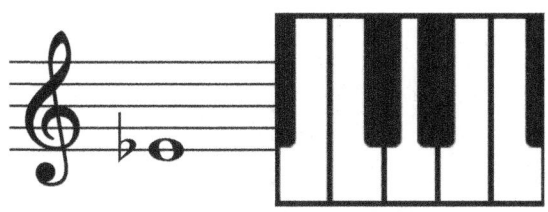

Note: _____

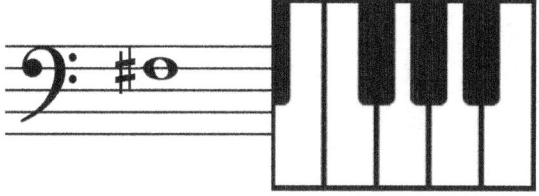

Note: _____

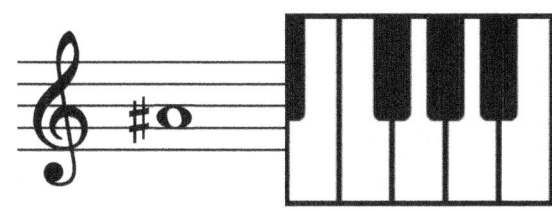

Note: _____

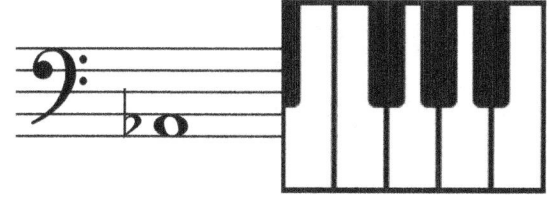

Note: _____

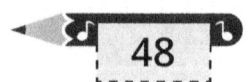

1. Clef 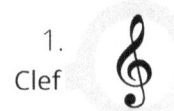 2. Accidental 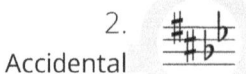 3. Name 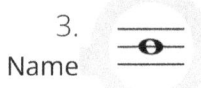 4. Keyboard

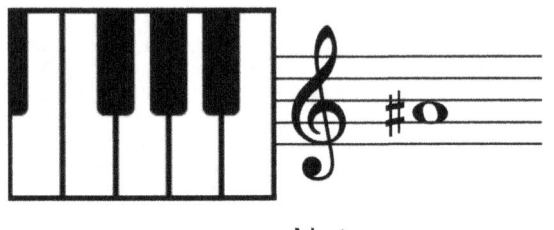

Note: _____

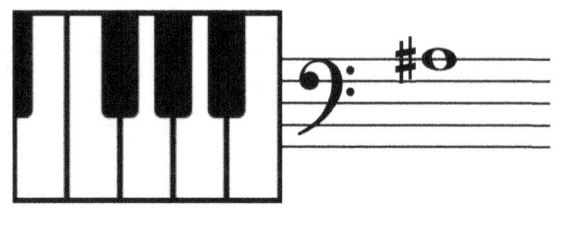

Note: _____

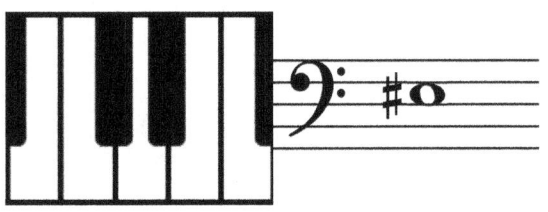

Note: _____

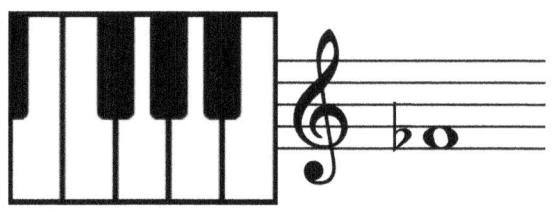

Note: _____

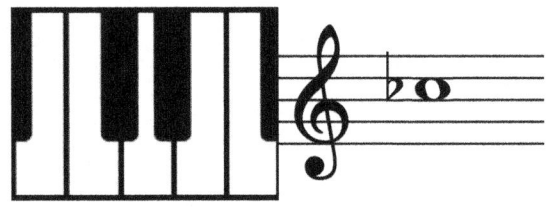

Note: _____

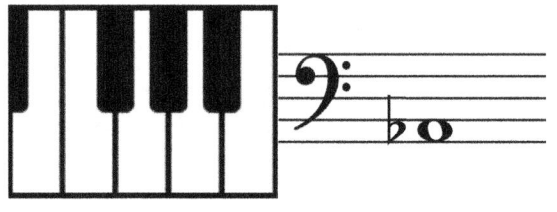

Note: _____

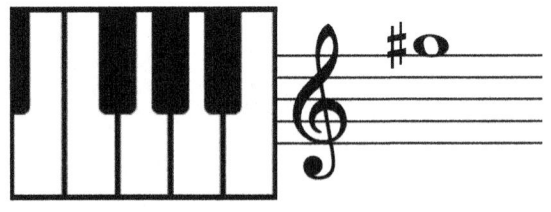

Note: _____

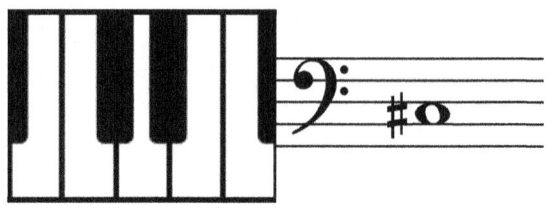

Note: _____

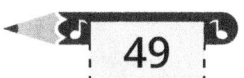

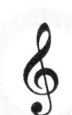 1. Clef   2. Accidental   3. Name   4. Keyboard

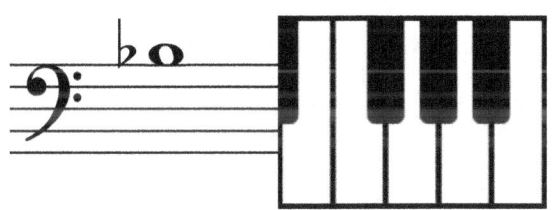

Note: _____

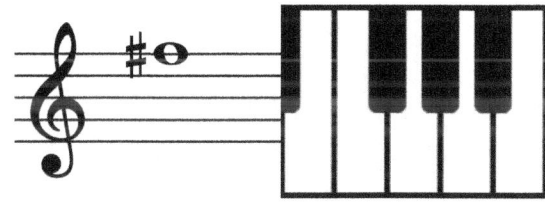

Note: _____

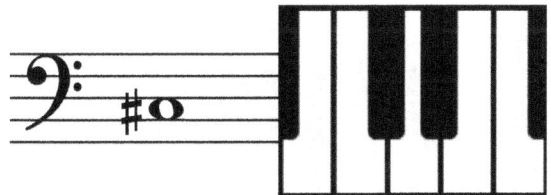

Note: _____

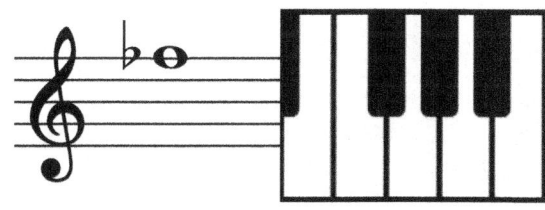

Note: _____

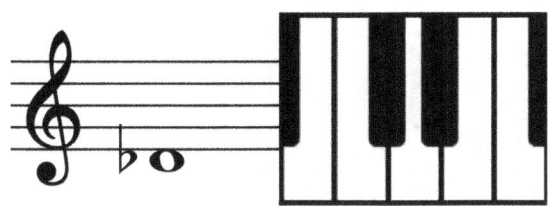

Note: _____

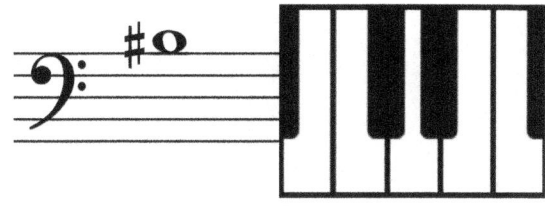

Note: _____

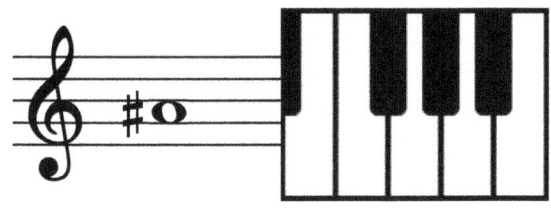

Note: _____

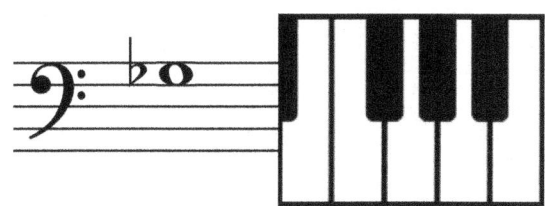

Note: _____

1. Clef 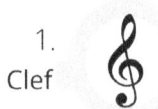 2. Accidental 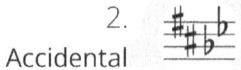 3. Name 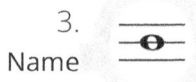 4. Keyboard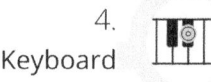

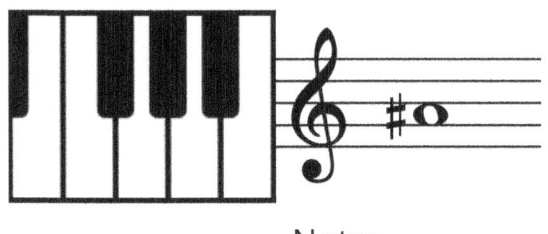

Note: _____

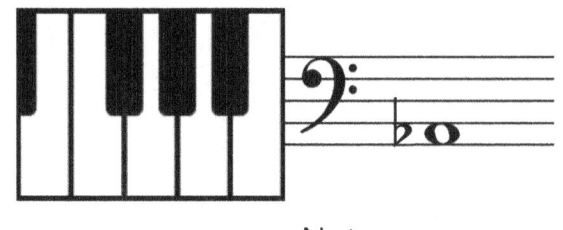

Note: _____

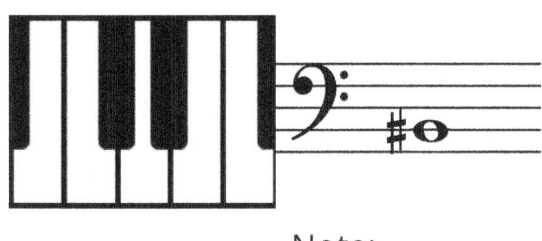

Note: _____

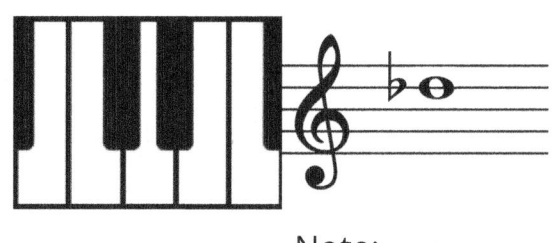

Note: _____

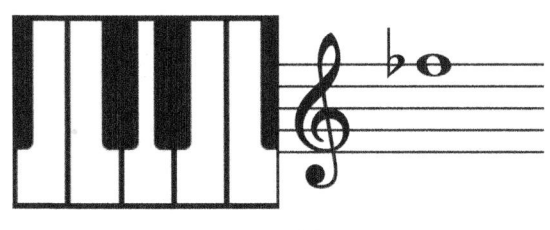

Note: _____

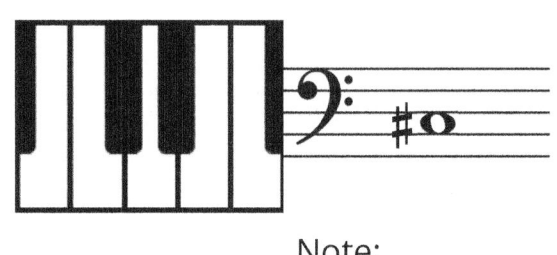

Note: _____

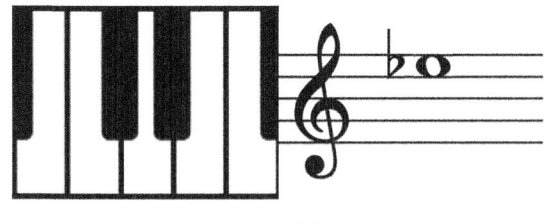

Note: _____

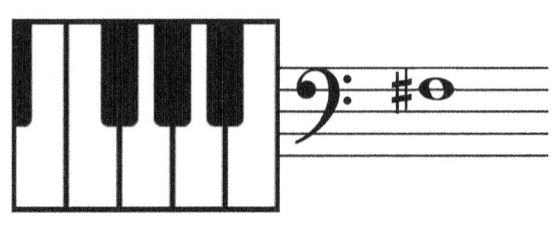

Note: _____

Chapter 4
Key Signatures

Instructions with Example

Practice in the Grand Staff

Practice on Keyboard & Staff

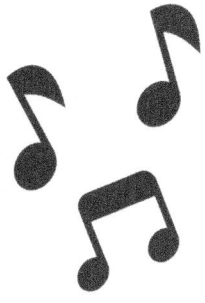

Instructions with Example

Three easy steps to complete the exercises:

1. 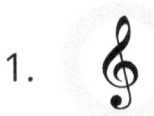 **Clef:** Look at the clef, which tells you what note belongs to each line or space on the staff. In the bass clef, the note **A** is in the lowest space. In the treble clef, the note **A** is one whole step higher.

2. **Key Signature:** The accidentals show the key. Key Signatures follow the Circle of Fifths, and the sharps and flats always appear in a special, set order

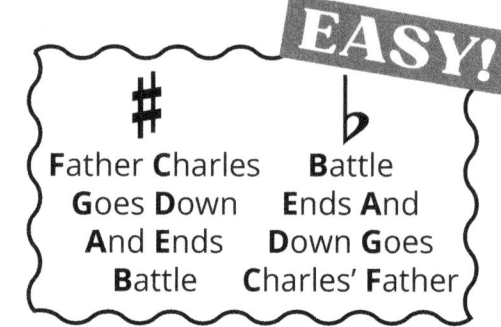

Father Charles **Battle**
Goes Down **Ends And**
And Ends **Down Goes**
Battle **Charles' Father**

3. **Name: Find the note name.** Ask yourself: Which line or space is the note on? Then, figure out the name of that note.

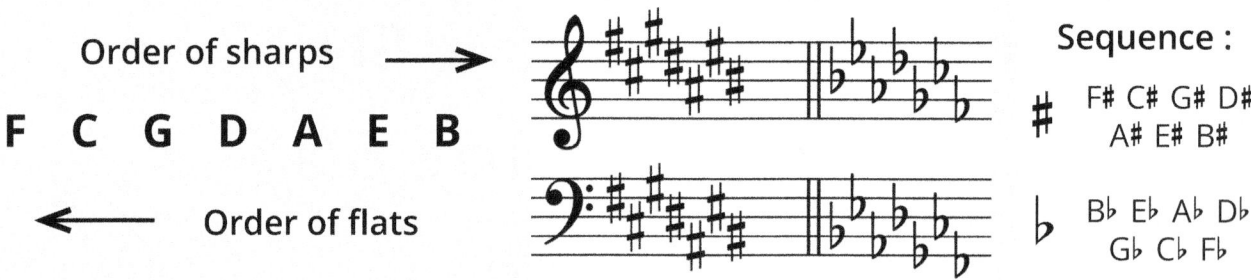

Order of sharps →

F C G D A E B

← Order of flats

Sequence :

♯ F# C# G# D#
A# E# B#

♭ B♭ E♭ A♭ D♭
G♭ C♭ F♭

Sharps and flats follow the same order in both treble and bass clef. **Sharps and flats are opposites**. The order of sharps is simply the reverse of the order of flats. Tip: Once you learn the order, you'll recognize key signatures quickly; no matter which clef you're using!

Example:

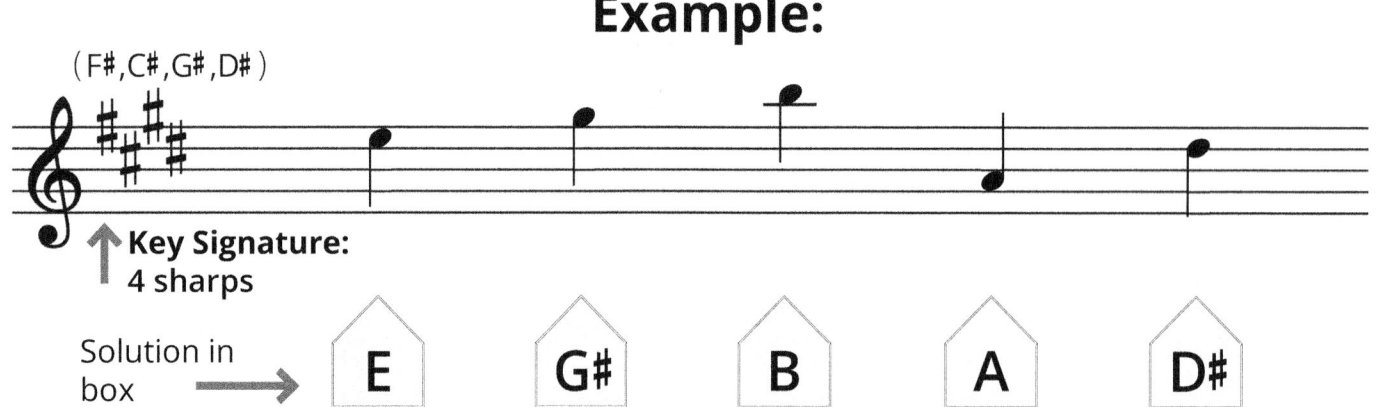

- 79 -

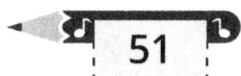

1. Clef
2. Key Signature
3. Name

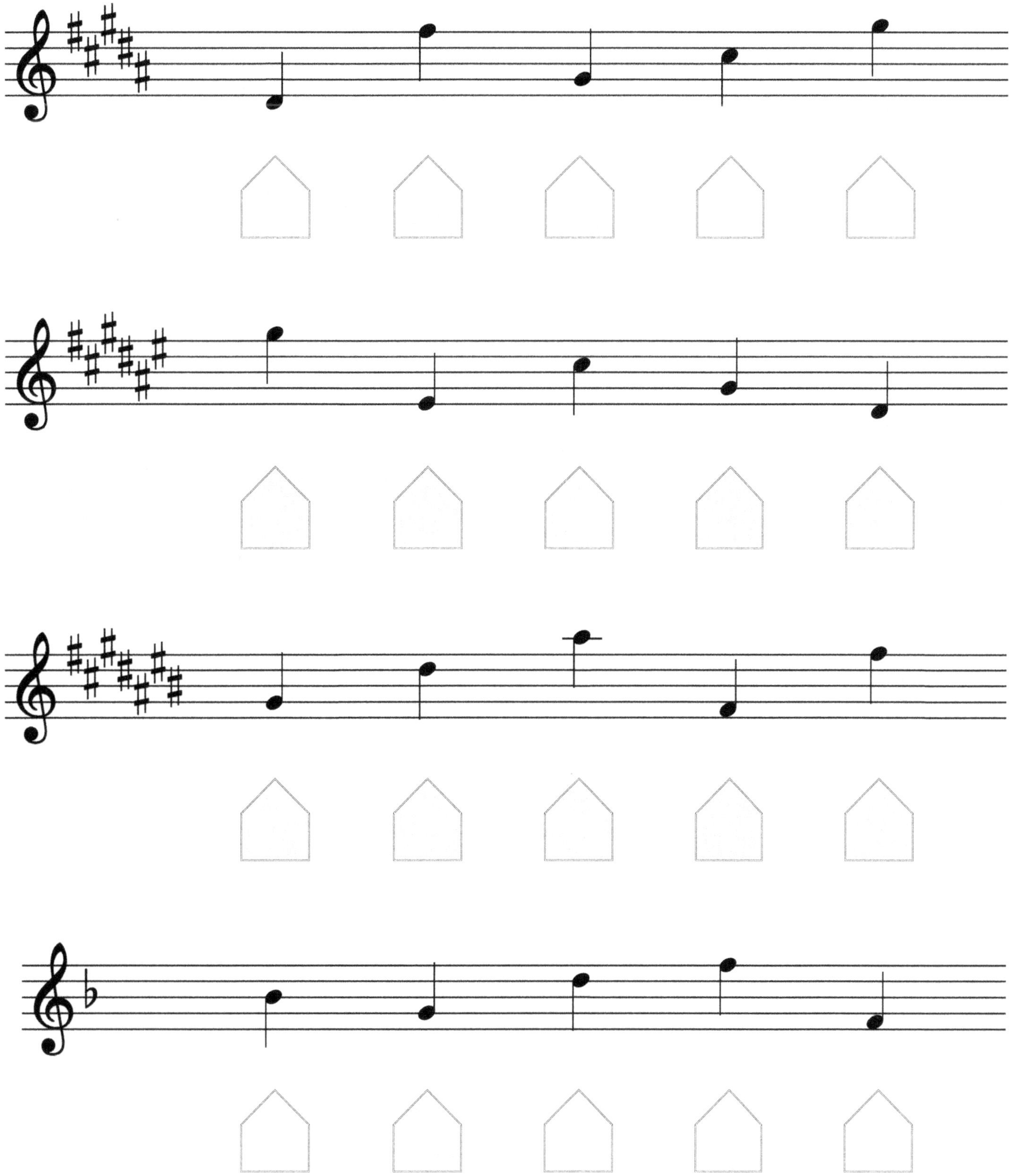

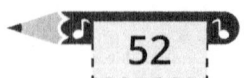

1. Clef 𝄞   2. Key Signature   3. Name

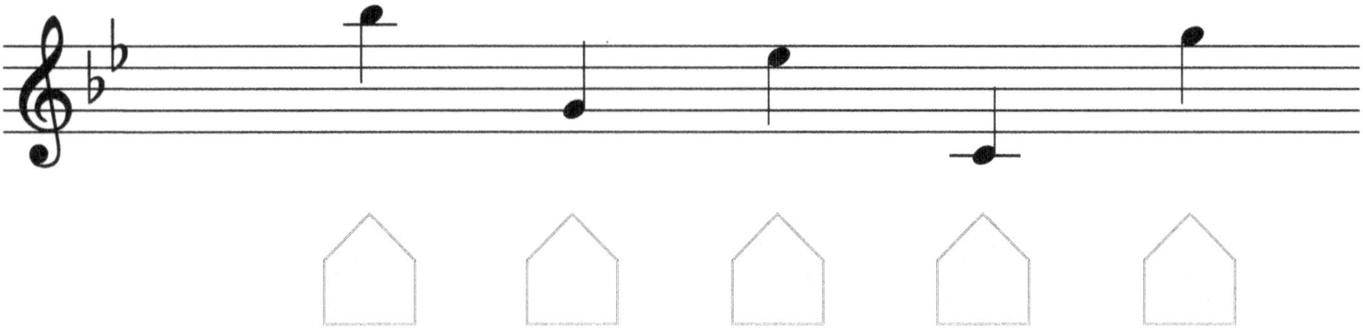

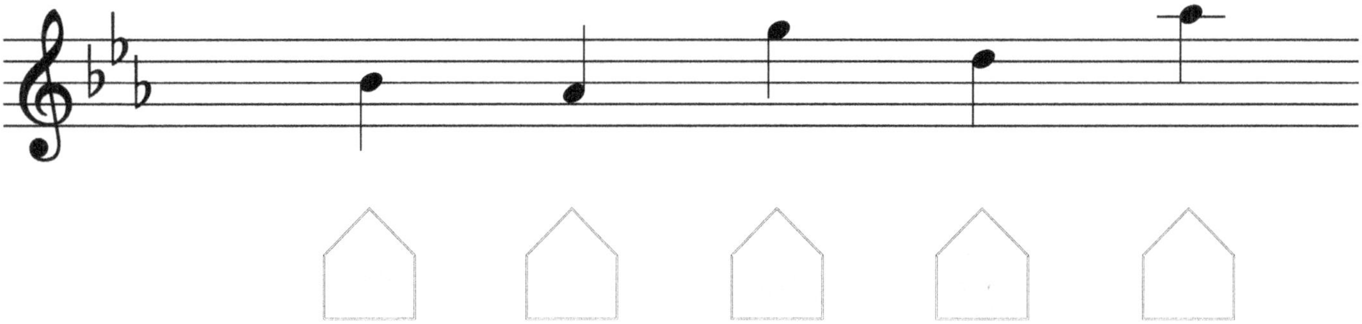

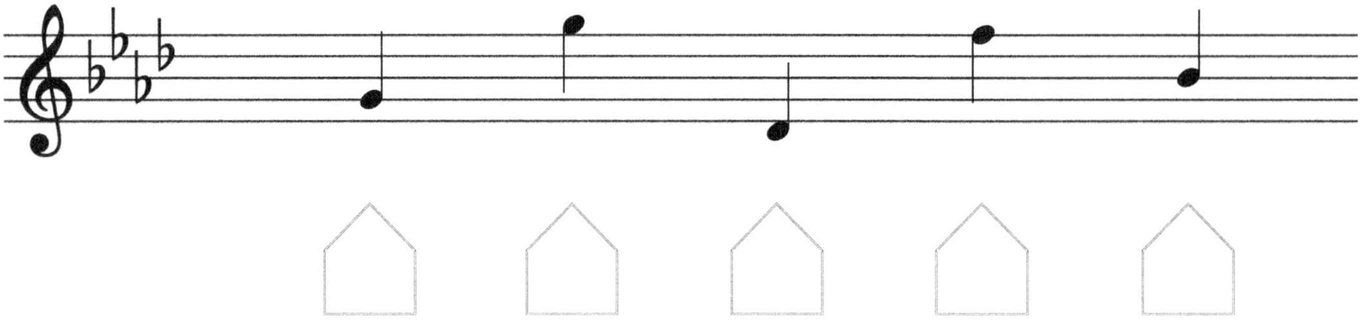

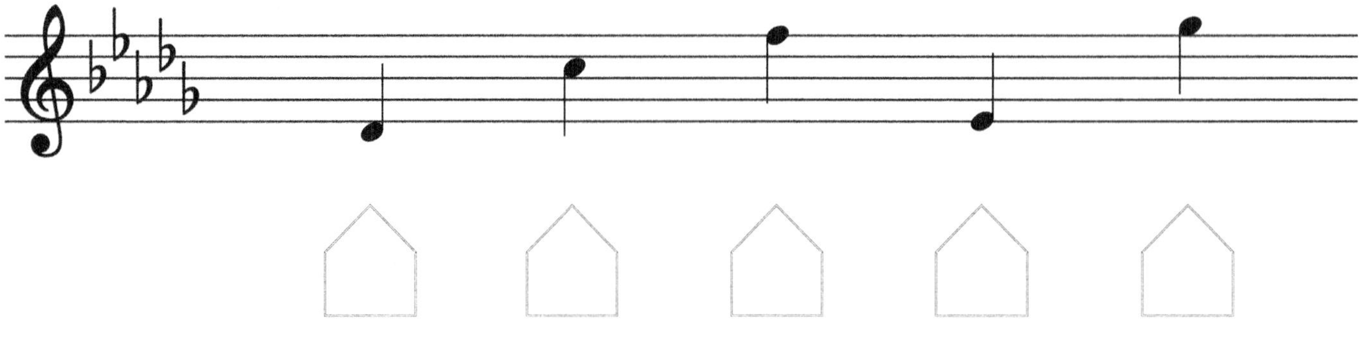

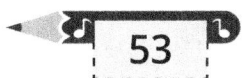

1. Clef 2. Key Signature 3. Name

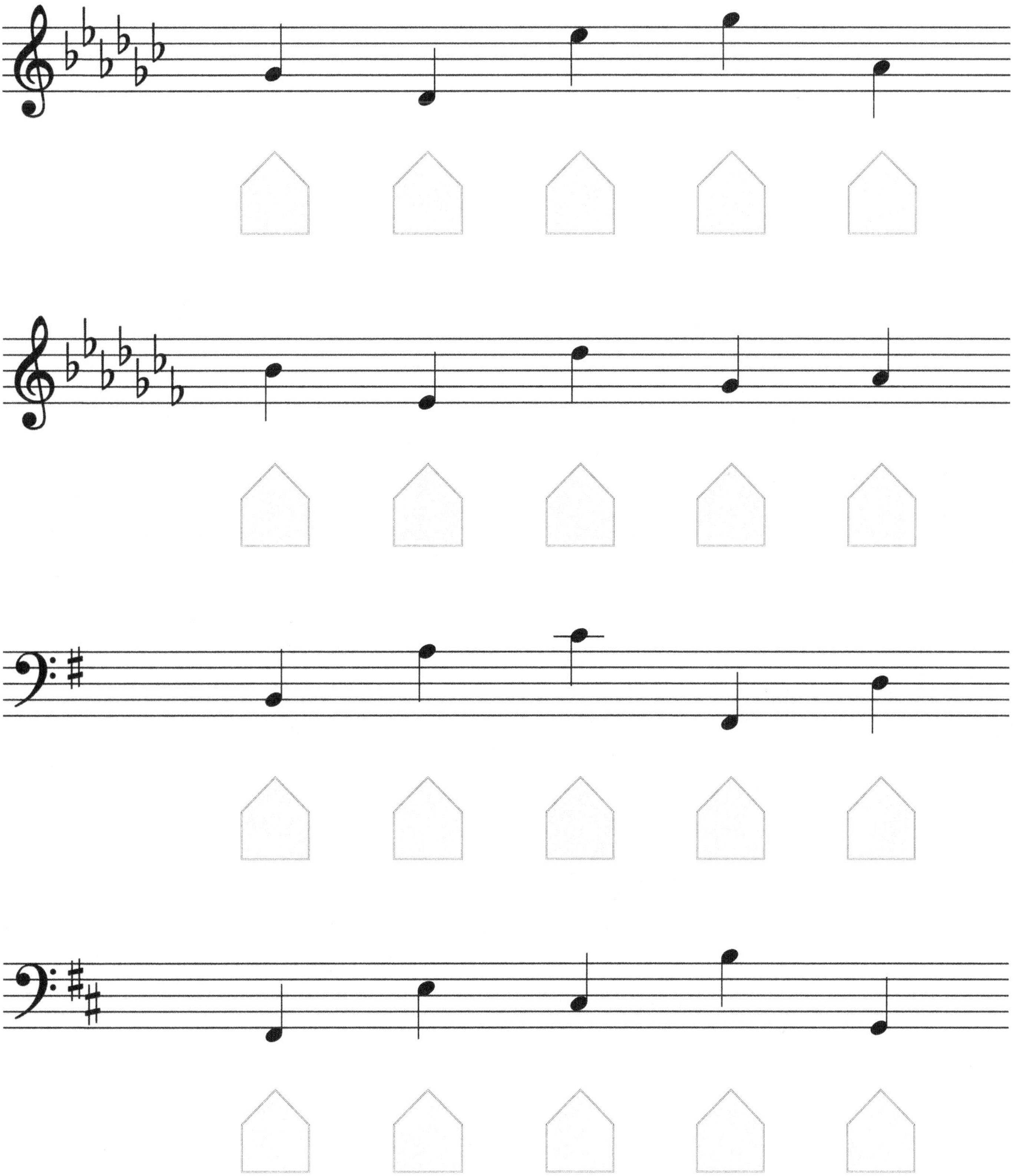

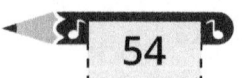

1. Clef
2. Key Signature
3. Name

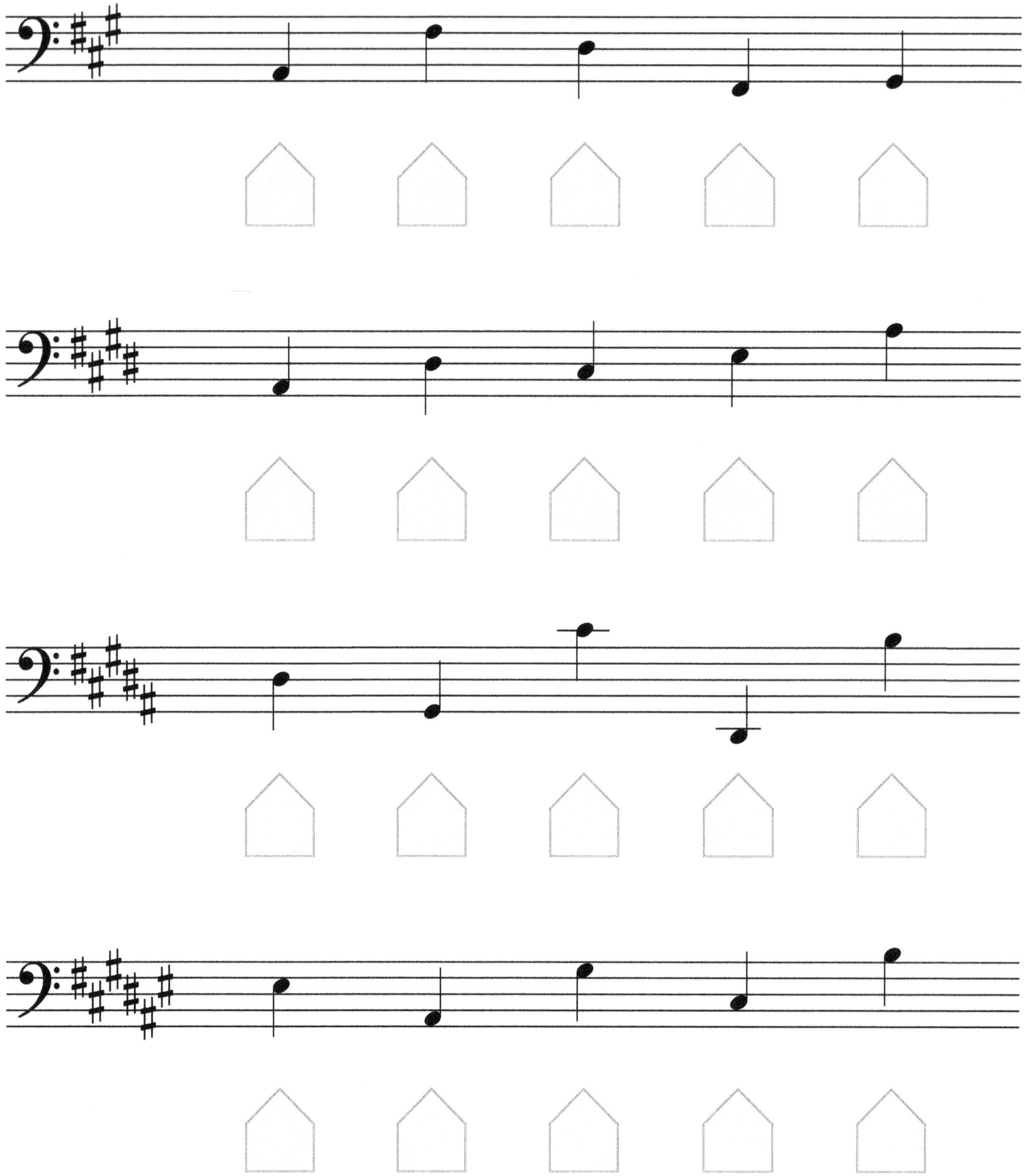

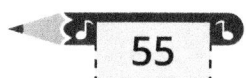

1. Clef　　2. Key Signature　　3. Name

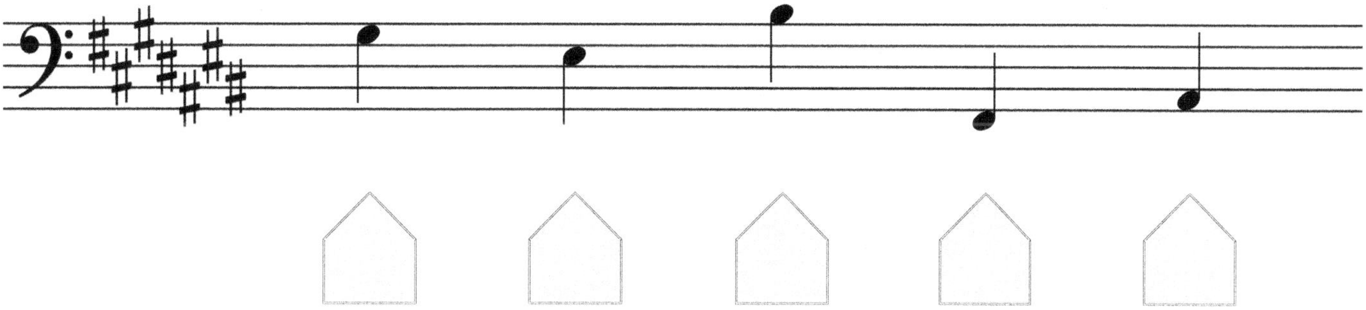

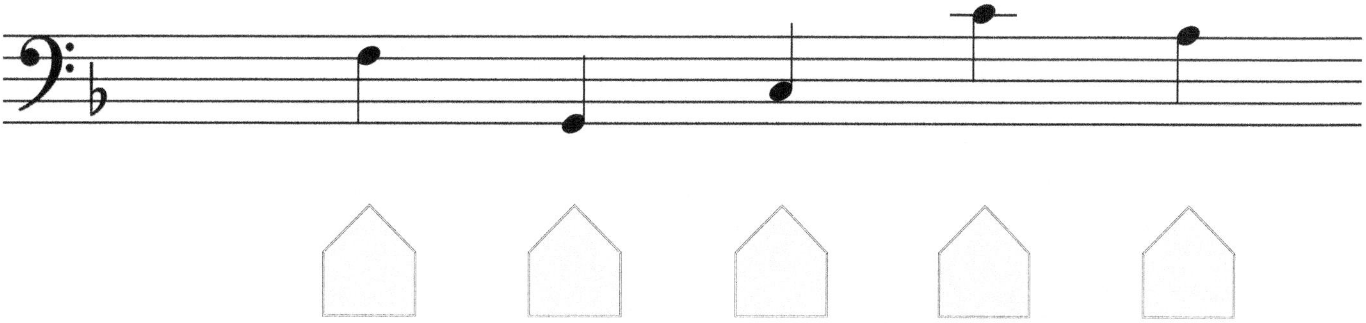

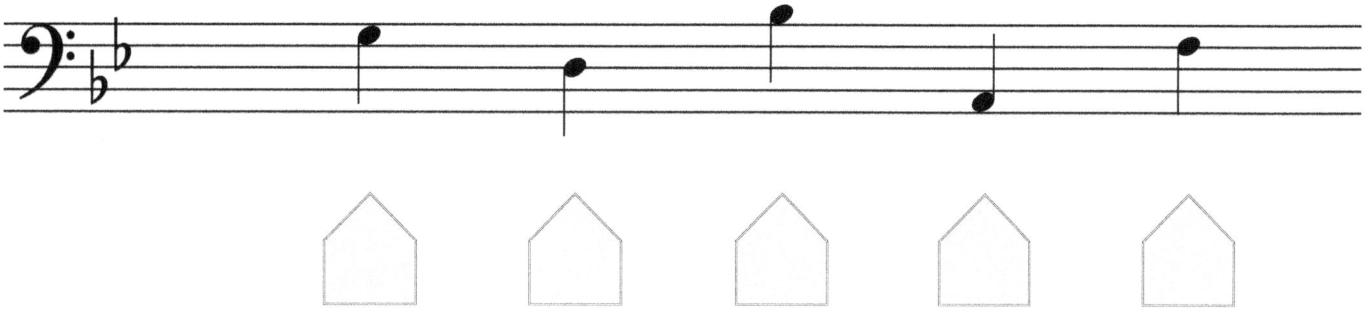

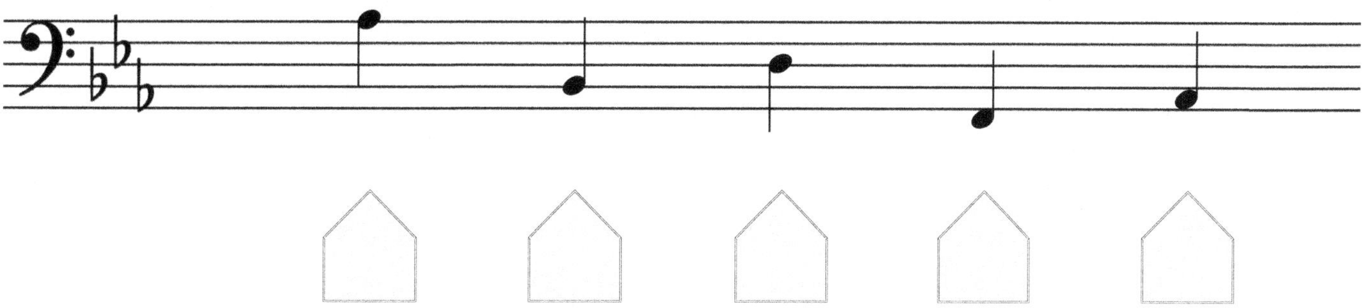

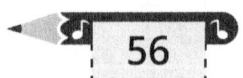

1. Clef   2. Key Signature   3. Name

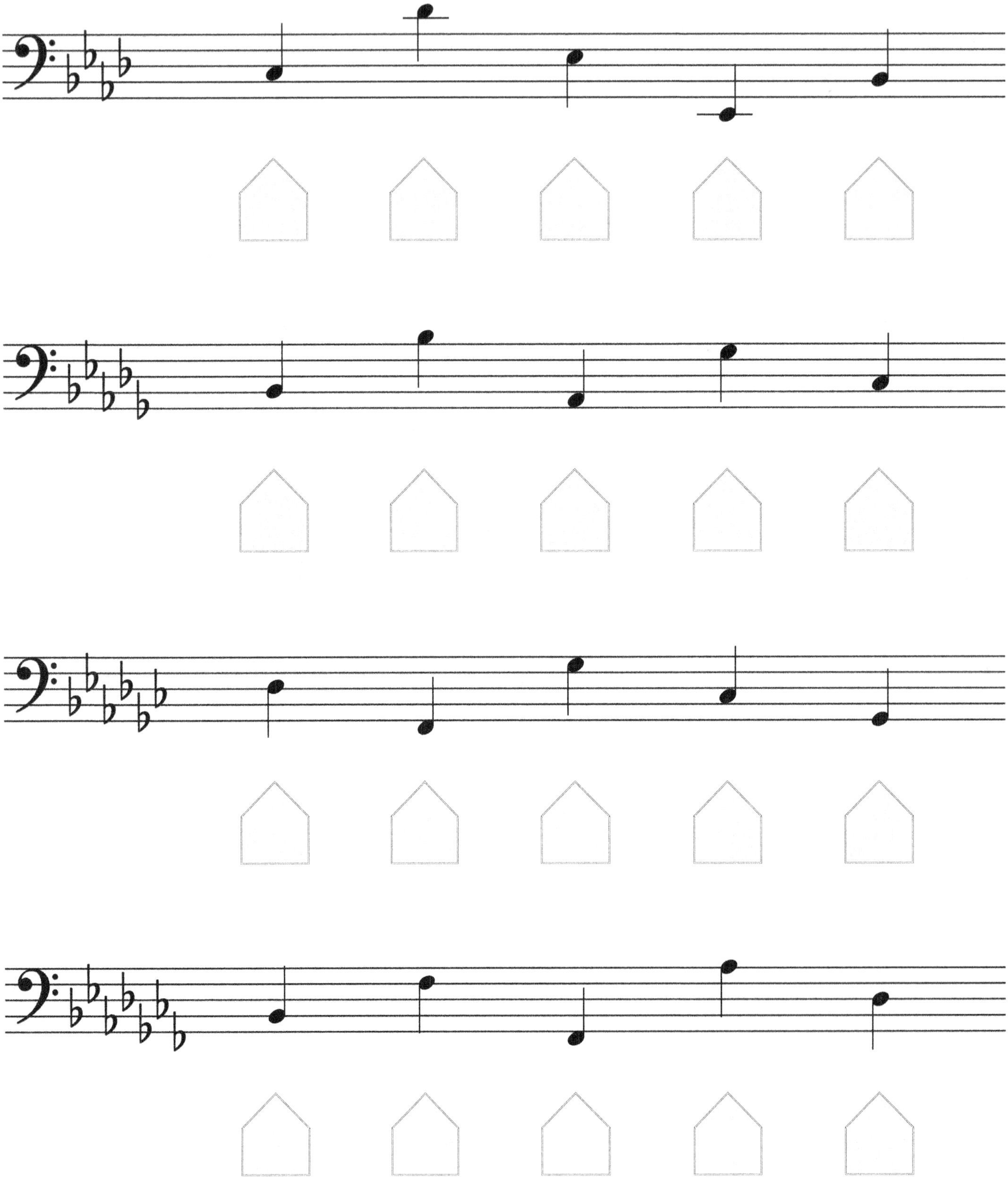

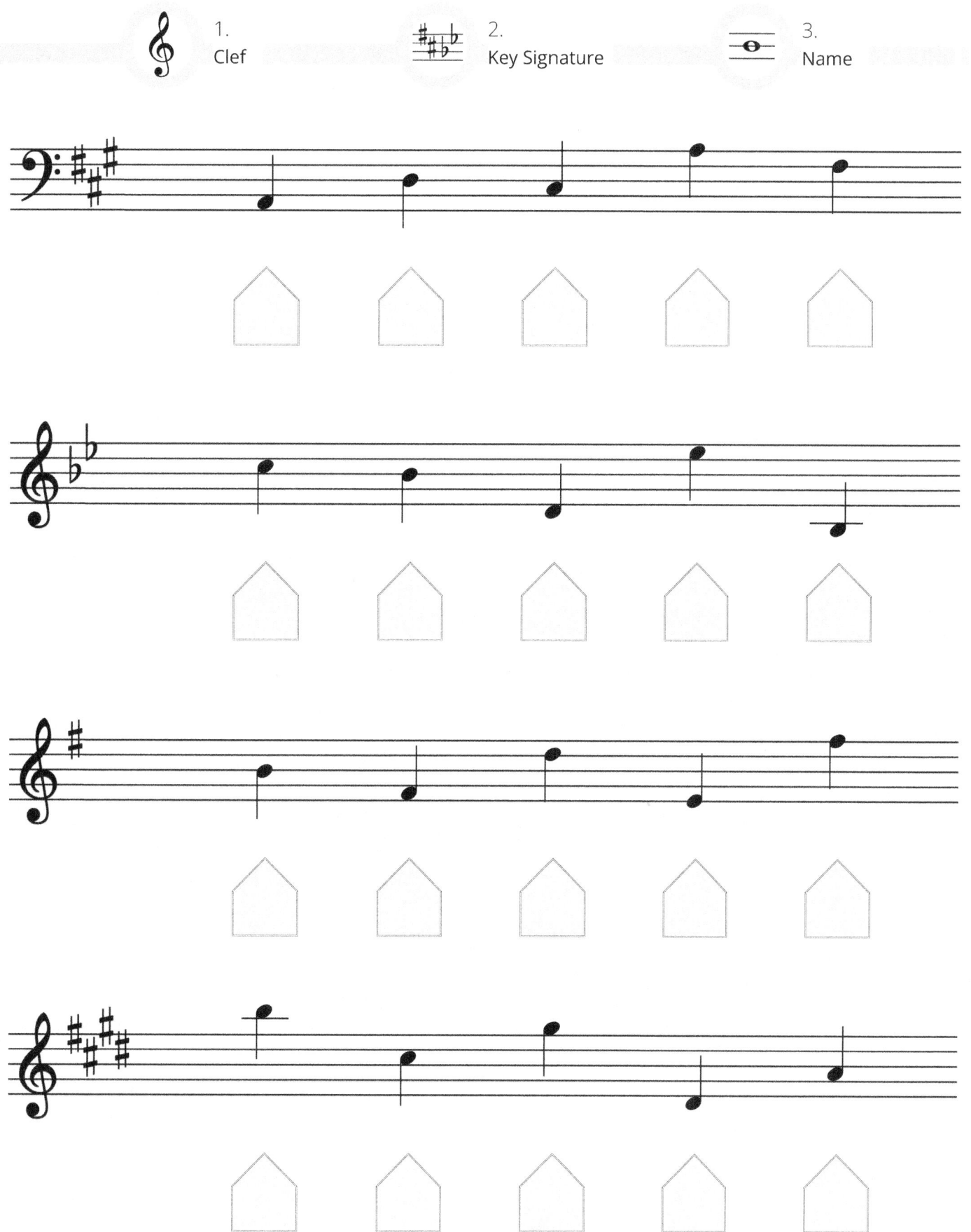

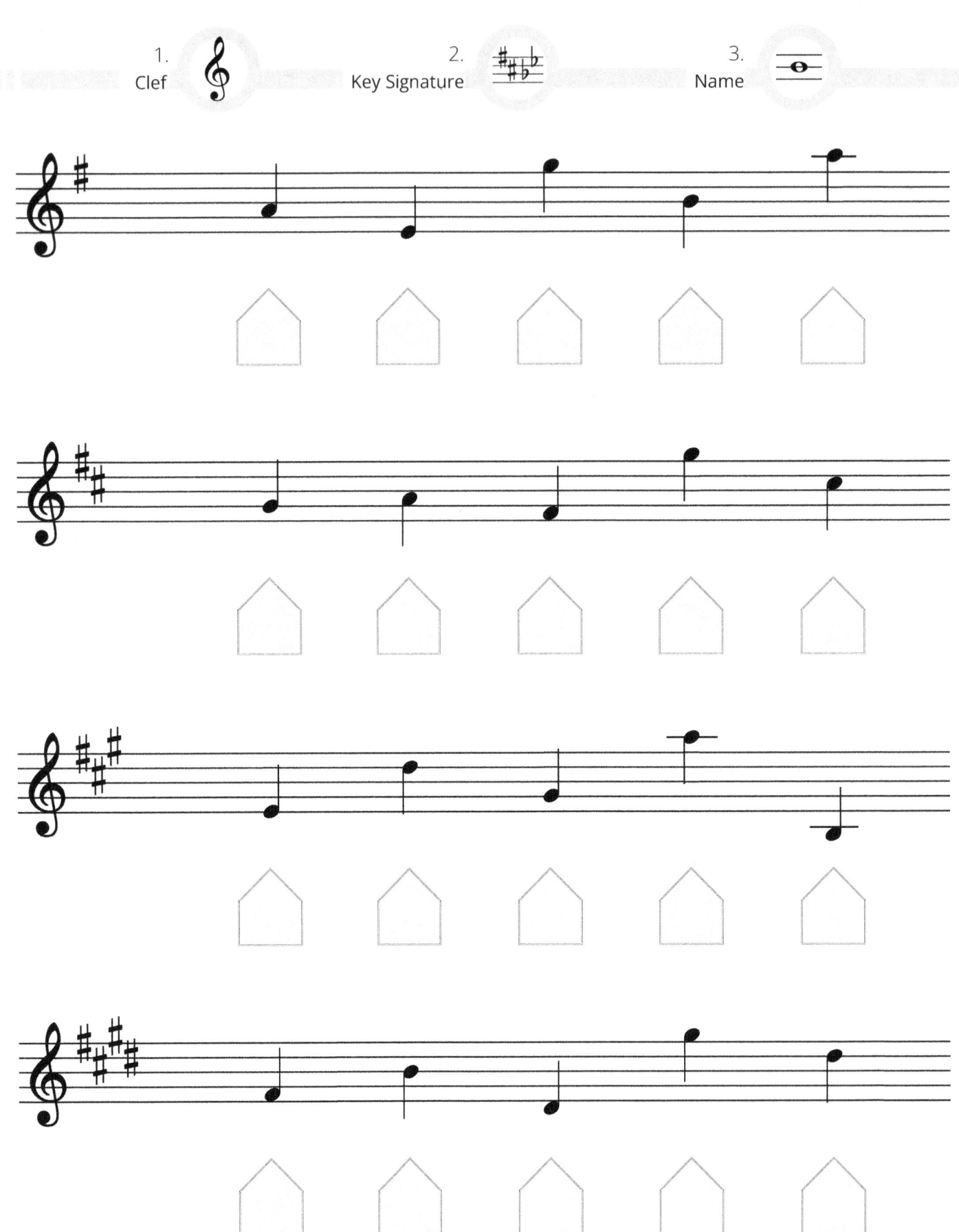

1. Clef
2. Key Signature
3. Name

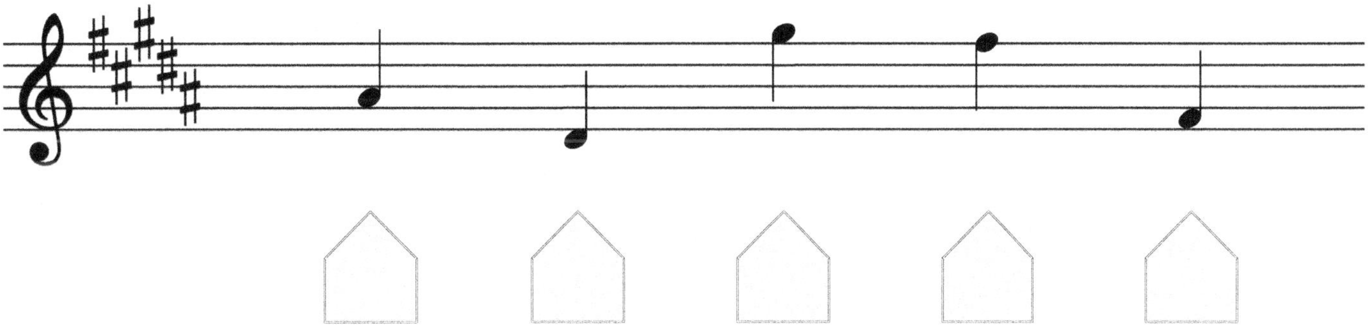

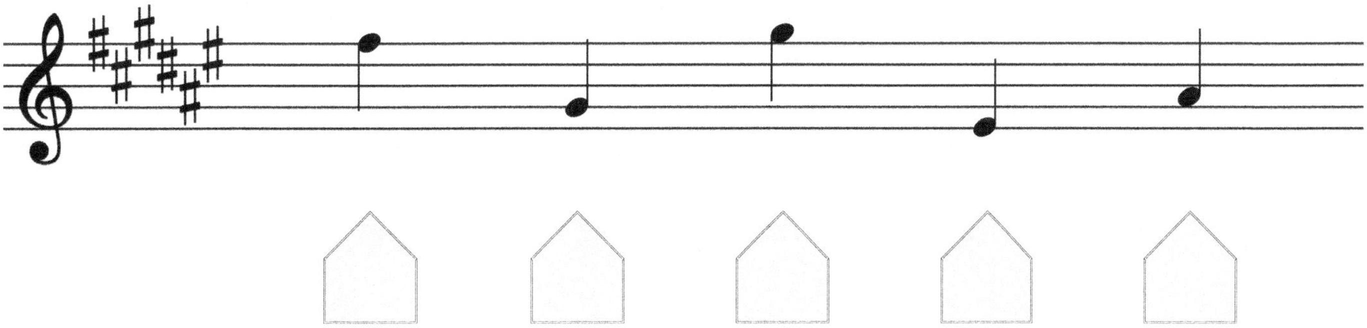

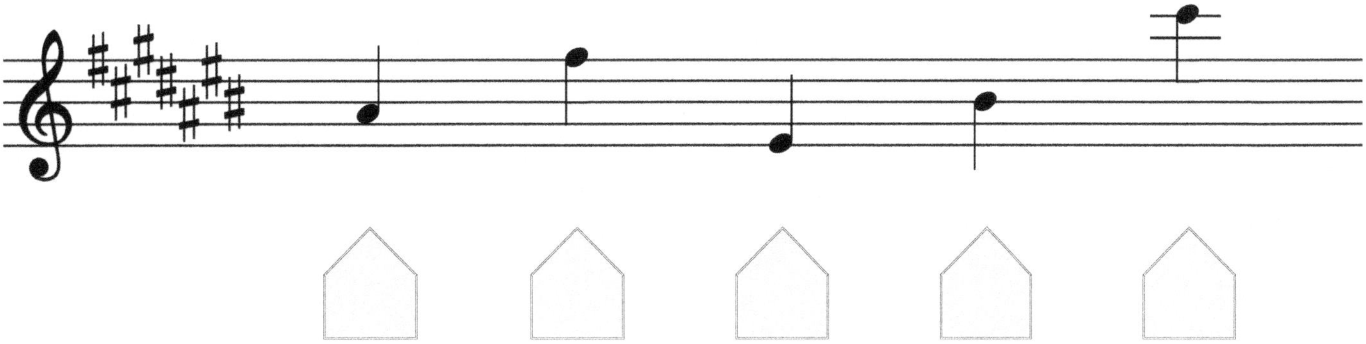

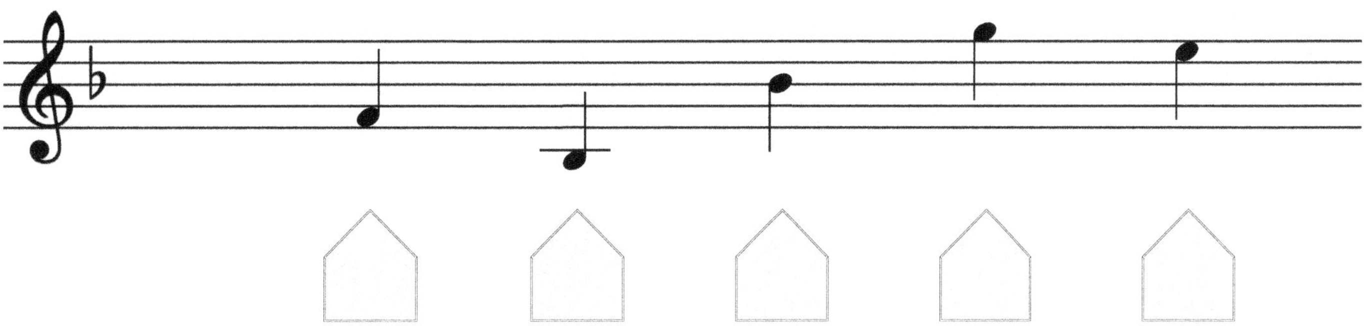

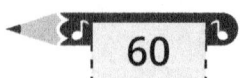

1. Clef 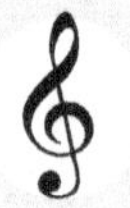
2. Key Signature 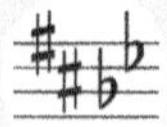
3. Name

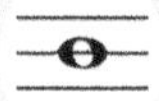

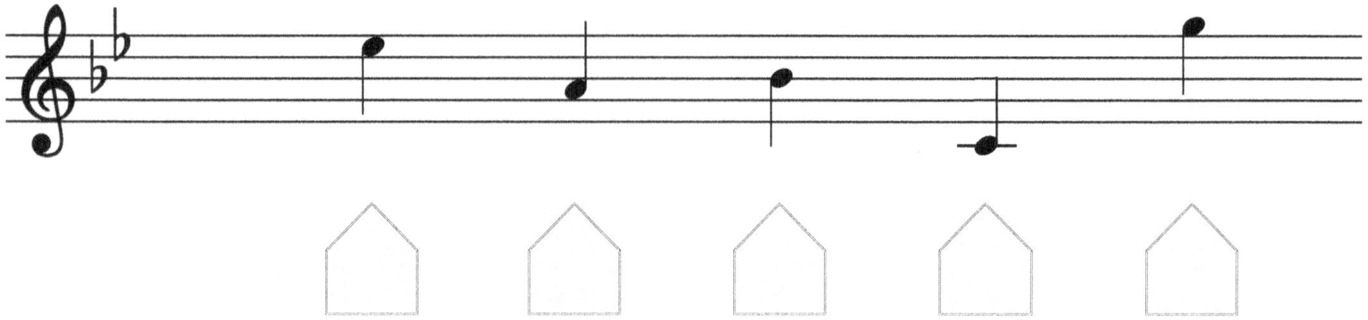

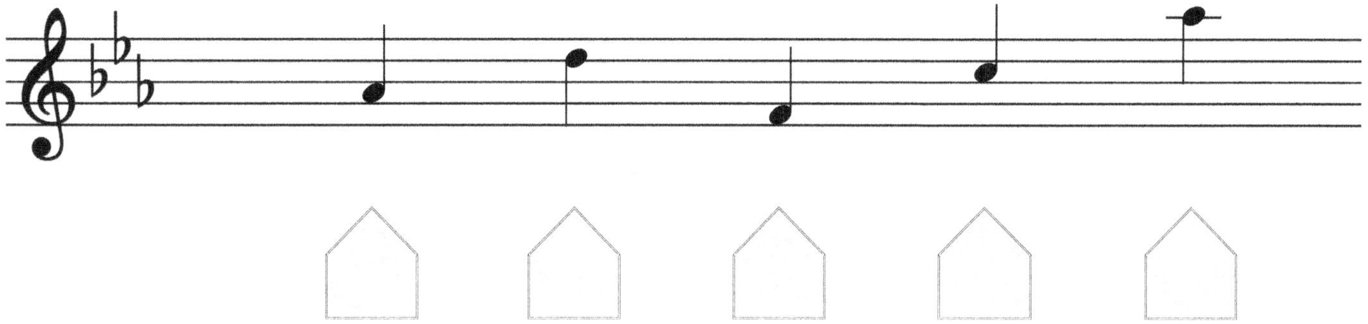

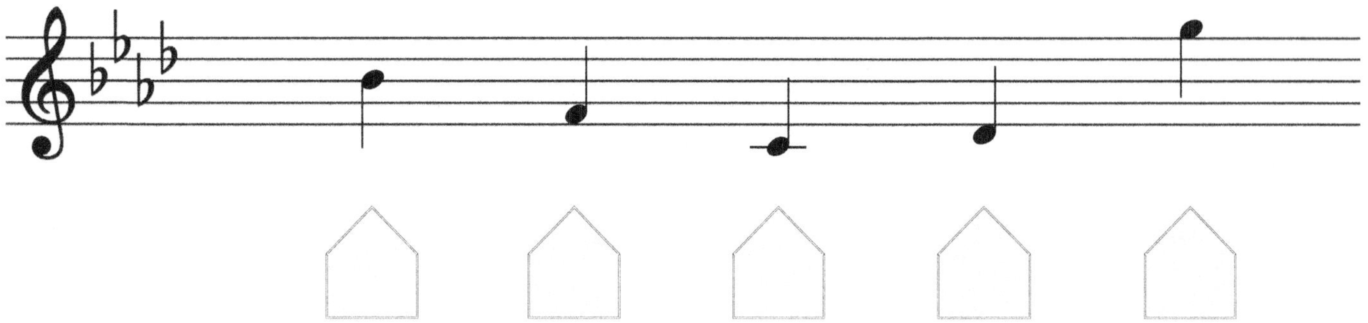

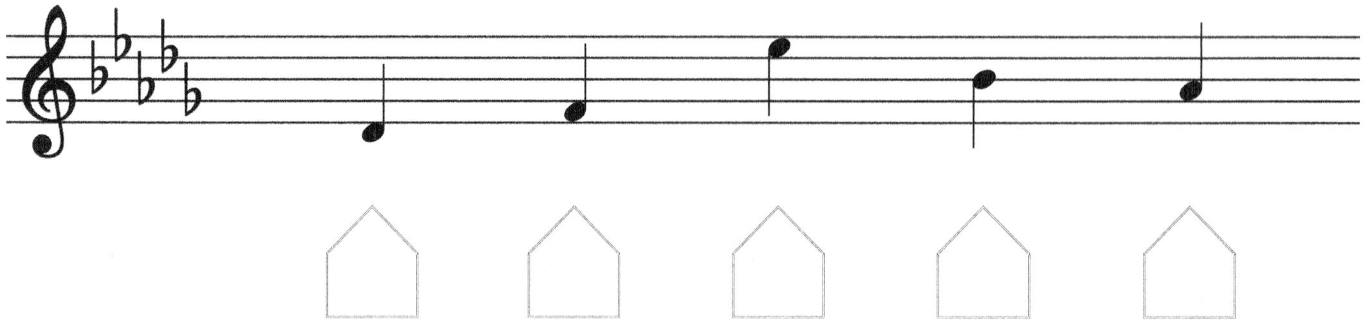

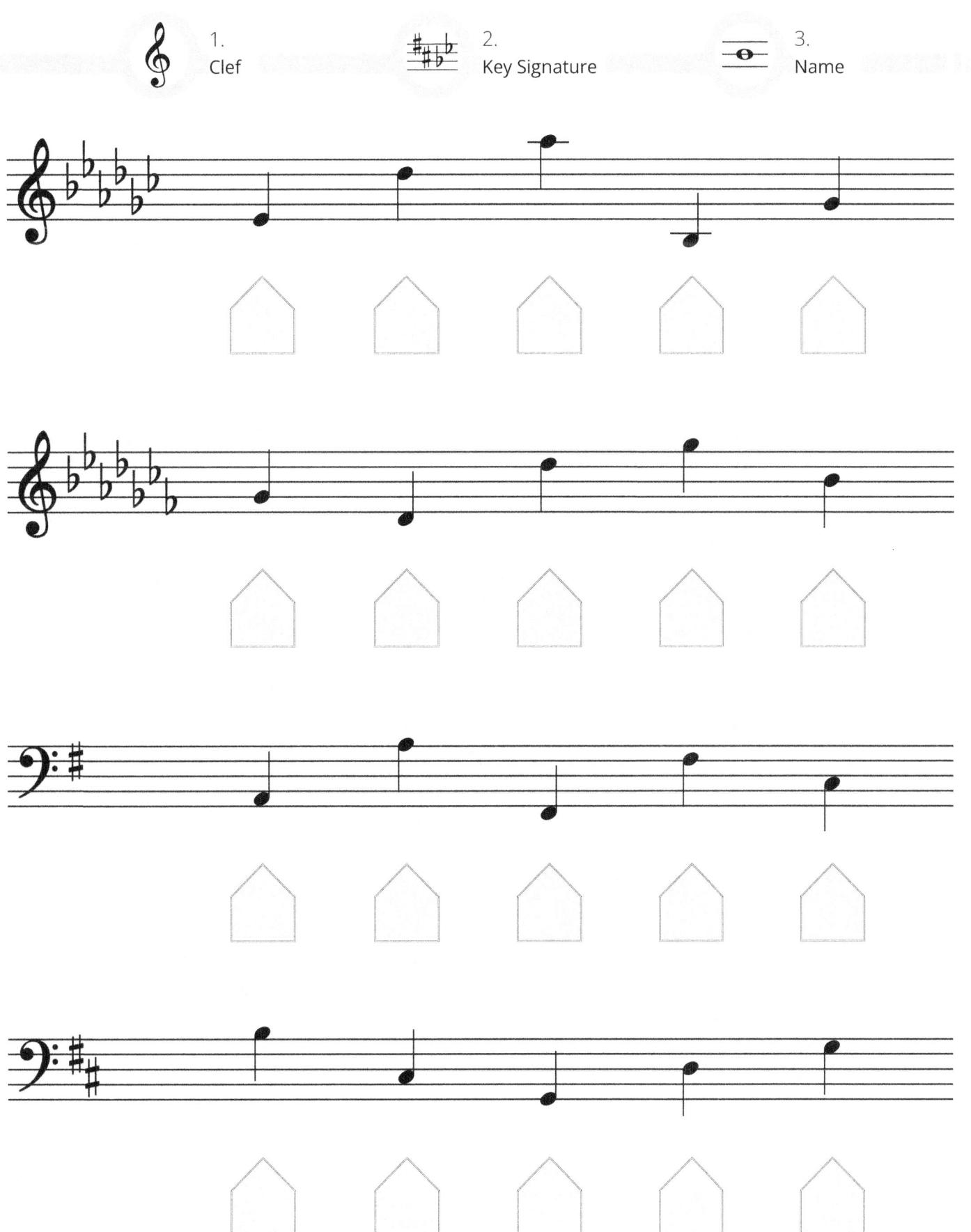

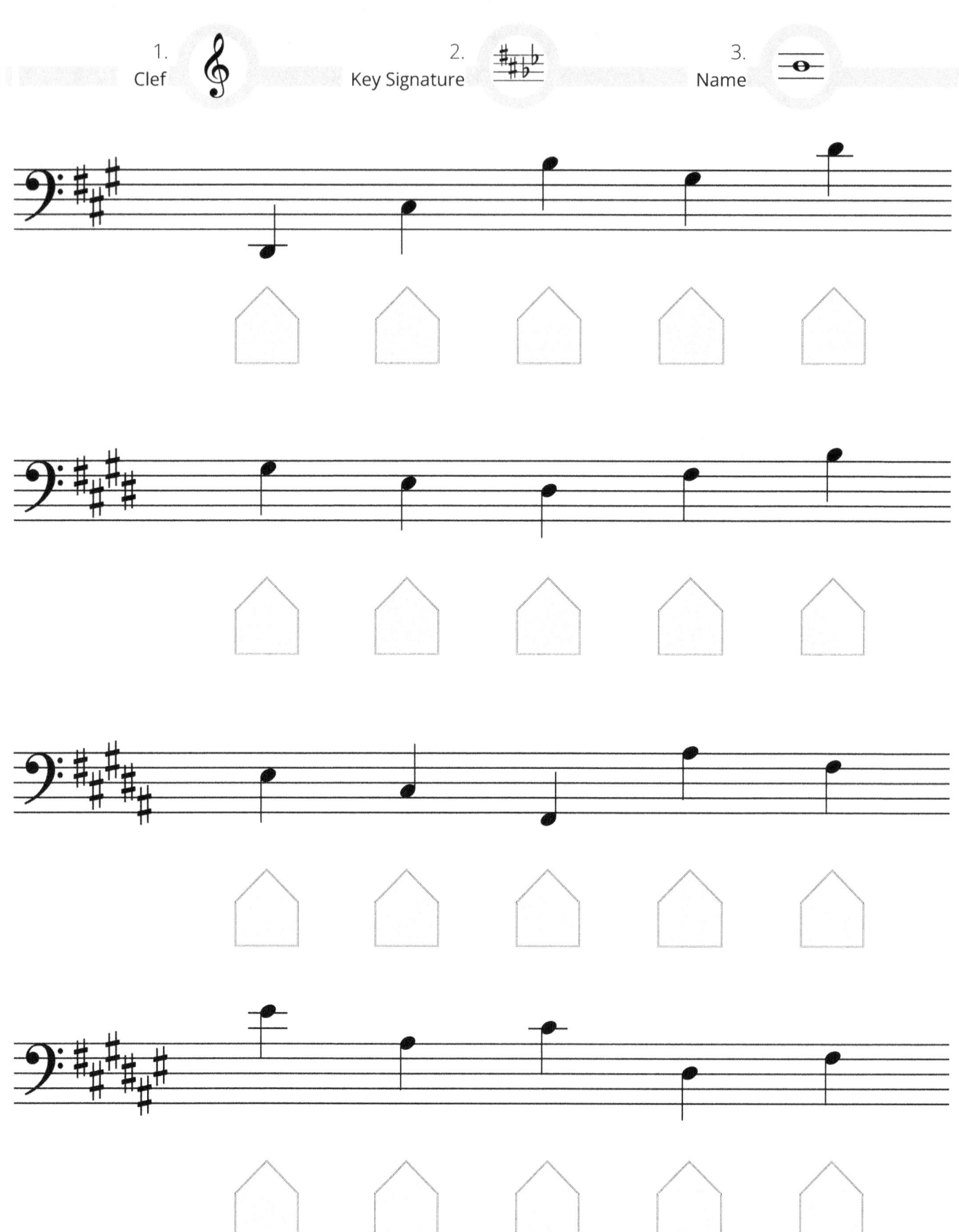

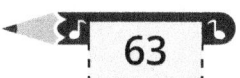

1. Clef
2. Key Signature
3. Name

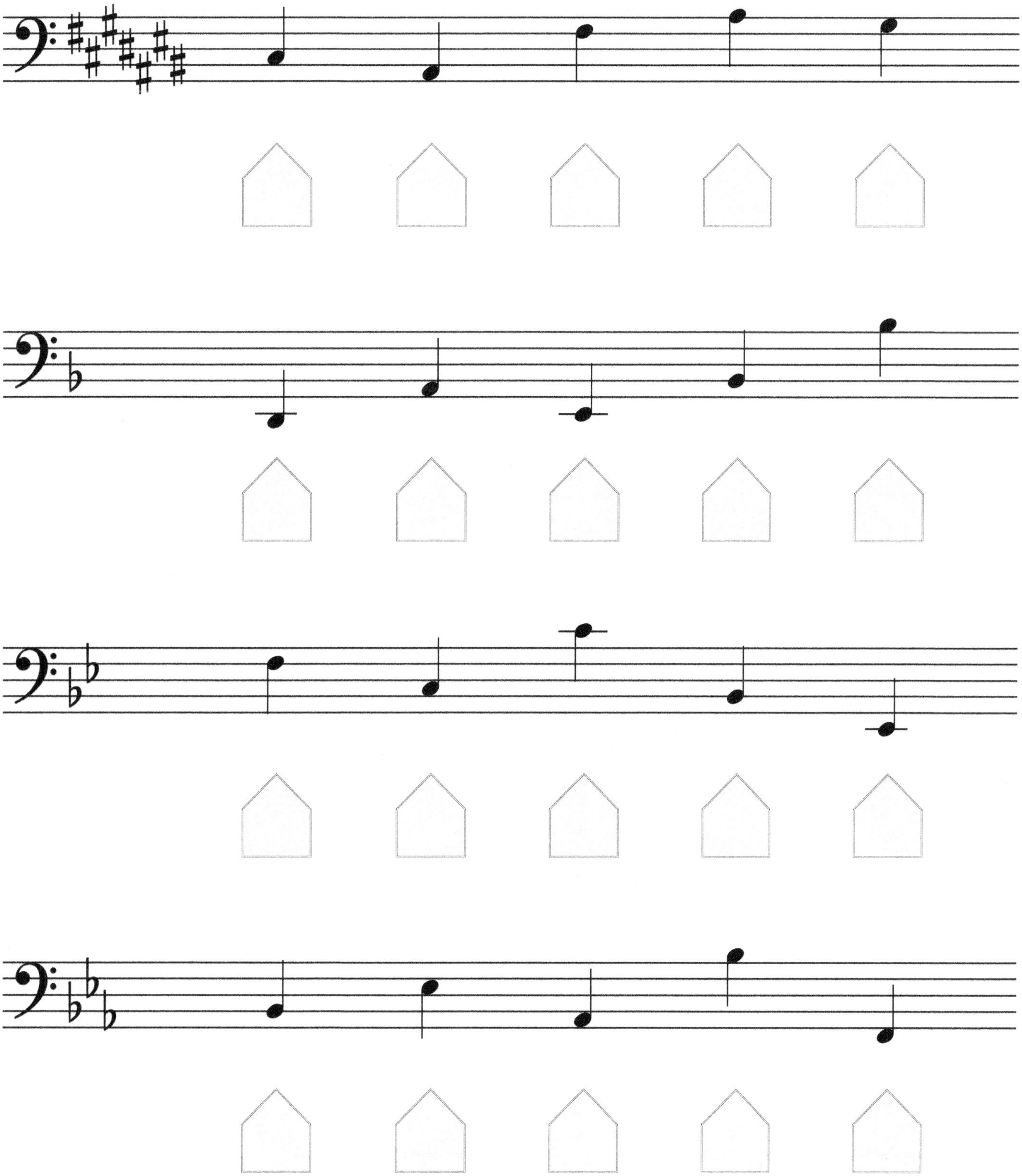

Keyboard Exercises

Four simple steps to complete the exercises:

1. 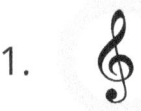 **Clef:** **Look at the clef**, which tells you what note belongs to each line or space on the staff. In the bass clef, the note **A** is in the lowest space. In the treble clef, the note **A** is one whole step higher.

2. 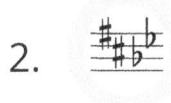 **Key Signature:** The accidentals show the key. Key Signatures follow the Circle of Fifths, and the sharps and flats always appear in a special, set order (see below).

3. 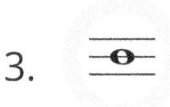 **Name: Find the note name.** Ask yourself: Which line or space is the note on? Then, figure out the name of that note.

4. 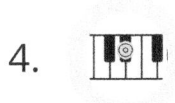 **Keyboard:** Look at the keyboard section and figure out which key goes with the note from the staff. Each keyboard diagram shows a group of **2 or 3 black keys** to help you find your way more easily.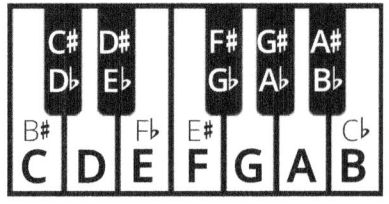

Sharps and flats follow the same order in both the treble and bass clef; each sharp or flat goes on a specific line or space in the clef, always in the same way.

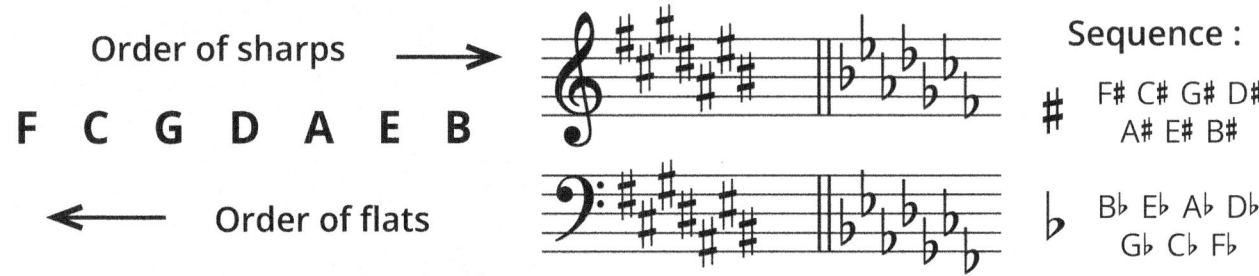

Example:

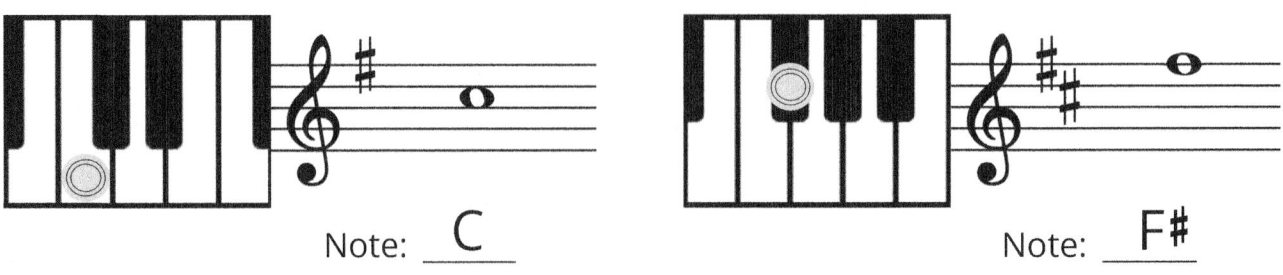

- 93 -

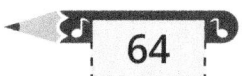

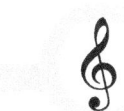 1. Key   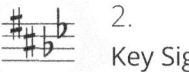 2. Key Signature   3. Name   4. Keyboard

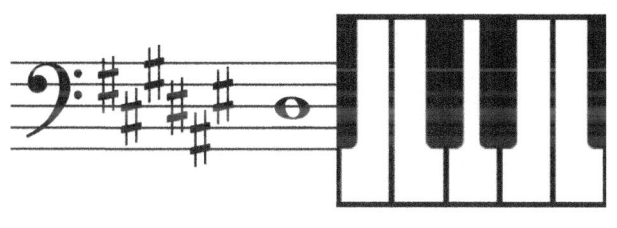

Note: _____

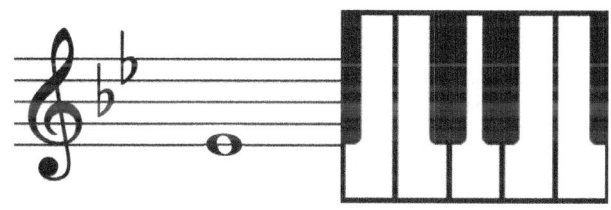

Note: _____

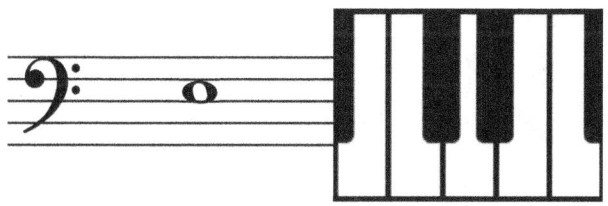

Note: _____

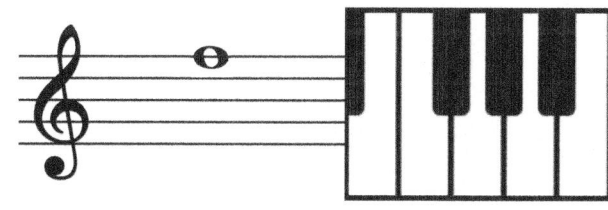

Note: _____

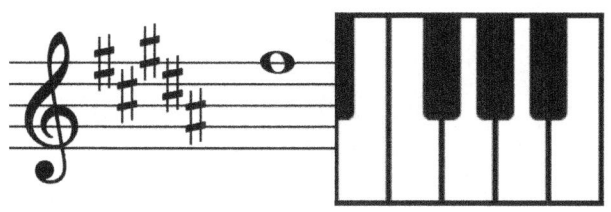

Note: _____

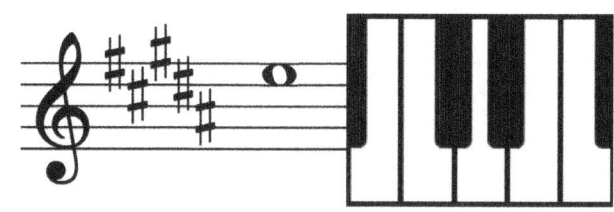

Note: _____

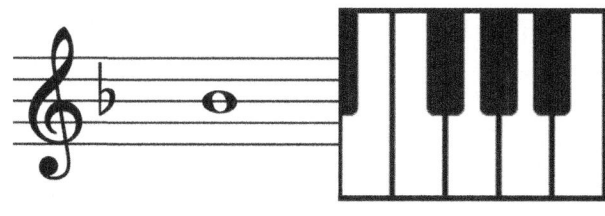

Note: _____

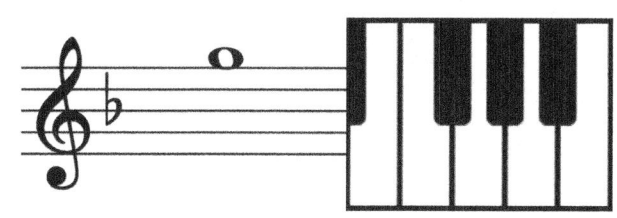

Note: _____

1. Clef 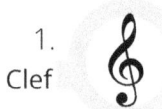   2. Key Signature 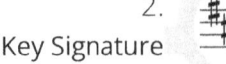   3. Name 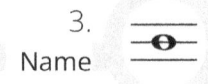   4. Keyboard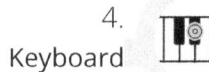

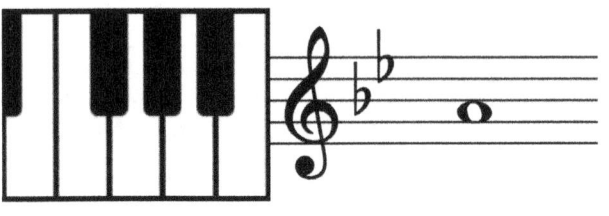

Note: _____

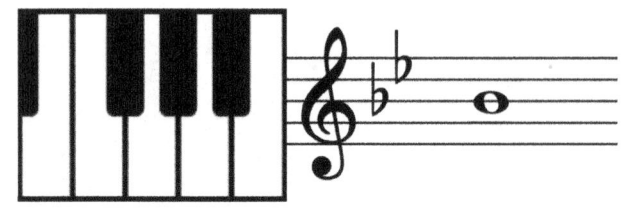

Note: _____

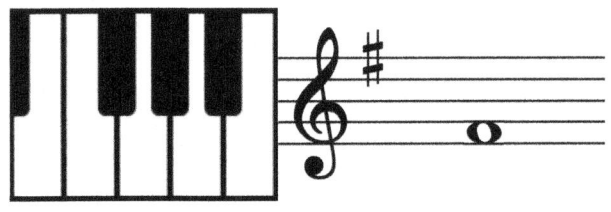

Note: _____

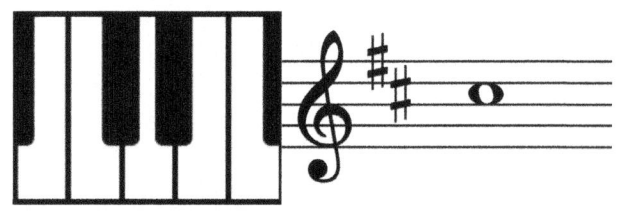

Note: _____

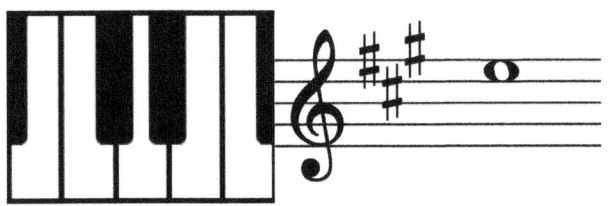

Note: _____

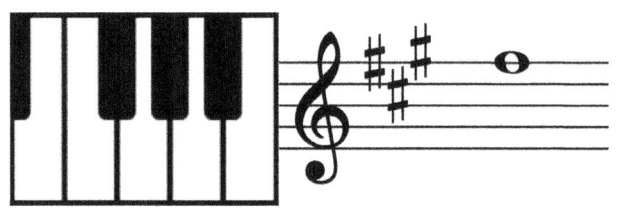

Note: _____

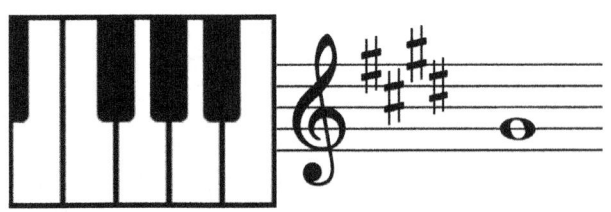

Note: _____

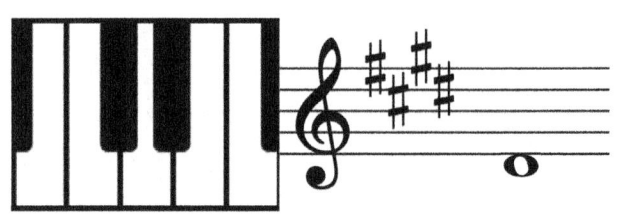

Note: _____

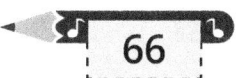

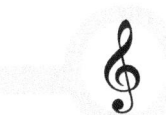 1. Key   2. Key Signature 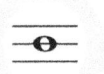 3. Name   4. Keyboard

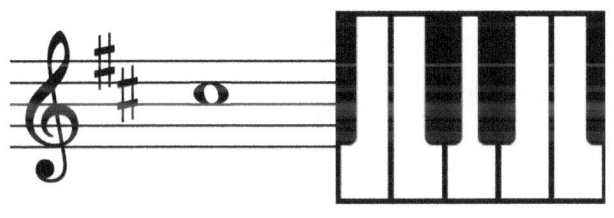

Note: _____

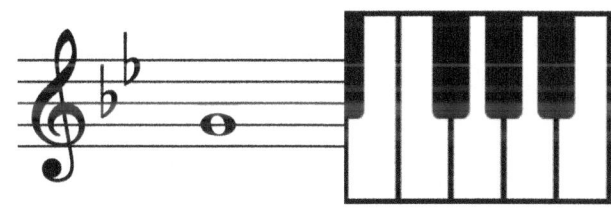

Note: _____

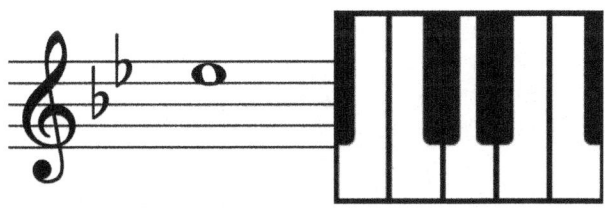

Note: _____

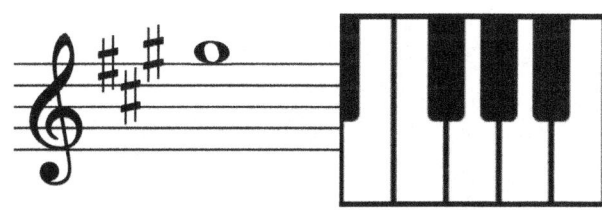

Note: _____

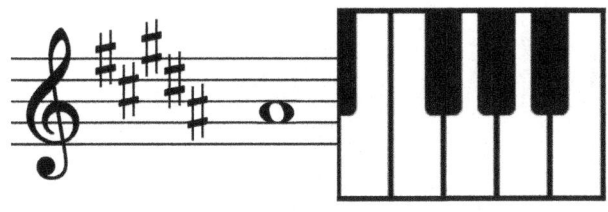

Note: _____

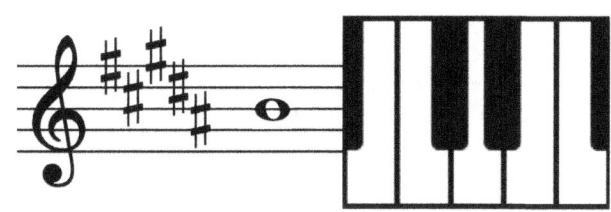

Note: _____

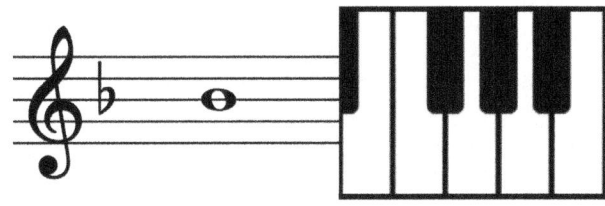

Note: _____

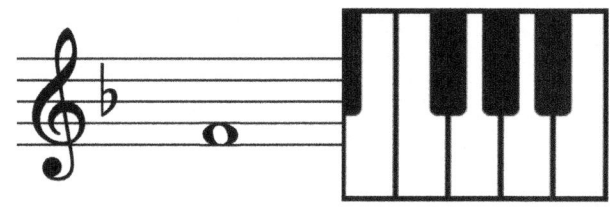

Note: _____

1. Clef 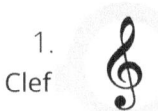　2. Key Signature 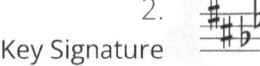　3. Name 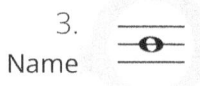　4. Keyboard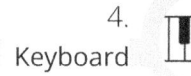

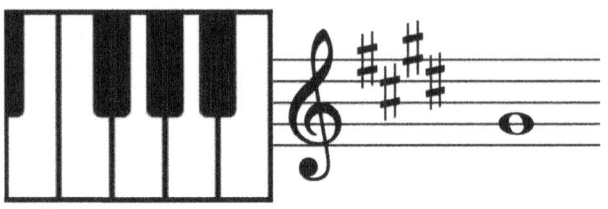

Note: _____

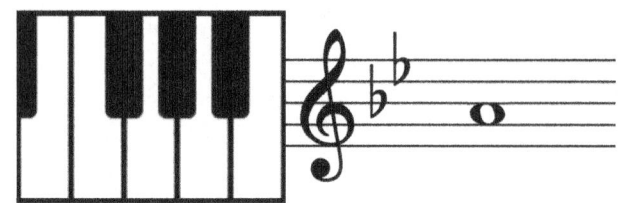

Note: _____

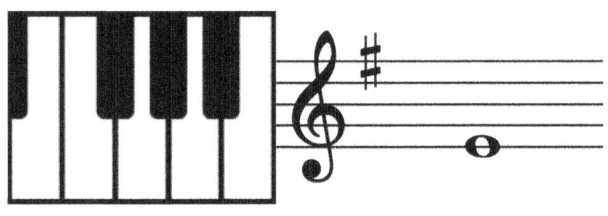

Note: _____

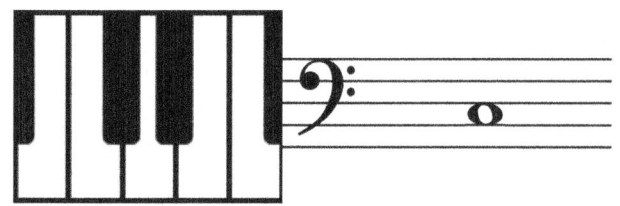

Note: _____

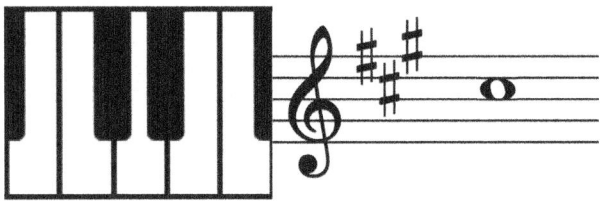

Note: _____

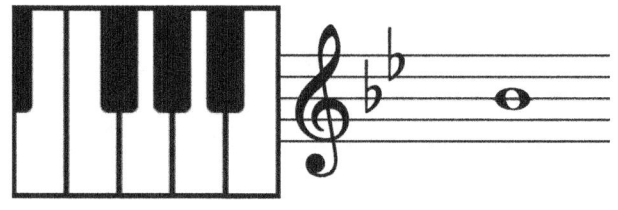

Note: _____

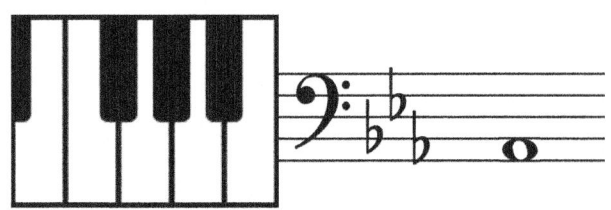

Note: _____

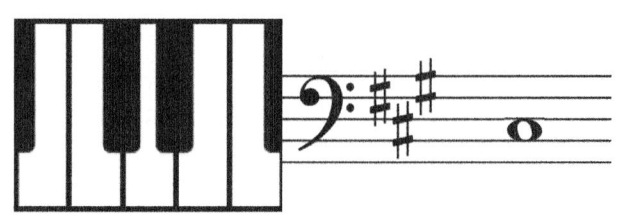

Note: _____

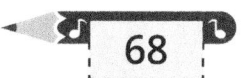

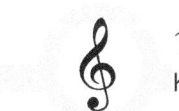 1. Key 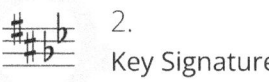 2. Key Signature 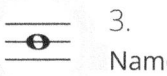 3. Name 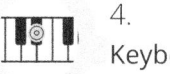 4. Keyboard

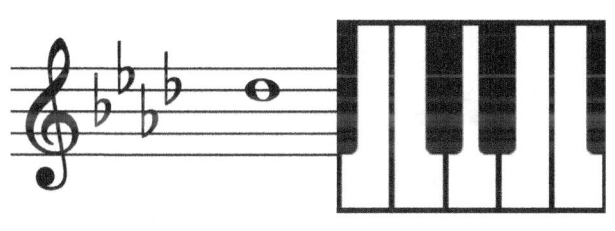

Note: _____

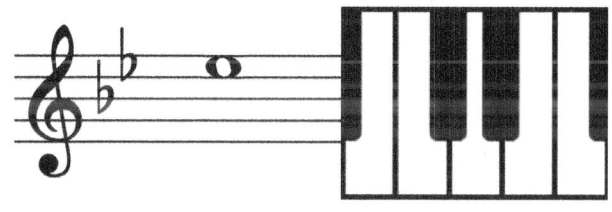

Note: _____

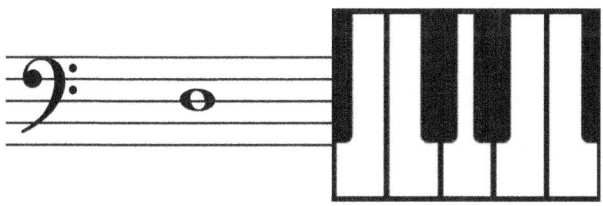

Note: _____

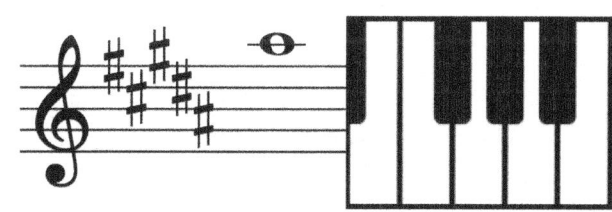

Note: _____

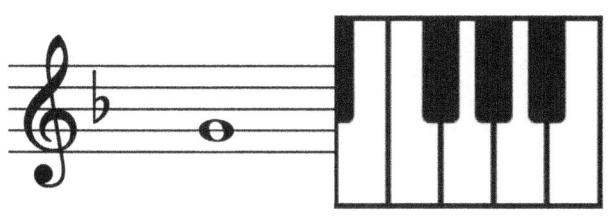

Note: _____

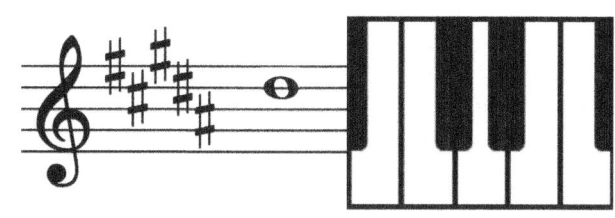

Note: _____

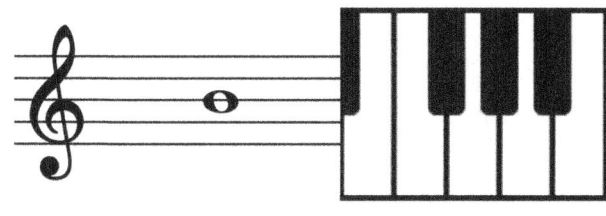

Note: _____

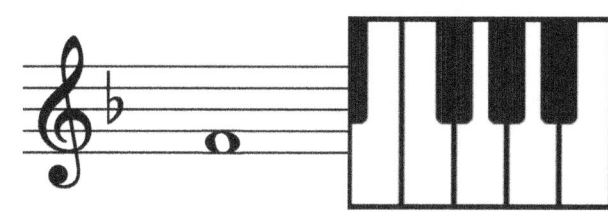

Note: _____

1. Clef 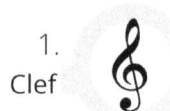   2. Key Signature 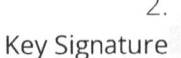   3. Name   4. Keyboard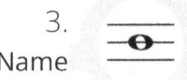

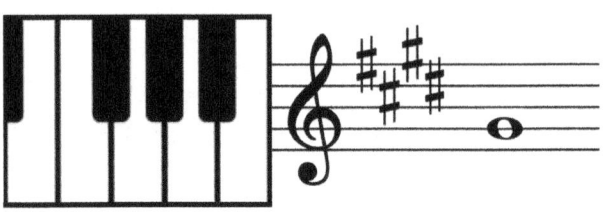

Note: _____

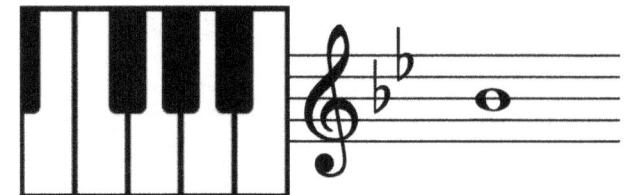

Note: _____

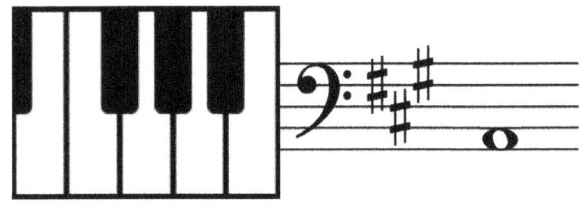

Note: _____

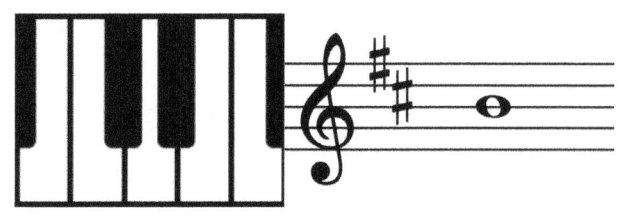

Note: _____

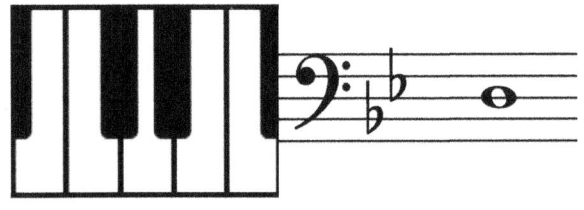

Note: _____

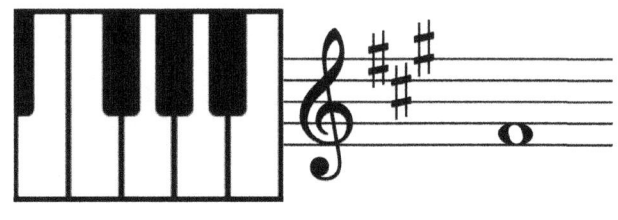

Note: _____

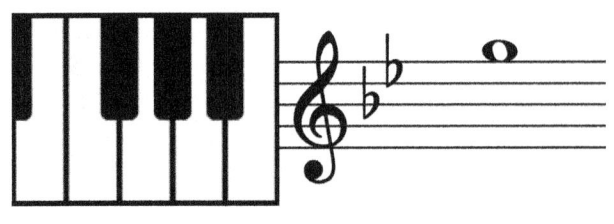

Note: _____

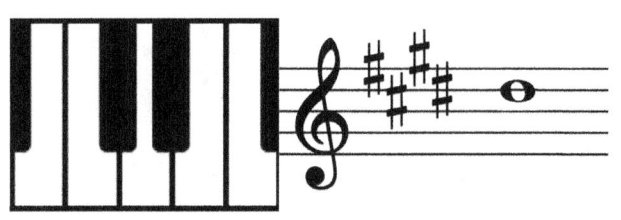

Note: _____

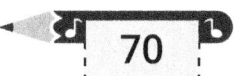

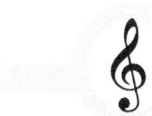 1. Key   2. Key Signature   3. Name   4. Keyboard

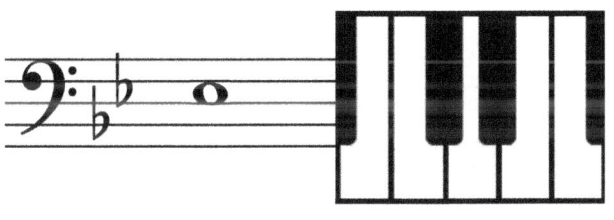

Note: _____

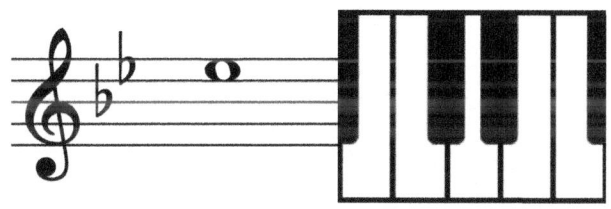

Note: _____

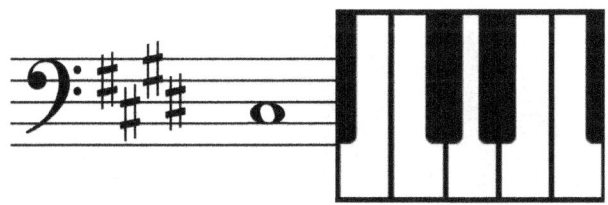

Note: _____

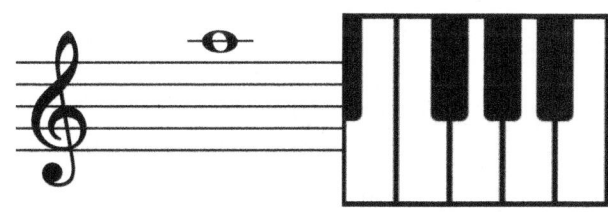

Note: _____

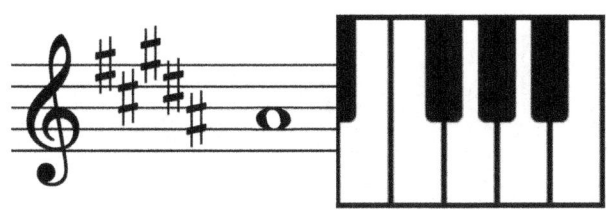

Note: _____

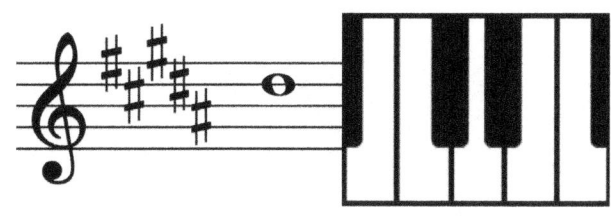

Note: _____

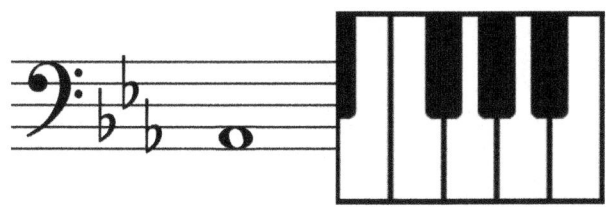

Note: _____

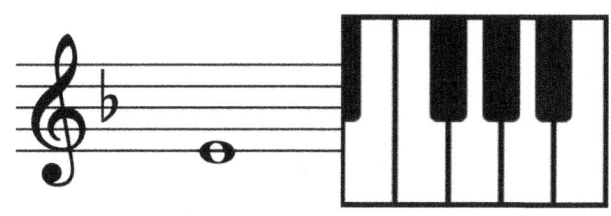

Note: _____

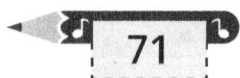

1. Clef 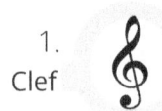   2. Key Signature 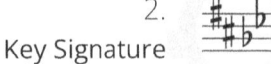   3. Name 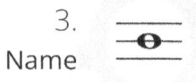   4. Keyboard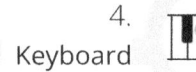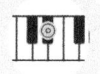

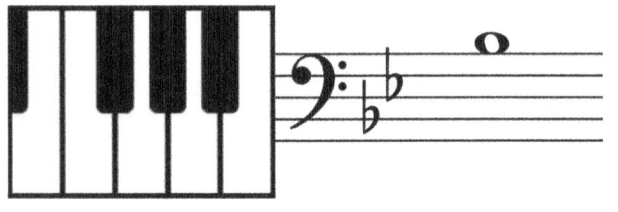

Note: _____

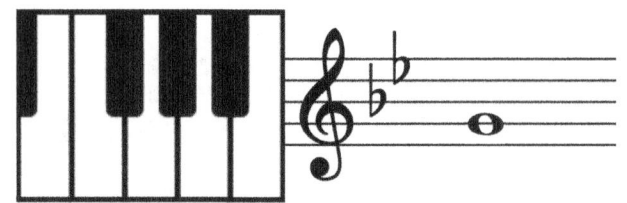

Note: _____

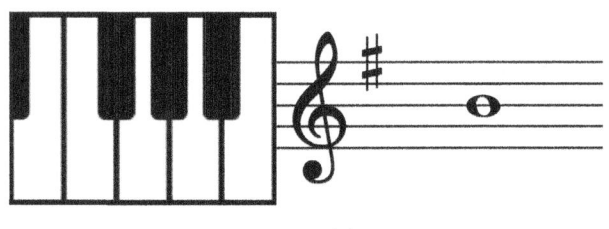

Note: _____

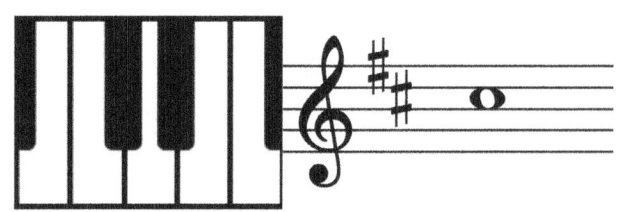

Note: _____

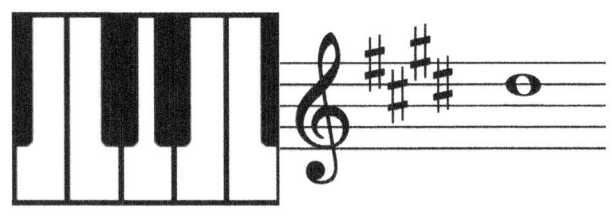

Note: _____

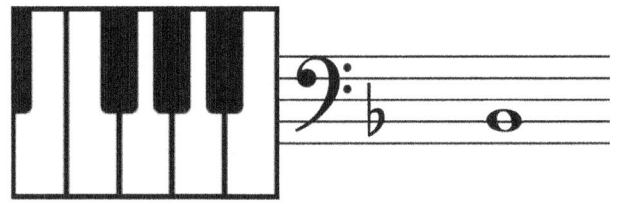

Note: _____

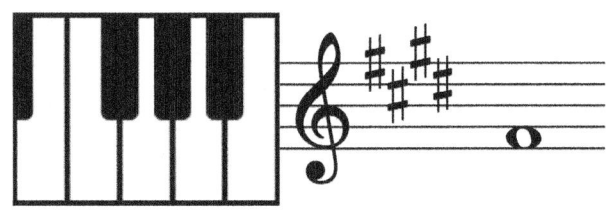

Note: _____

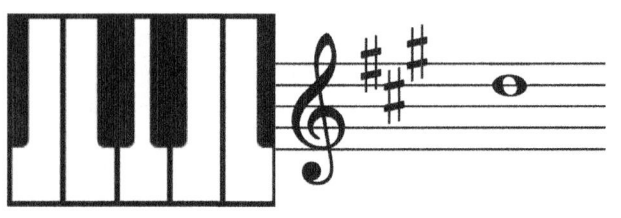

Note: _____

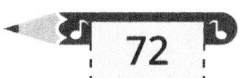

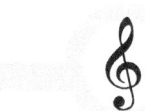 1. Key   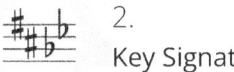 2. Key Signature   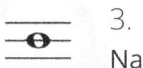 3. Name   4. Keyboard

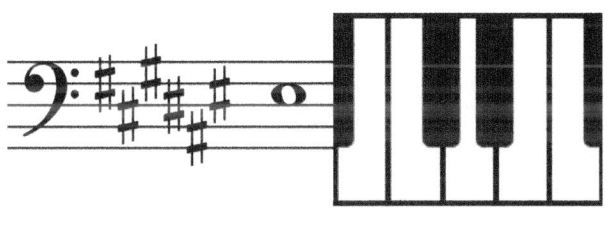

Note: _____

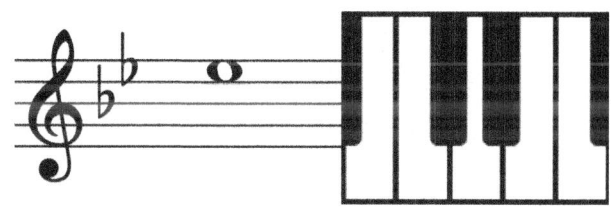

Note: _____

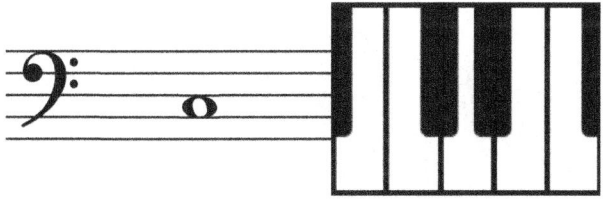

Note: _____

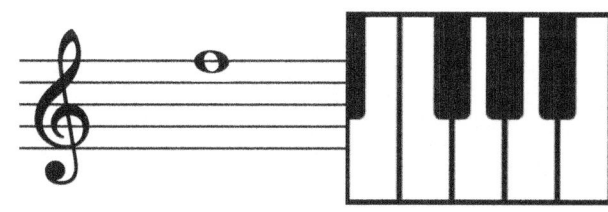

Note: _____

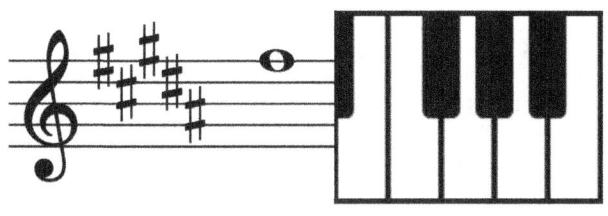

Note: _____

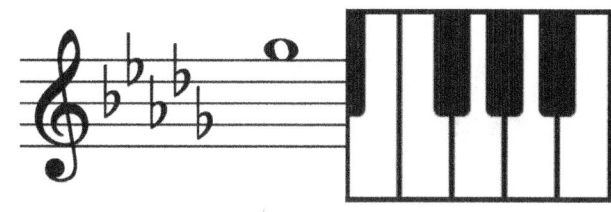

Note: _____

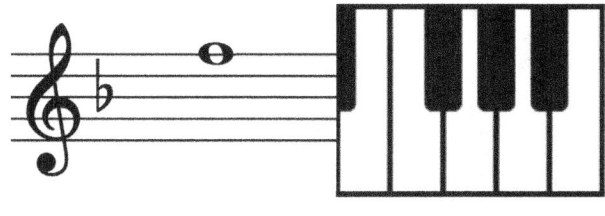

Note: _____

Note: _____

1. Clef 2. Key Signature 3. Name 4. Keyboard

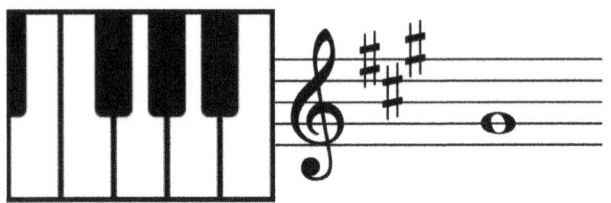
Note: _____

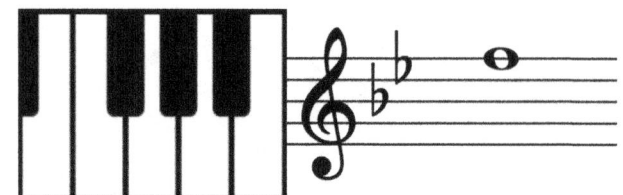
Note: _____

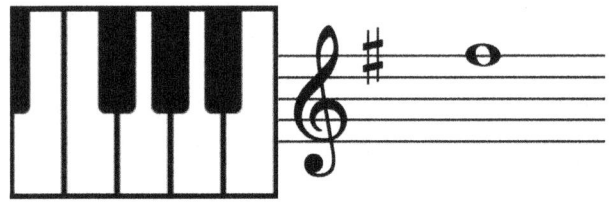
Note: _____

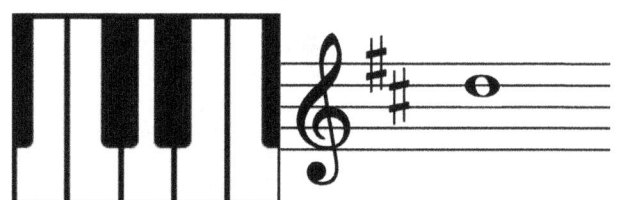
Note: _____

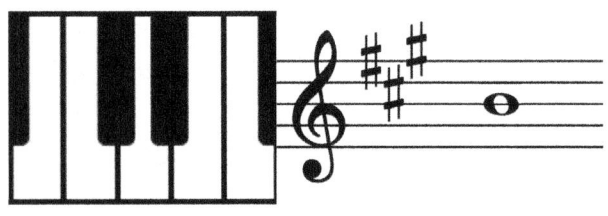
Note: _____

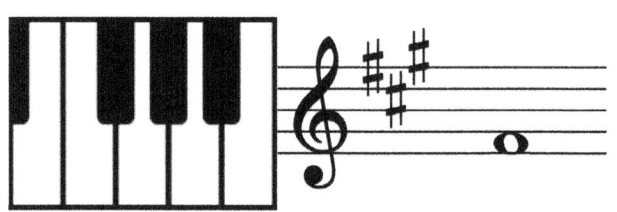
Note: _____

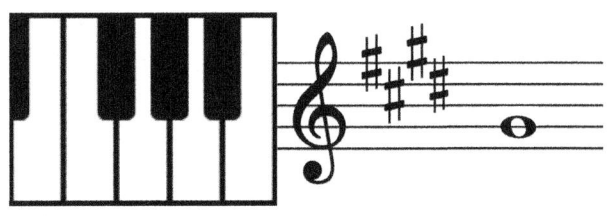
Note: _____

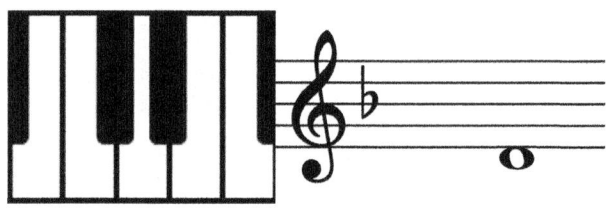
Note: _____

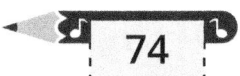

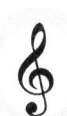 1. Key   2. Key Signature   3. Name   4. Keyboard

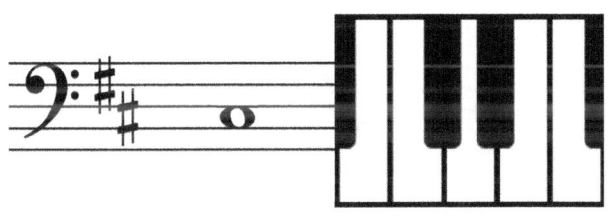

Note: _____

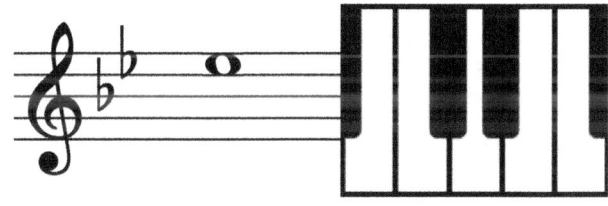

Note: _____

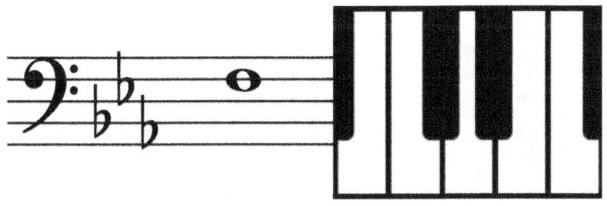

Note: _____

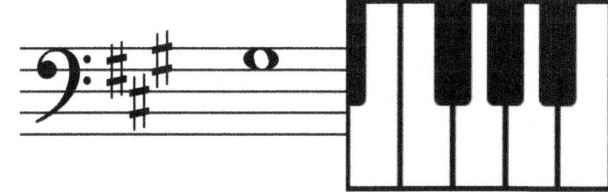

Note: _____

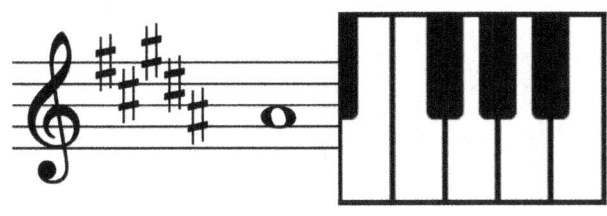

Note: _____

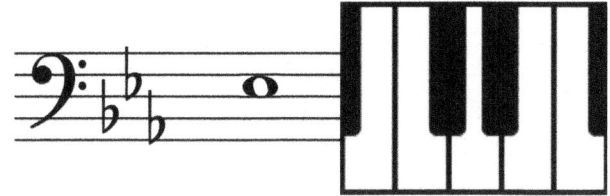

Note: _____

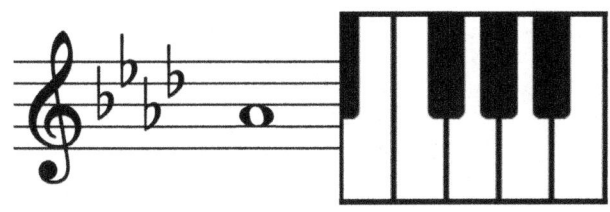

Note: _____

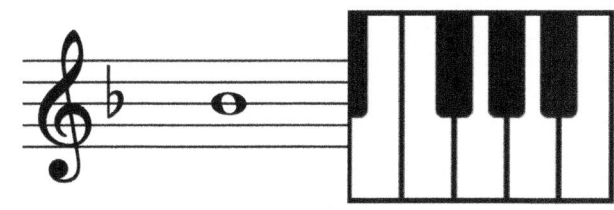

Note: _____

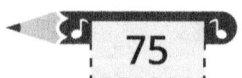

1. Clef 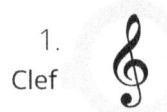 2. Key Signature 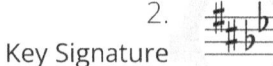 3. Name 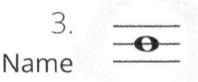 4. Keyboard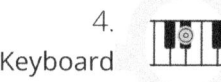

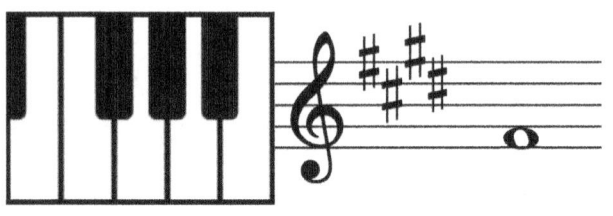
Note: _____

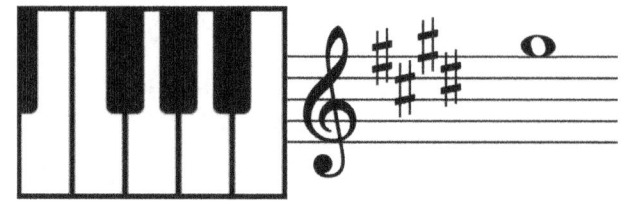
Note: _____

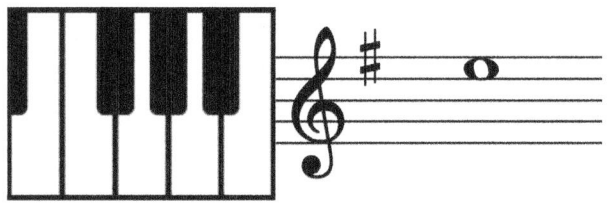
Note: _____

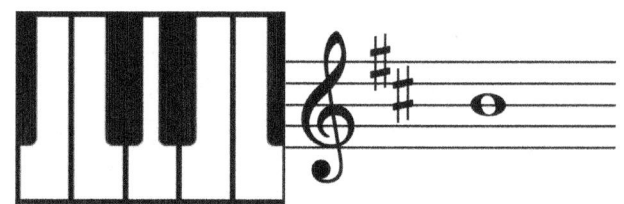
Note: _____

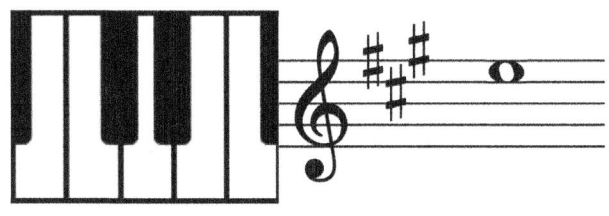
Note: _____

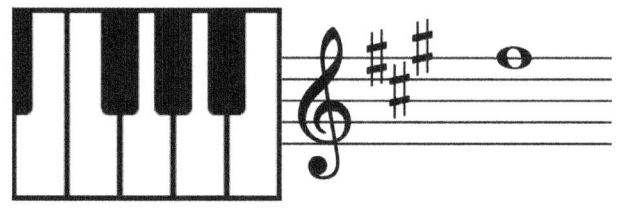
Note: _____

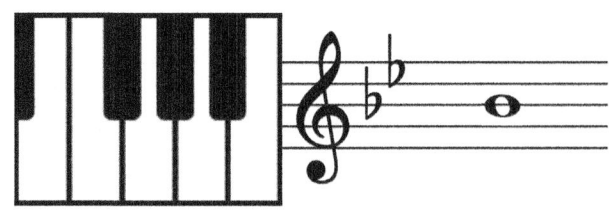
Note: _____

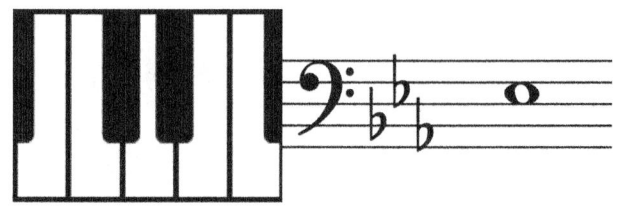
Note: _____

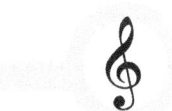 1. Key 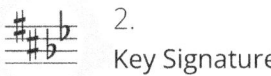 2. Key Signature 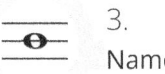 3. Name 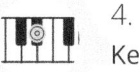 4. Keyboard

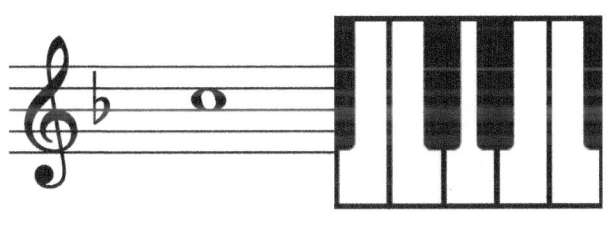

Note: _____

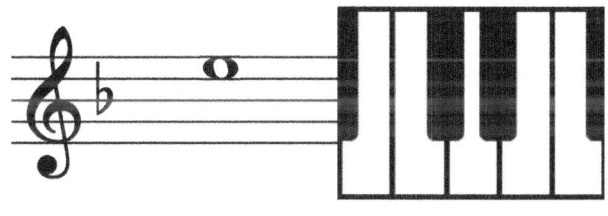

Note: _____

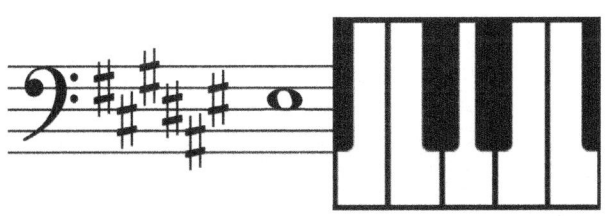

Note: _____

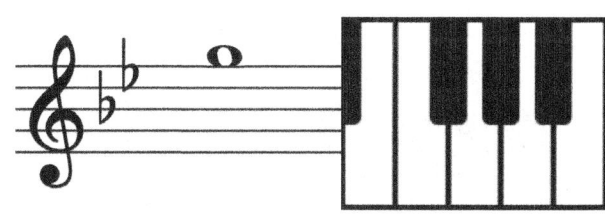

Note: _____

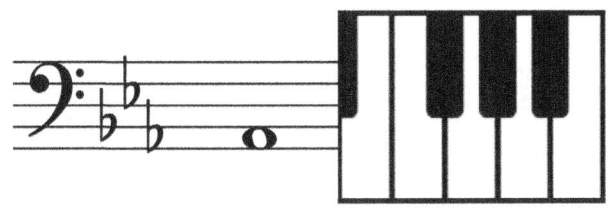

Note: _____

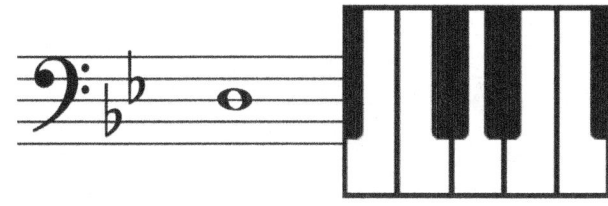

Note: _____

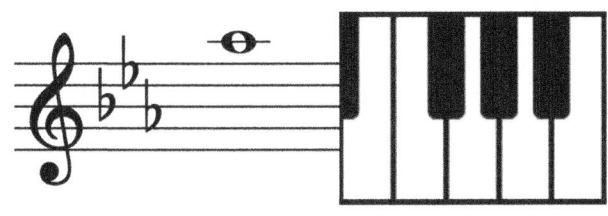

Note: _____

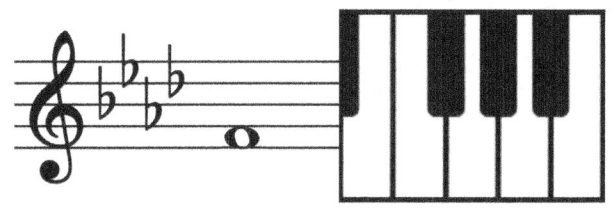

Note: _____

Tips for Note Reading

1. Focus on the Sheet Music

When playing the piano or keyboard, develop the habit of not looking at your fingers while reading the sheet music. This practice enhances your skills and makes you a more effective note reader.

2. Watch for Sharps, Flats & Patterns

Accidentals like sharps (♯) and flats (♭) tell you how the notes change. Always pay attention to the key signature and look for helpful patterns as scales, chords, and arpeggios.

3. Count Your Beats and Feel the Rhythm

The time signature tells you how many beats are in each measure. To get the rhythm right, tap gently on the piano; right hand for the top line, left for the bottom, and count out loud.

4. Clap it Out First

Before playing a new piece, clap the rhythm and say it out loud. Noting the rhythm above the notes can be very helpful. Counting from the start builds string ryhthm skills.

5. One Hand at a Time

Focus on one hand at a time while learning a new section. Once each hand is confident on its own, you can combine them.

6. Learn in Small Sections

Always practice small parts at a time. In the beginning, stick to four measures or less. Think of the saying: How do you eat an elephant? One bite at a time. Practicing large sections too soon can lead to frustration.

7. Try Not to Stop

Try not to pause or stop. Keep going even if you make mistakes; keeping a steady beat is more important than playing every note perfectly.

8. Everything Takes Time

Relax and stay positive. It can be frustrating when your hands don't do what your mind tells them. But remember: **Practice makes progress!**

Solutions

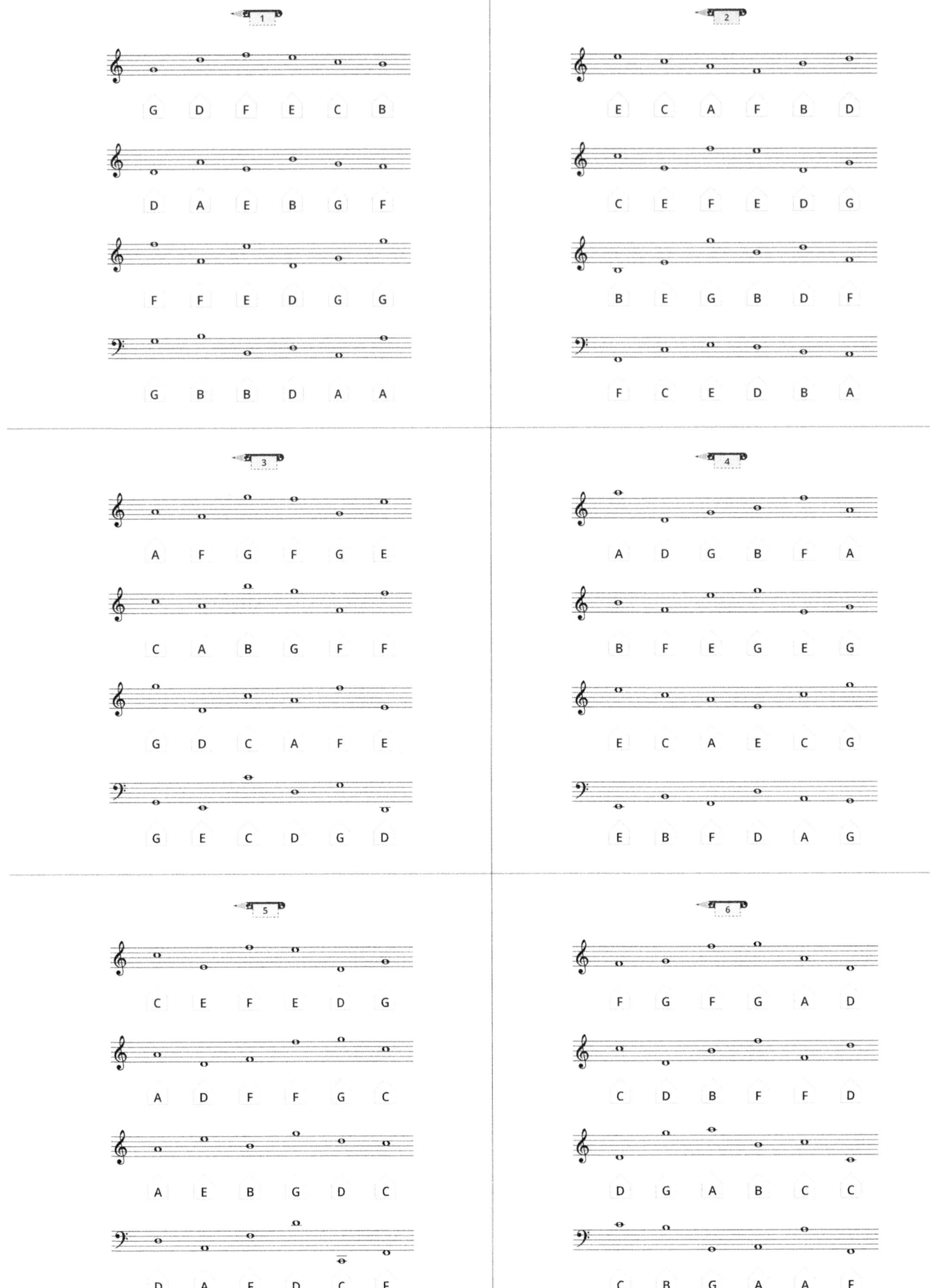

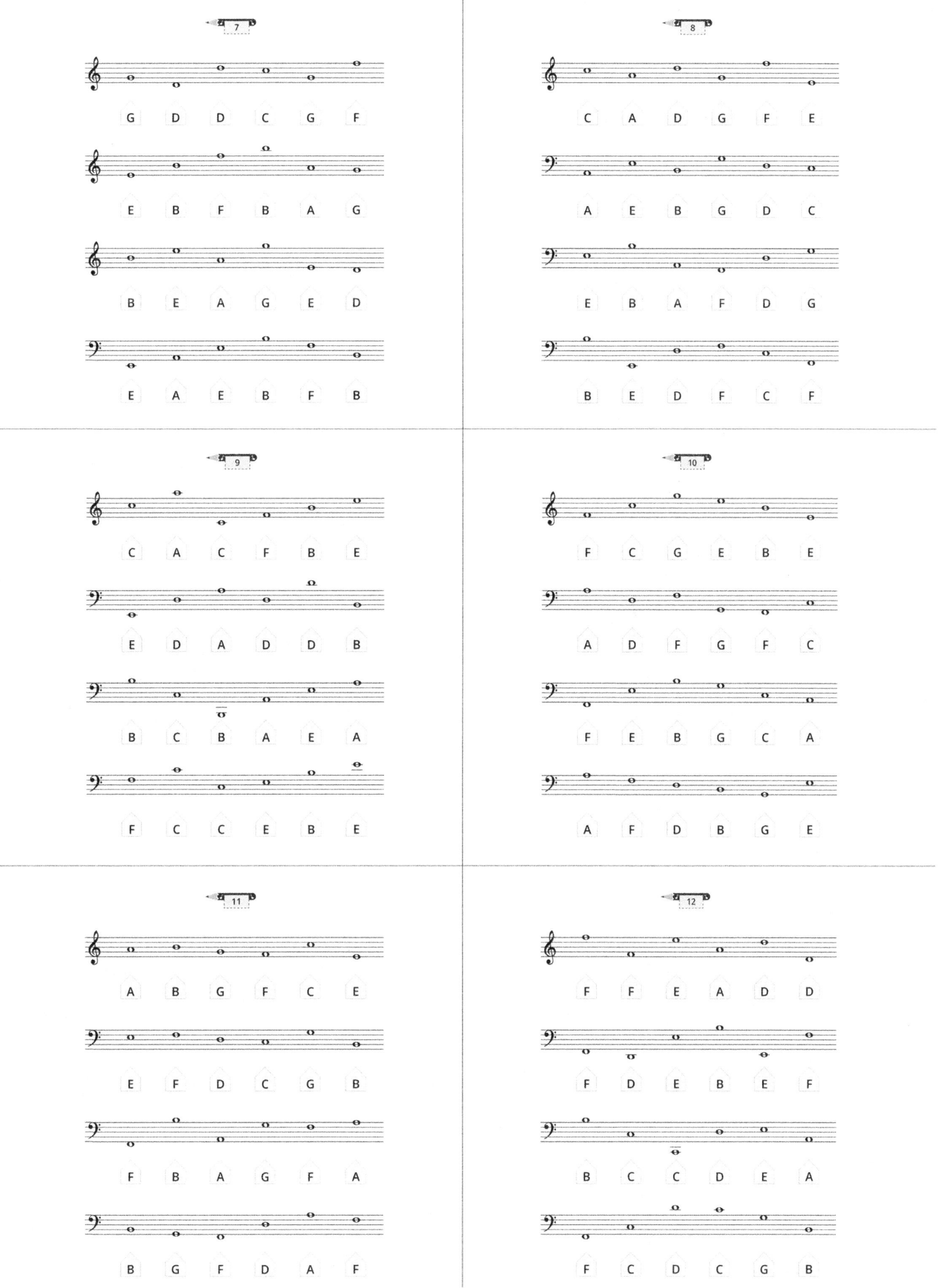

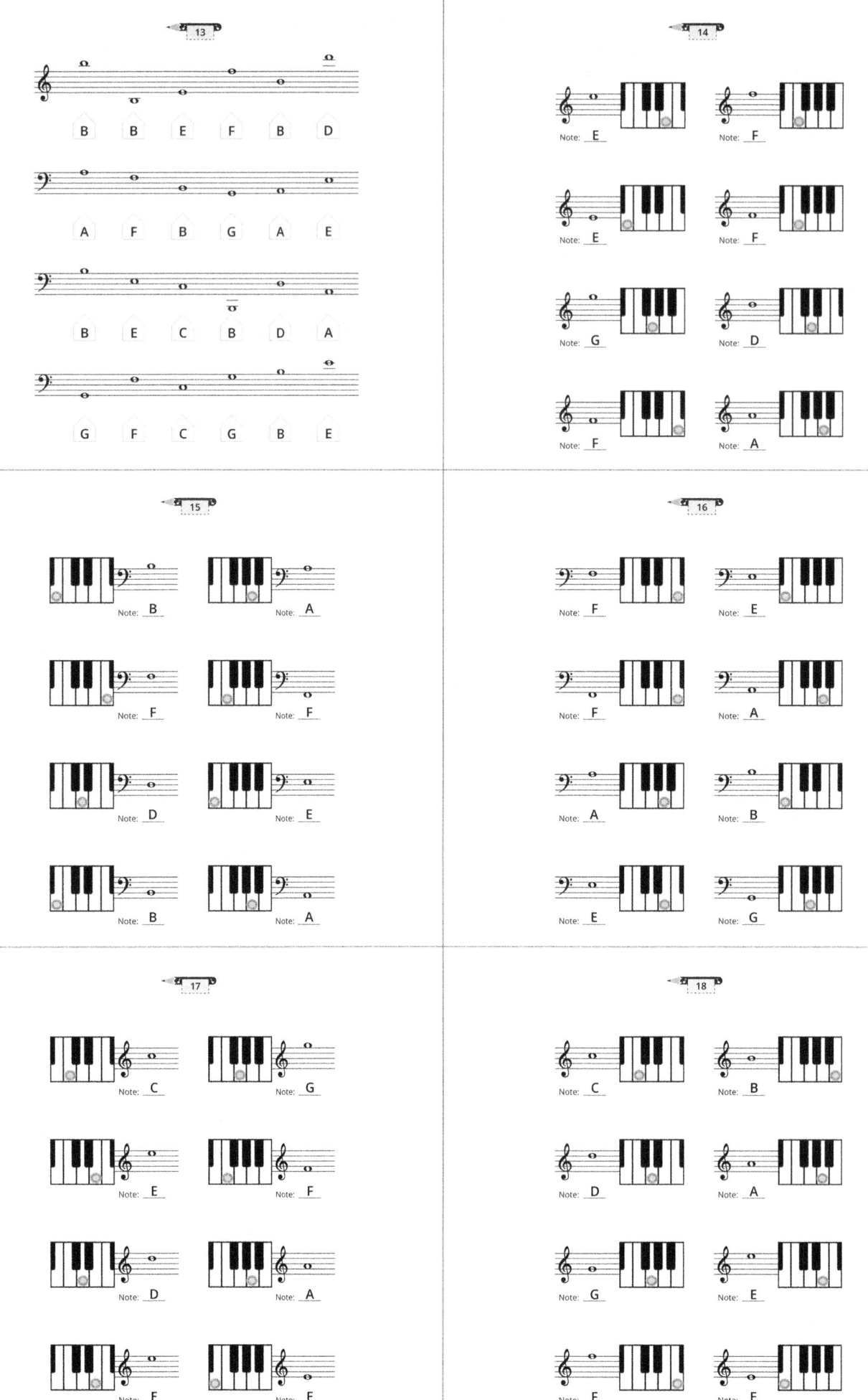

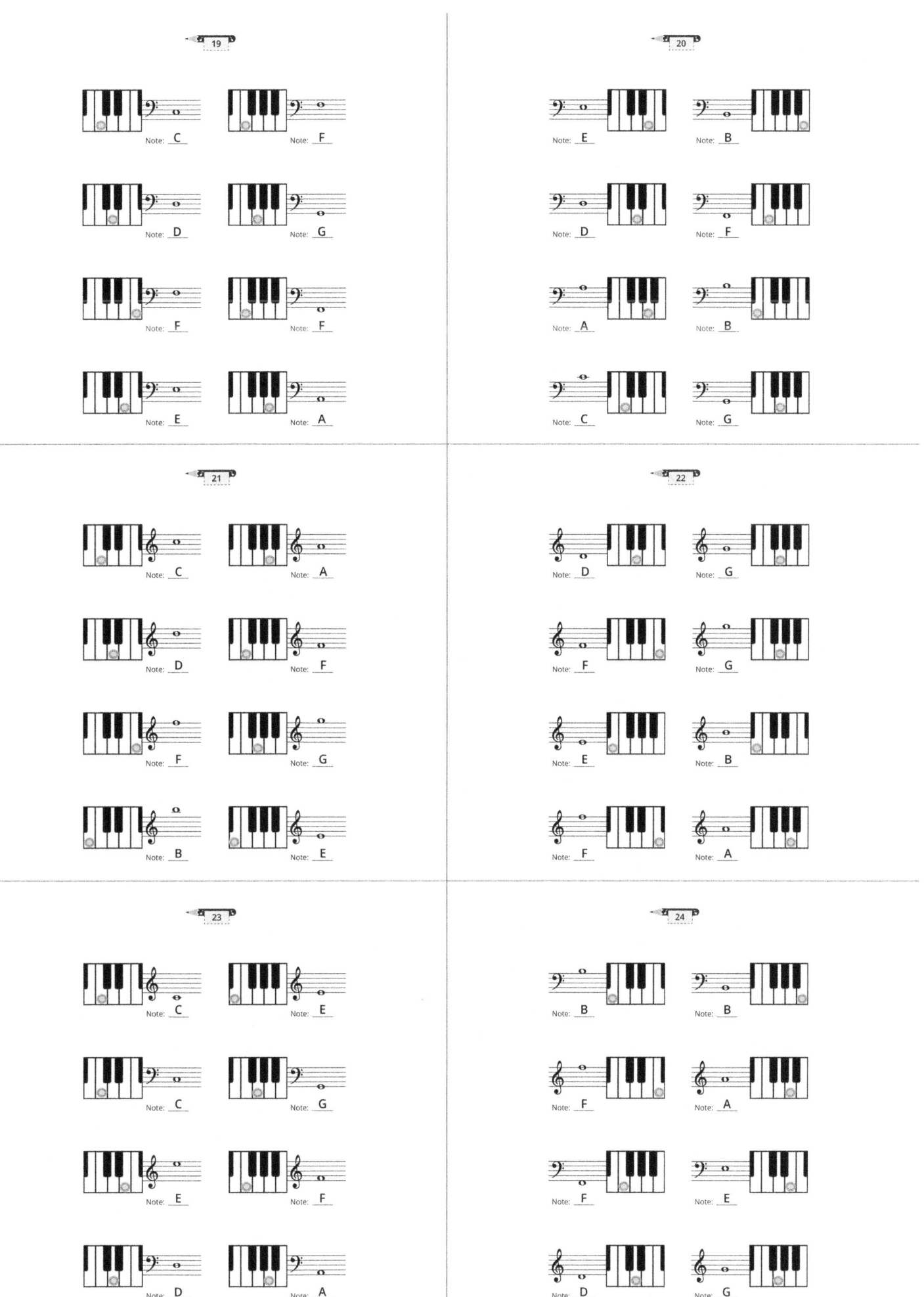

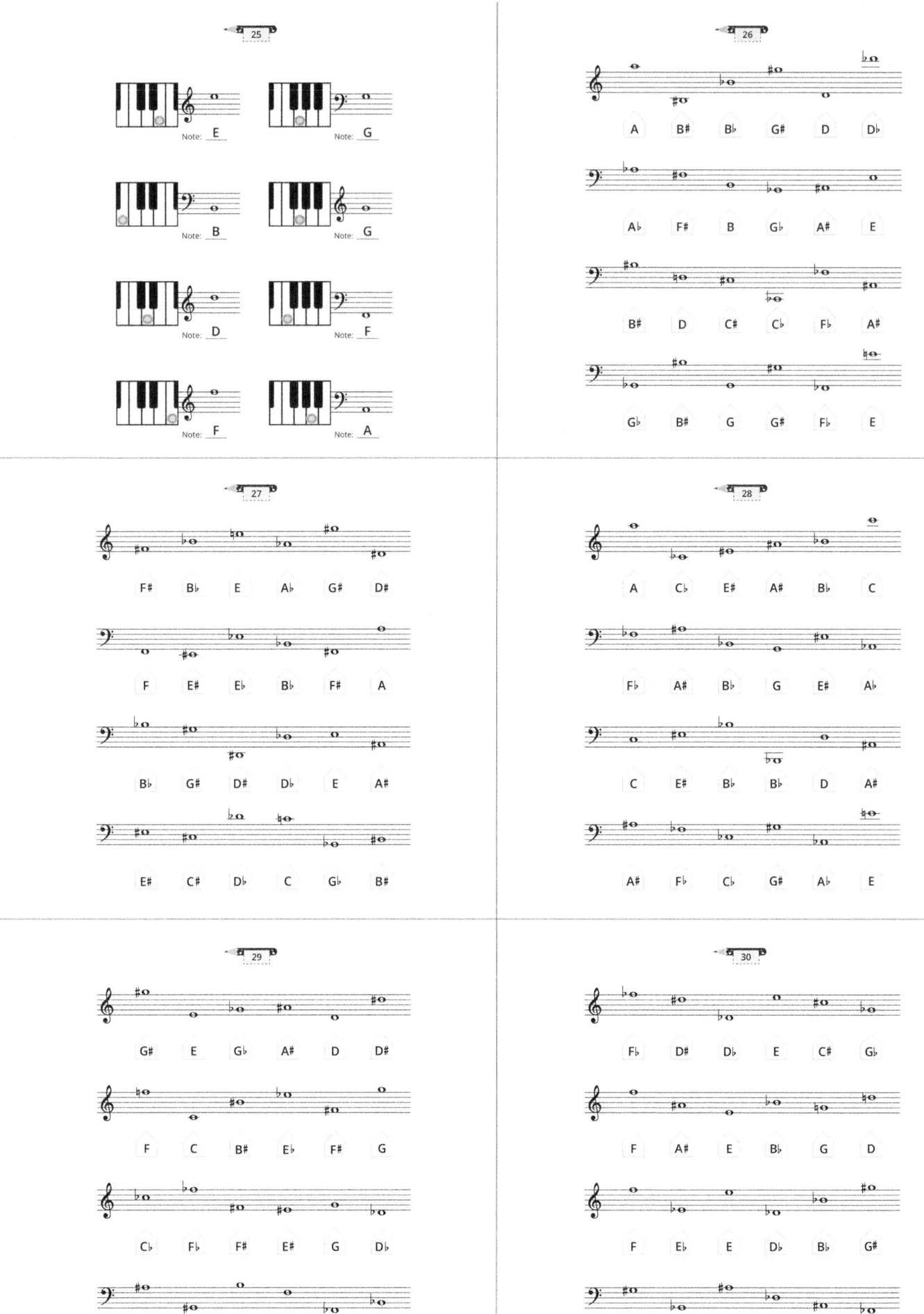

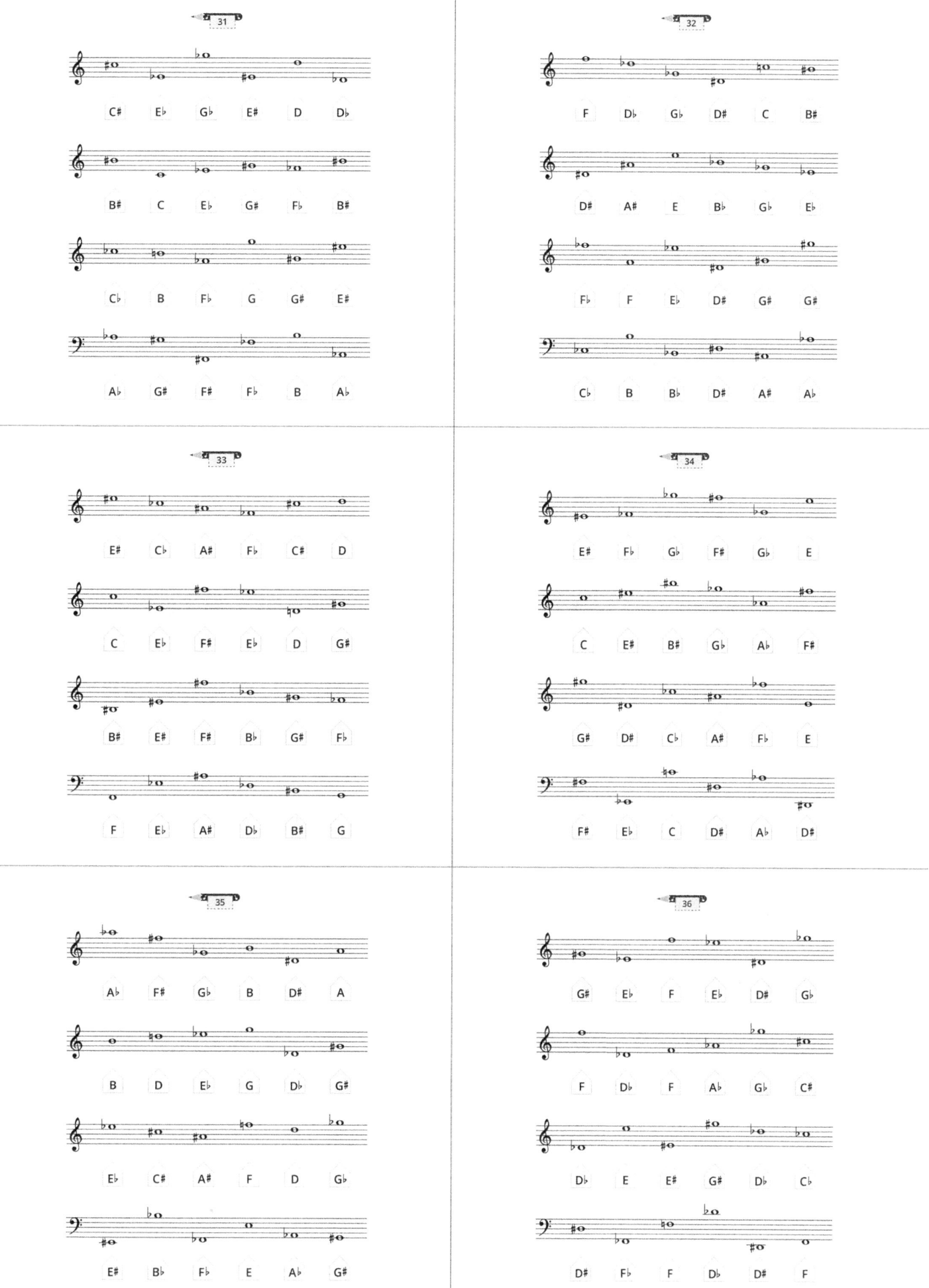

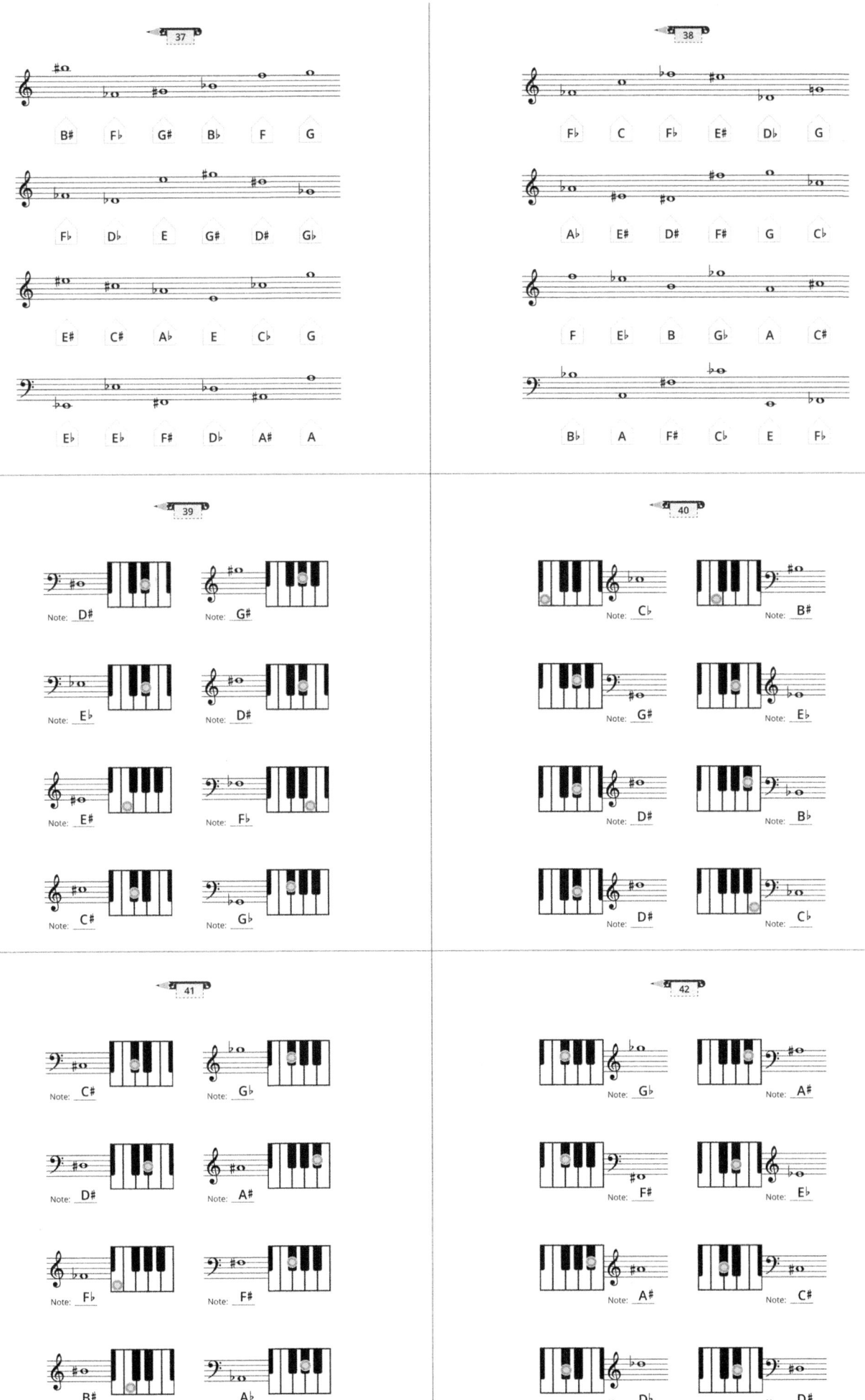

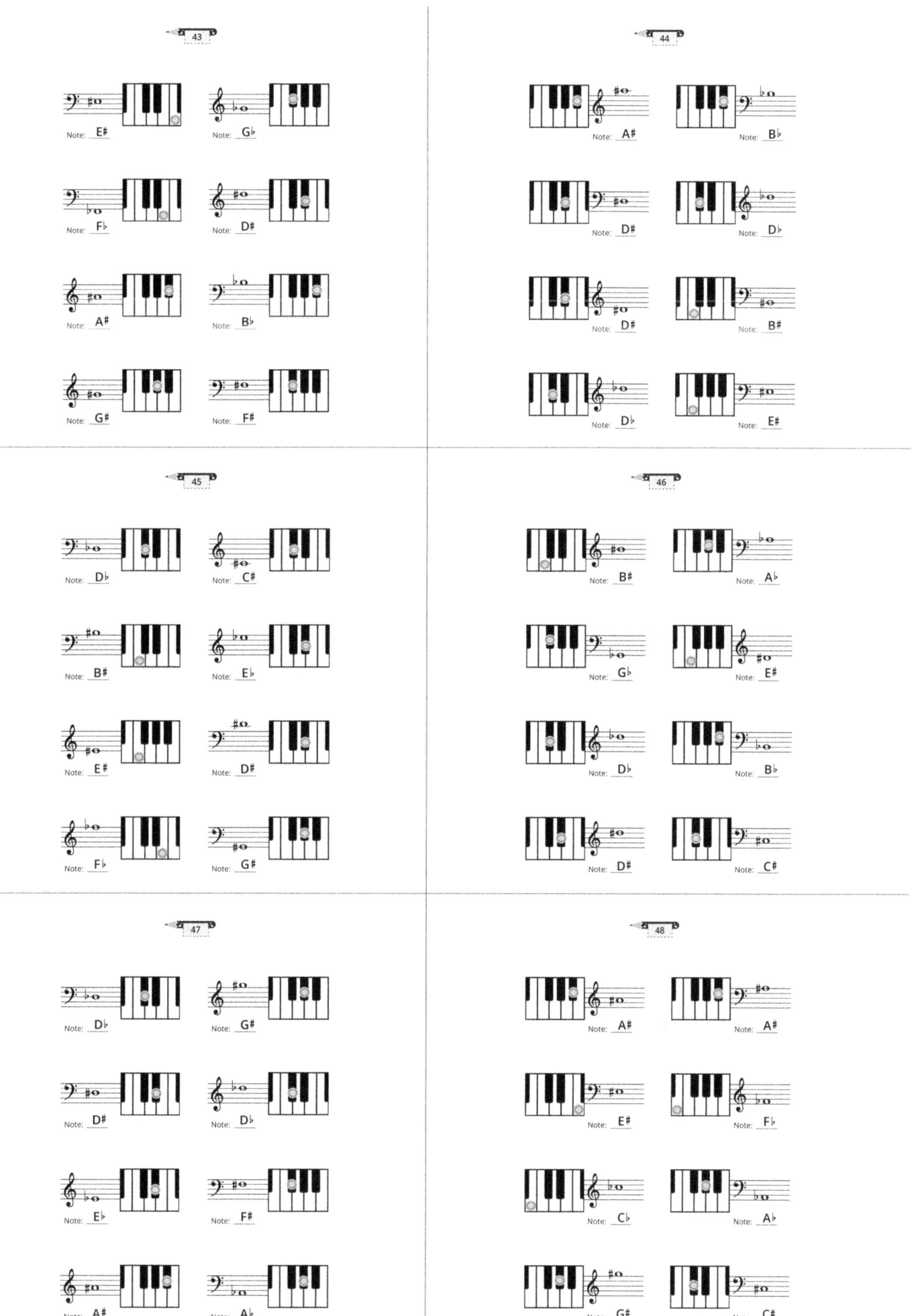

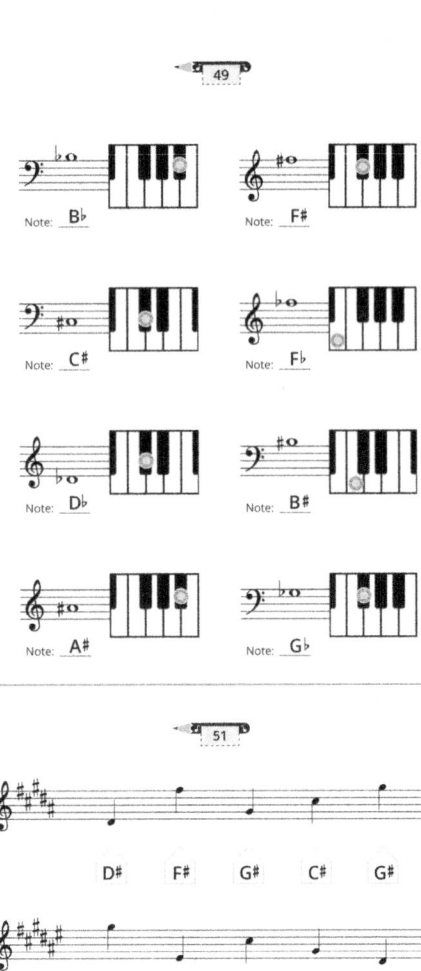
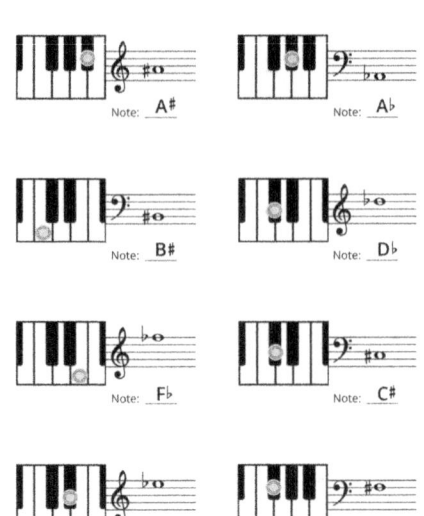
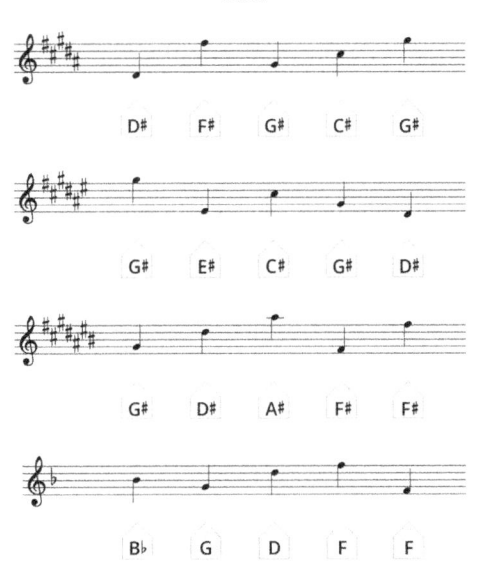
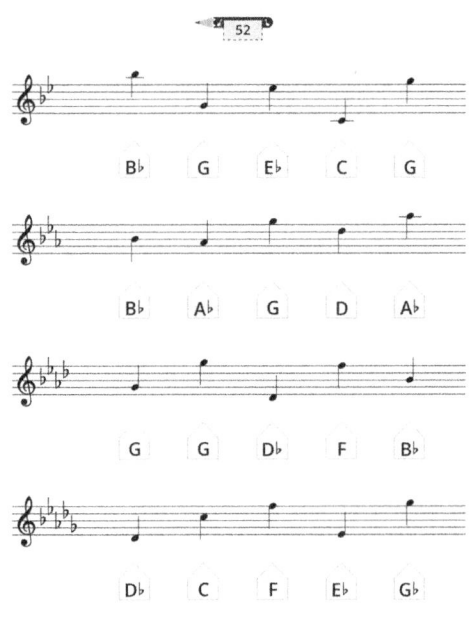
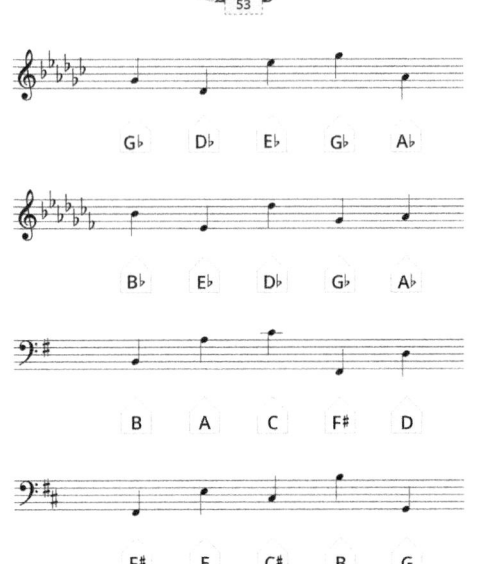
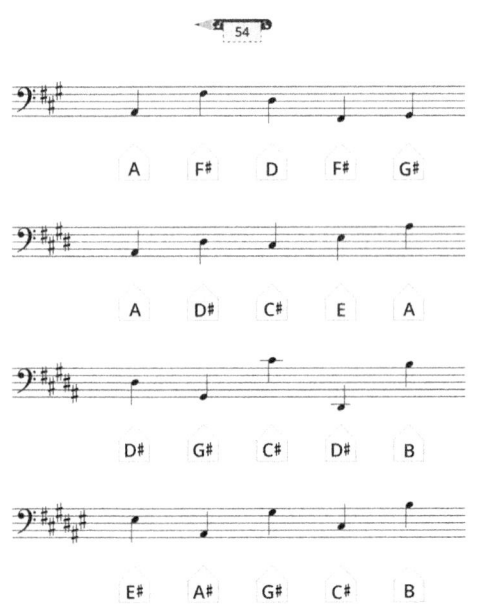

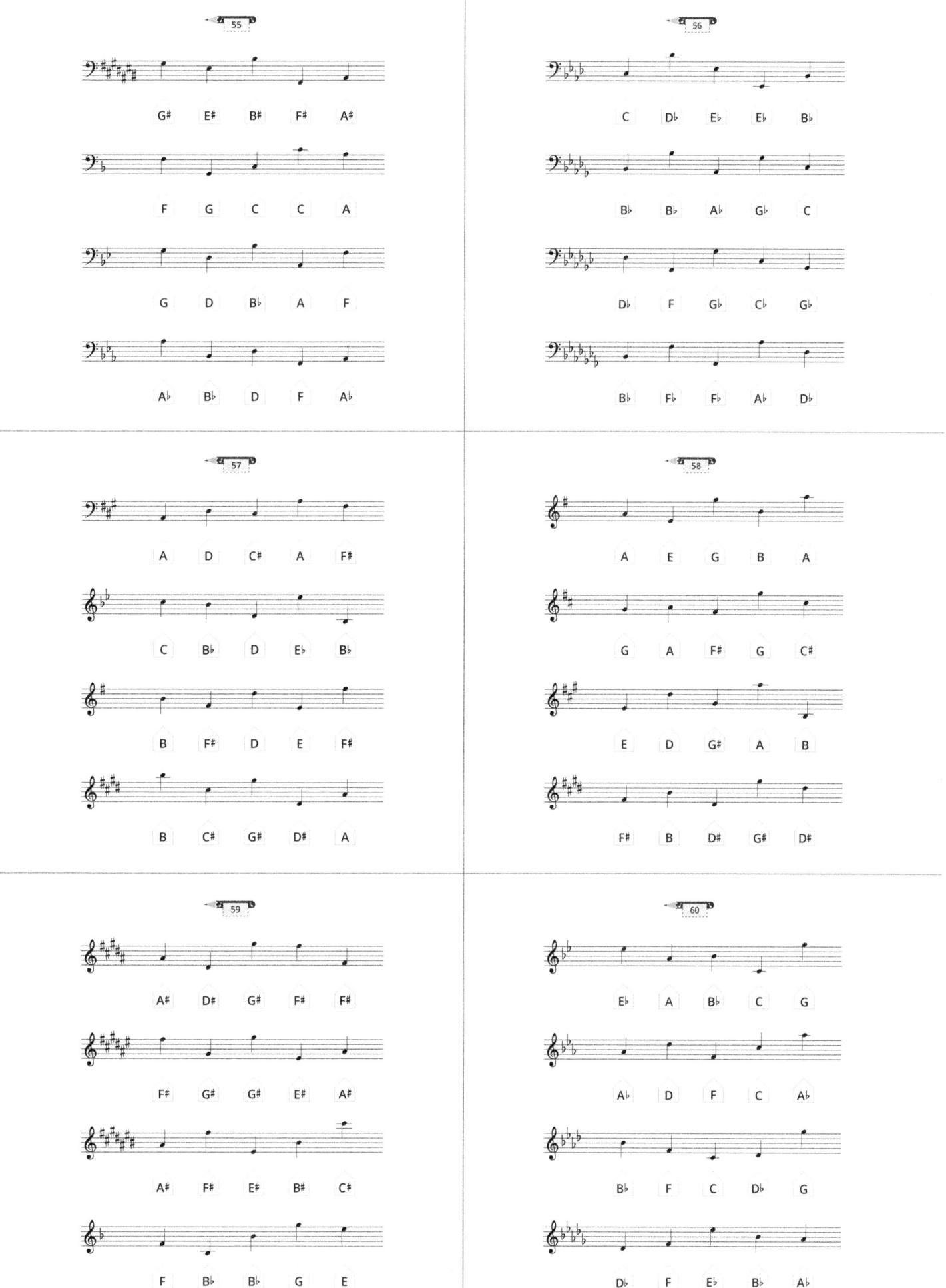

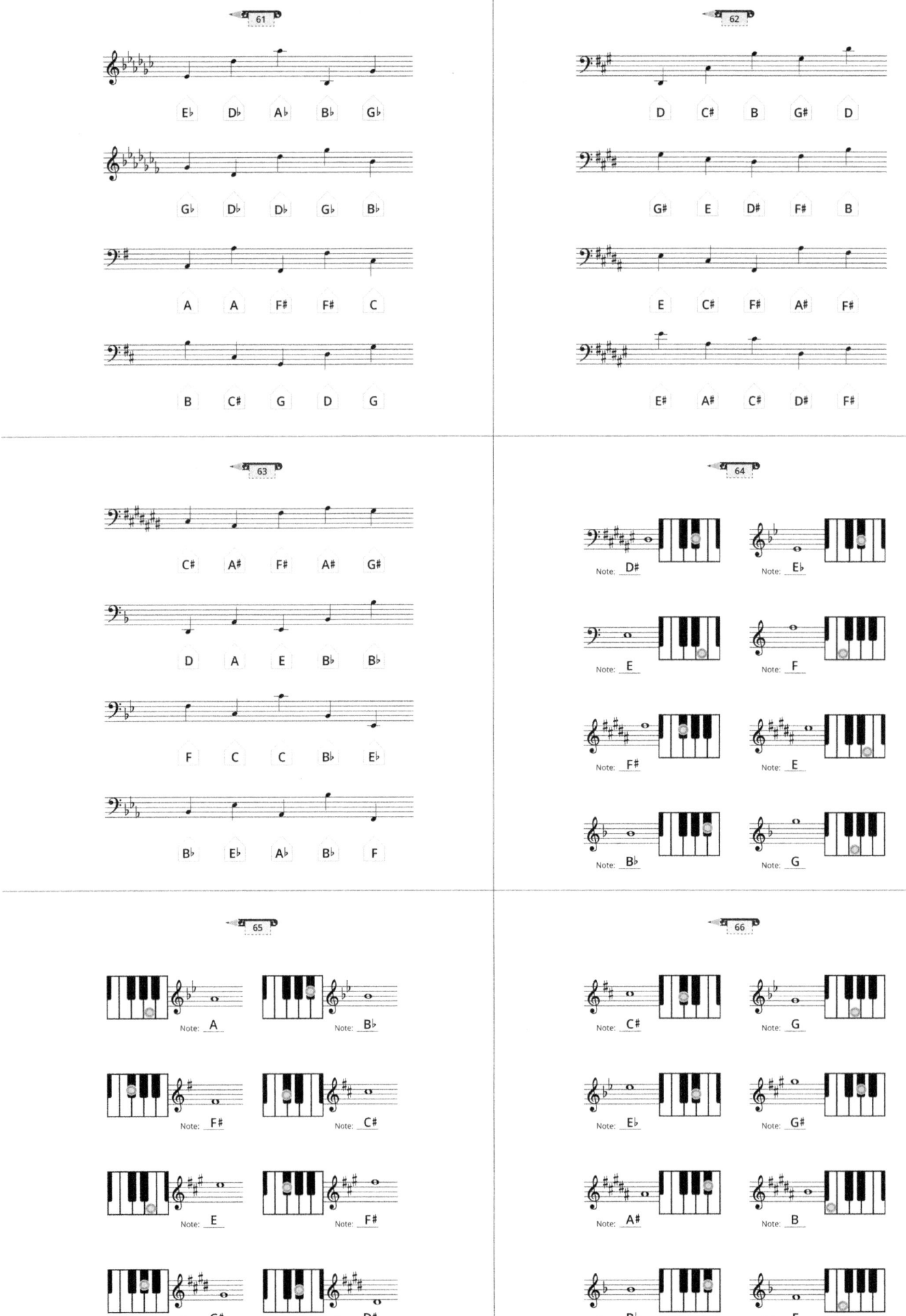

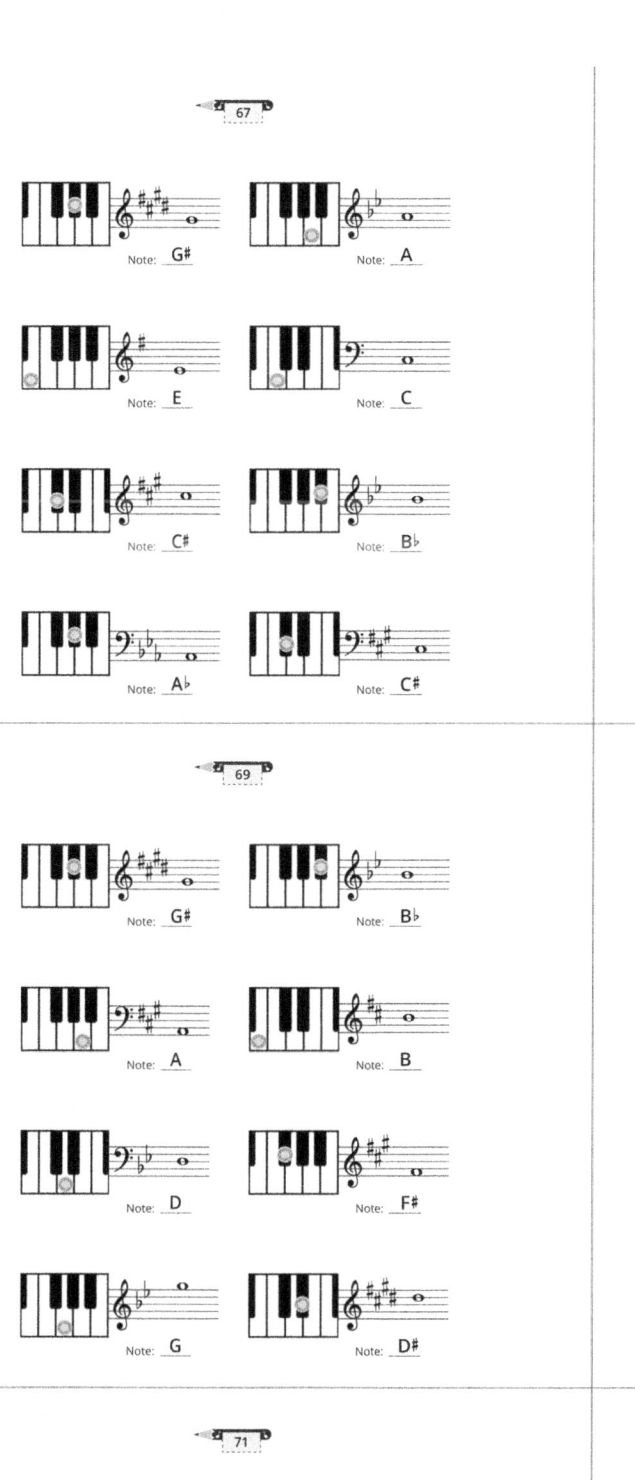
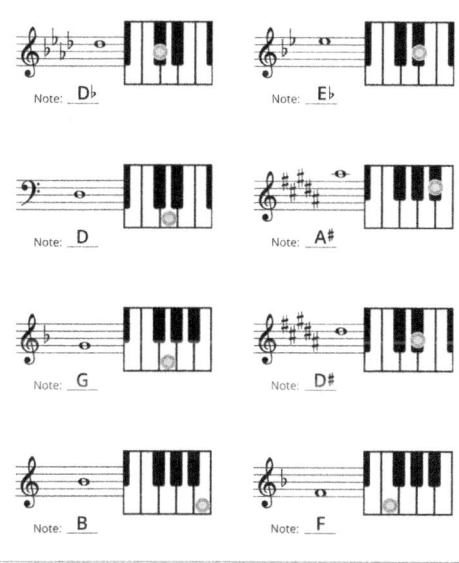
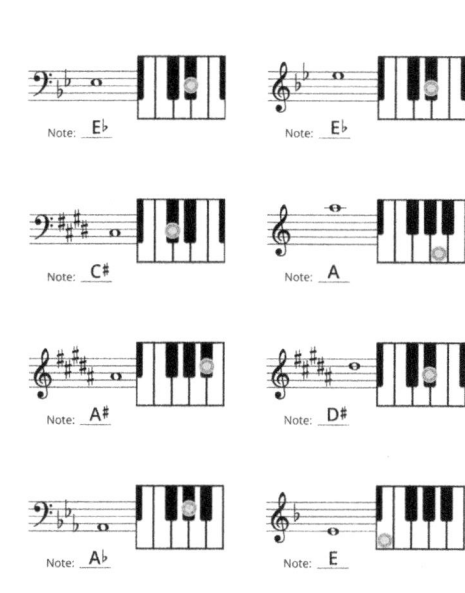
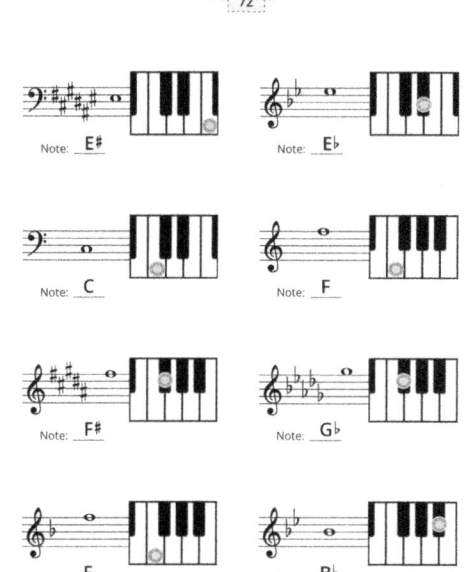

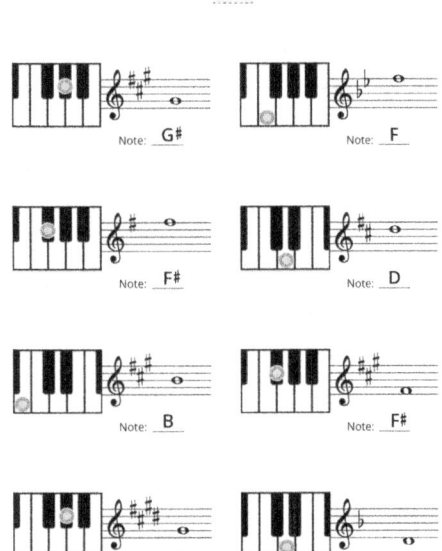
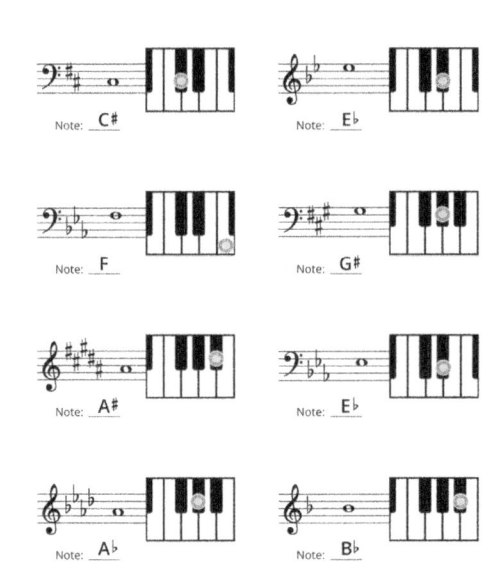
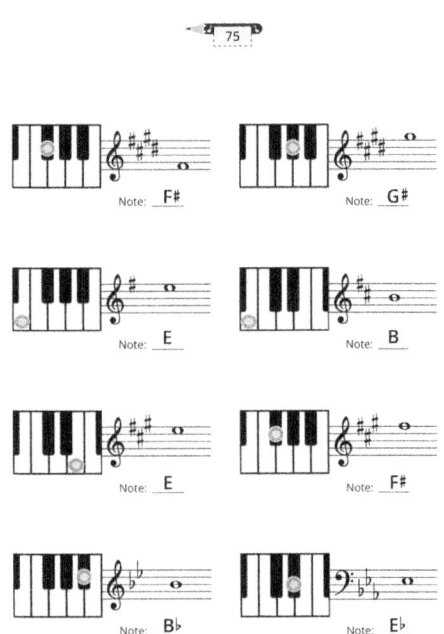
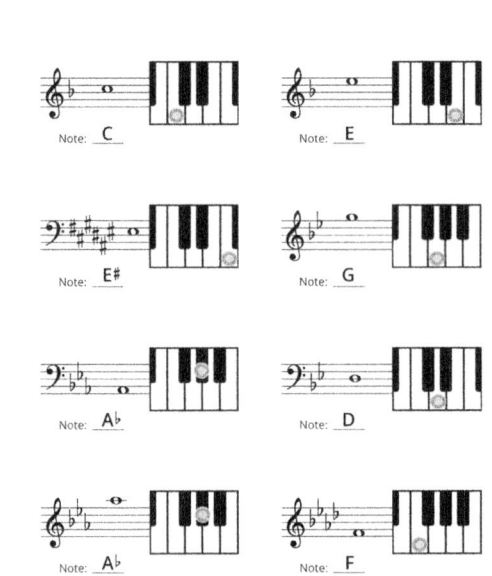

Congratulations!

I hope you've learned a lot from this book, and I'd be truly grateful if you could recommend it to others.

A **feedback on amazon** would also be very helpful. We use your feedback to continually improve our books and bring you the best possible learning experience in the world of music. Thank you!

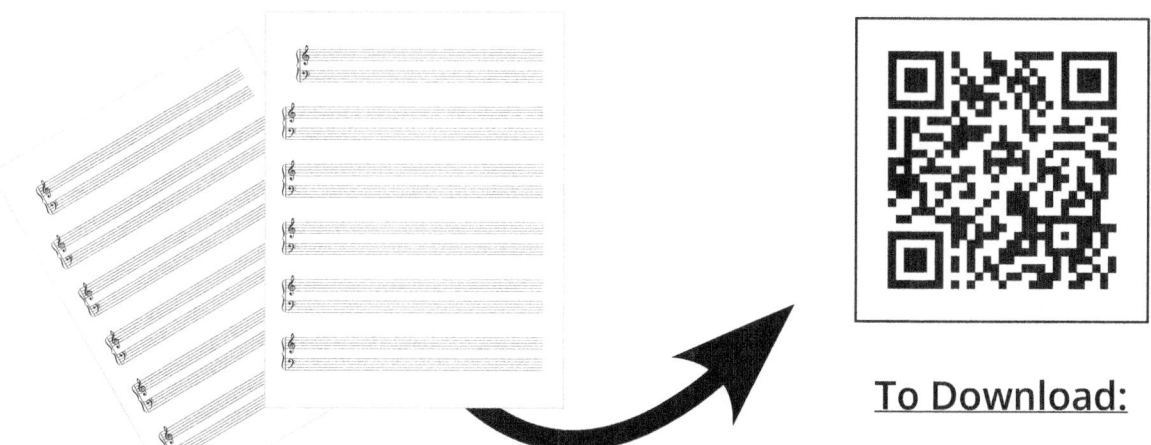

To Download:

https://hermannpress.kit.com/e373b00c11

Thank you for using our educational material!

At **Hermann Press**, we're commited to offering you even more learning tools and practice material—**completely free**.

Visit the link above or simply scan the **QR code** with your phone to download your **free staff paper and charts**.

Use the printable templates for your own exercises, and you'll also receive more helpful resources and exciting updates directly to your inbox.
If you have any questions, suggestions, or feedback, feel free to contact us at **hello@hermannpress.com**.

www.hermannpress.com

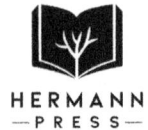

Printed in Dunstable, United Kingdom